Rooted Cosmopolitanism

Will Kymlicka and Kathryn Walker

Rooted Cosmopolitanism
Canada and the World

UBCPress · Vancouver · Toronto

21 20 19 18 17 16 15 14 13 12   5 4 3 2 1

Printed in Canada on FSC-certified ancient-forest-free paper
(100% post-consumer recycled) that is processed chlorine- and acid-free.

Library and Archives Canada Cataloguing in Publication

Rooted cosmopolitanism : Canada and the world / edited by Will Kymlicka
and Kathryn Walker.

Includes bibliographical references and index.
ISBN 978-0-7748-2260-2

1. Canada – Foreign relations. 2. Cosmopolitanism – Canada. 3. Nationalism
– Canada. 4. World citizenship. 5. Internationalism. I. Kymlicka, Will II. Walker,
Kathryn

FC242.R66 2012   327.71   C2011-907430-3

Canada

UBC Press gratefully acknowledges the financial support for our publishing program
of the Government of Canada (through the Canada Book Fund), the Canada Council
for the Arts, and the British Columbia Arts Council.

This book has been published with the help of a grant from the Canadian Federation
for the Humanities and Social Sciences, through the Aid to Scholarly Publications
Program, using funds provided by the Social Sciences and Humanities Research
Council of Canada.

UBC Press
The University of British Columbia
2029 West Mall
Vancouver, BC V6T 1Z2
www.ubcpress.ca

Contents

Acknowledgments

This book has been published with the help of a grant from the Canadian Federation for the Humanities and Social Sciences, through the Aid to Scholarly Publications Programme, using funds provided by the Social Sciences and Humanities Research Council of Canada. Kathryn Walker's work on this project was supported by the Social Sciences and Humanities Research Council of Canada, la Chaire du Canada en Mondialisation, citoyenneté, et démocratie at the Université du Québec à Montréal, and the Queen's University Postdoctoral Fellowship in Democracy and Diversity funded by the Canadian Institute for Advanced Research.

We would also like to thank Anna Drake for her editorial work, and Cecil Foster for his ongoing support and inspiration.

Rooted Cosmopolitanism

1
Rooted Cosmopolitanism: Canada and the World

Will Kymlicka and Kathryn Walker

In the contemporary world, human beings often combine profound local, ethnic, religious, or national attachments with a commitment to cosmopolitan values and principles that transcend those more local boundaries. The aim of this volume is to explore the interplay between local attachments and cosmopolitan values, through a critical exploration of the idea of "rooted cosmopolitanism." Cosmopolitanism itself is a theory originating in the fourth century BCE. It posits that our political and moral existence should be played out on a world stage and that each of us belongs to a community of human beings that transcends the particularities of local affiliation. Although cosmopolitanism is usually understood as requiring us to set aside our more local attachments, a new school of thought argues that the outward-bound cosmopolitan perspective requires and involves the very roots it claims to transcend. This idea of rooted cosmopolitanism was popularized by Kwame Anthony Appiah (1996, 2006) in the mid-1990s, and has since been adopted in various forms by a range of political theorists and philosophers. The essays in this volume examine rooted cosmopolitanism using Canada as a test case, exploring how the local attachments and identities that characterize Canadians facilitate or impede cosmopolitan concerns.

Canada provides particularly fertile ground for exploring these ideas. As we discuss below, the idea that "being Canadian" includes or entails "being a good citizen of the world" has a long history in Canadian public debate and academic discourse, and is underpinned by several structural features of Canada's internal political dynamics and its position in the world. We can therefore learn a great deal about the potential for rooted cosmopolitanism, and its limits, by examining the Canadian case.

In the process, we hope to bring into dialogue three bodies of scholarship that have remained relatively isolated from each other. There is considerable work in the social sciences devoted to how nations and national identities have adapted to processes of globalization, but this is rarely linked to the normative debates about rooted cosmopolitanism. Similarly, there is a great deal of important work by normative theorists on ideas of cosmopolitanism and global justice, but few attempts have been made to study how these ideas are manifested (or not) in particular national contexts. Finally, although much has been written on Canadian nationalism, it tends to focus on either our internal ethnic/linguistic diversity or our relations with the United States rather than on its links to cosmopolitanism. Our aim is to link these debates so as to enrich and deepen our understandings of national identity, cosmopolitan values, and Canadian studies.

Why Rooted Cosmopolitanism? Why Now?
Since the 1990s, there has been a dramatic revival in philosophical discussions of cosmopolitanism. Commenting on this trend, David Miller (2008, 23) claims that "'cosmopolitan' is probably now the preferred self-description of most political philosophers who write about global justice." It is no accident that this renewed interest in global conceptions of humanity coincides with concrete trends of globalization in economic, political, technological, cultural, and social sectors. Indeed, we could say that globalization has made some form of cosmopolitanism virtually inevitable. The pressures of globalization – environmental concerns, refugees, the migration of peoples, awareness of the crimes of genocidal regimes, terrorism, multinational trade, and advances in communication technology – have made older ideas of national autarky or isolation increasingly untenable. There is growing recognition of the need for some normative conception of global community, responsibility, and governance.

However, if current realities have made some form of cosmopolitanism inevitable, these realities have also made clear that we need to revise our inherited ideas of cosmopolitanism. In the past, self-styled cosmopolitans typically endorsed an amalgam of moral, political, and cultural cosmopolitanism. *Moral* cosmopolitanism holds that all human beings are subject to a common moral code and that birthplace is morally irrelevant to someone's moral worth. *Political* cosmopolitanism maintains the need for institutions of global governance. *Cultural* cosmopolitanism emphasizes the idea of a common global culture, and/or the ability of individuals to move freely and comfortably between different cultures, so that people feel culturally at home wherever they are in the world. For many Enlightenment cosmopolitans, these dimensions were strongly interconnected: we should recognize the equal moral worth of all human beings by creating a single world political order united around a single common language and global culture. (For Condorcet, for example, the language and culture of this cosmopolitan order would of course be French.)

Today, however, these Enlightenment images of cosmopolitanism seem paradoxically both utopian and dystopian. They are utopian in their expectations of a democratic world state, but dystopian in their suppression of cultural and linguistic diversity and in the way they open the door to imperialism. Indeed, European colonialism was often justi-fied as a means of spreading a cosmopolitan order and ethos. The core idea of cosmopolitanism may be to recognize the moral worth of people beyond our borders, particularly the poor and needy, but its historical practice has often been to extend the power and influence of privileged elites in the wealthy West while doing little if anything to benefit the truly disadvantaged. In this sense, cosmopolitanism has been aptly described by Craig Calhoun as the "class consciousness of the frequent flier" (Calhoun 2002).

Any defensible conception of cosmopolitanism for today's world must avoid these connotations. It must be a postcolonial cosmopolitanism, divorced from ideas of either cultural homogenization or political uni-fication, accepting of cultural diversity and of the rights of the world's peoples to local autonomy. And it is in this context that ideas of rooted cosmopolitanism have emerged. (Some authors prefer slightly different terminology, such as "anchored cosmopolitanism" [Dallmayr 2003], "situated cosmopolitanism" [Baynes 2007], "embedded cosmopolitan-ism" [Erskine 2008], "vernacular cosmopolitanism" [Werbner 2006], or "republican cosmopolitanism" [Chung 2003], to express a similar idea.) Rooted cosmopolitanism attempts to maintain the commitment to moral cosmopolitanism, while revising earlier commitments to a world state or a common global culture, and affirming instead the enduring reality and value of cultural diversity and local or national self-government.

Even as rooted cosmopolitanism affirms the legitimacy of national self-government, however, it also entails revising our traditional under-standing of "nationhood." For many rooted cosmopolitans, the nation can no longer be seen as the locus of unqualified sovereignty, exclusive loyalty, or blind patriotism. People's attachment to their ethnic cultures and national states must be constrained by moral cosmopolitan com-mitments to human rights, global justice, and international law. Rooted cosmopolitanism, in short, attempts to redefine our traditional under-standings of both cosmopolitanism and nationhood.

Rooted cosmopolitanism is not a monolithic doctrine, and it is worth distinguishing weaker and stronger forms of the claim that cosmopolitanism requires roots. The weakest form merely argues that rooted attachments (to local self-government and to cultural diversity) are not inherently inconsistent with global responsibilities. In this view, cosmopolitanism leaves room for meaningful rooted attachments and vice versa. A stronger form argues that rooted attachments are functionally required to achieve cosmopolitan goals. For example, it is often argued that the achievement of cosmopolitan goals requires the existence of political units capable of engaging in legitimate collective decisions and effective agency, and this requires building a sense of membership in and attachment to bounded political communities. To achieve any political goals, including cosmopolitan goals, there must be cohesive and legitimate political units, and such cohesion and legitimacy in turn requires building a sense of belonging or, if you prefer, patriotism. Without bounded communities that inspire feelings of patriotism, there will be no political units with the functional capacity to pursue cosmopolitan commitments.

An even stronger form of rooted cosmopolitanism holds that particularist attachments can be the moral sources of cosmopolitan commitments. Particularist attachments can serve as "sources" in at least two different senses. One version of this argument states that particularist attachments are epistemologically required even to understand cosmopolitan goals. In this view, we can come to understand the moral significance of "the other" only because we have first been immersed in our own particular communities and ways of life, which give us a "thick" or "deep" sense of moral value and moral responsibility. If we lacked these particularist attachments, and hence saw the world only as a collection of abstract and undifferentiated human beings with their universal human rights, we would lack the concepts, virtues, and practices needed to understand truly why the lives of others matter, or what justice requires of us. People must first be successfully socialized into the habits and practices of moral particularism before they are epistemologically or psychologically capable of morally engaging with the claims of distant others.[1]

Rooted attachments may serve as moral sources in a second and even stronger sense: namely, they may contain within them the seeds of more universalistic commitments, such that we can appeal to people's sense of rooted attachments to help motivate cosmopolitan commitments. In this view, people pursue cosmopolitan commitments because this is what their particular attachments require of them. For example, people become good citizens of the world because this is part of what it means to be a good Canadian: being Canadian motivates being or becoming a cosmopolitan. Immersion in the loyalties and attachments of "being Canadian" does not just help to develop certain moral capacities that are presupposed by cosmopolitanism, such as a sense of responsibility; rather, Canadianness itself may impel people toward cosmopolitanism, as people attempt to more fully explore or express their sense of being Canadian.

Of these different formulations, it is this final and strongest articulation of rooted cosmopolitanism that is the most controversial.[2] As various essays in this volume discuss, the idea that cosmopolitan commitments leave room for more particularistic attachments is widely accepted, although how much room is very much open to debate. Similarly, the idea that bounded communities can provide the effective collective agency necessary for the attainment of cosmopolitan goals is widely recognized, particularly given the dystopian nature of older ideas of a single world state. And the idea that immersion in particularistic attachments precedes more abstract or impartial reasoning is familiar – it is widely recognized, for example, that if children do not form bonds of love and trust within the family, they are unlikely to develop an effective sense of justice later in life.

But to argue that our rooted attachments – including our national attachments – are the very source of our cosmopolitan commitments is more controversial and counterintuitive. The fact that nation-states can draw on strong national identities and patriotisms makes them potentially effective vehicles of collective agency for achieving cosmopolitan goals, if and when citizens decide to pursue such goals, but can we really say that these strong national identifications and patriotisms *motivate* cosmopolitanism? Does not history tell us that the most serious obstacle to cosmopolitanism in the modern world is precisely the moral blinders and national egoism associated with nationalism?

Yet, as Alison Brysk (2009) notes, national identity politics can be constructive. Indeed, her empirical study of "global good Samaritans" suggests that countries that act as good global citizens do so precisely because of their national identities. It is worth quoting her summary in full:

In a world riven by resurgent nationalism, reactive fundamentalism, and constructed clash of civilizations, modernist social science counsels universalist materialism as a bulwark against parochial chaos. But political communities are inevitably constituted and oriented by some set of values, and national versions of cosmopolitan values can serve as an alternative to both neoliberal homogenization and the defensive, competitive particularism it evokes. Canadian soldiers sacrificing their lives in Afghanistan, or Swedish taxpayers bankrolling African refugees are not just trying to be better human beings – they take national pride in expressing their identity as Swedes or Canadians through these global contributions, and acting globally builds national identities as "Canadian peacekeepers" or "Swedish volunteers." The lesson of the post-Cold War world is that identities do not melt away with modernization, so that our best bet for global cooperation is to enhance and mobilize constructive national values, and promote national identification with positive aspects of global good citizenship. (Brysk 2009, 221)

This is the promise of rooted cosmopolitanism: that the very same national identities that bind people deeply to their own particular national community and territory can also mobilize moral commitment to distant others, and that inculcating and affirming a sense of Swedishness or Canadianness among co-nationals can simultaneously inculcate and affirm a sense of global citizenship.

This helps to clarify what is new and distinctive about the idea of rooted cosmopolitanism. Questions about how insiders should treat outsiders and strangers are as old as political philosophy, dating back to the ancient Greeks, and addressed in all the major world religions (Sullivan and Kymlicka 2007). But the idea of rooted cosmopolitanism is not just a new name for this old debate about duties toward insiders versus duties toward outsiders. Rooted cosmopolitanism is born of historically specific political circumstances, and is intimately tied to the evolving nature and function of modern democratic nation-states and the role they play in mediating moral and political cosmopolitanism.

Moral cosmopolitanism is a straightforward invitation to appreciate the moral equality of humanity in general, and many people throughout the ages have found this idea compelling, for the same basic reasons. Beliefs about how to translate this moral position into political practice are much more variable historically, however, and the rise of rooted cosmopolitanism reflects a specific set of political circumstances. In the immediate aftermath of the Second World War, it was widely assumed that the best hope of achieving moral cosmopolitan values lay in (1) overcoming national partialities and nationalist ideologies, and (2) creating new forms of transnational and global governance. Cosmopolitanism has often been defined as antagonistic to nationalism (see Beck 2006; Brighouse and Brock 2005; Cabrera 2004; Habermas 1998; Held 2002,

2005; Moellendorf 2005; Nussbaum 1996) and as requiring individuals to renounce national partialities, and the bloody history of twentieth-century Europe seemed to confirm that supremacist nationalist ideologies are prone to violence, aggression, and ultimately genocide against those who are seen as "not one of us." The hope for cosmopolitanism, therefore, lay in overcoming nation-based politics through the building of transnational global institutions, such as the United Nations and the European Union.

Today, however, many commentators have become both more pessimistic about the prospects of transnational governance and more optimistic about the transformative and constructive potential of nation-based politics. On the one hand, it has become increasingly clear that any attempt to put moral cosmopolitanism into political practice requires serious attention to issues of legitimacy and authority, and schemes of global governance fall short in this regard. For example, what legitimacy does the United Nations have, given that its members are not elected by the people they represent? Legitimate government must be democratic government, and democratic government appears to require bounded political communities. All schemes for global governance are faced with serious "democratic deficits," undermining their potential to advance moral cosmopolitan goals.

Conversely, the idea of the nation-state, which was widely discredited by the horrors of the Second World War, has regained (some of) its legitimacy, as (some) nation-states have proven their capacity to combine a commitment to the welfare of their own citizens with a commitment to good global citizenship. To be sure, nationalism needs to be moderated by commitments to human rights and global justice, but studies such as Brysk's (2009) suggest that a suitably chastened form of nationalism or patriotism can help provide sources of moral motivation, help identify and respect morally relevant particularities that are essential aspects of our moral lives, and help provide sites for effective political participation and democratic accountability.

It is this constellation of factors that helps to explain the specificity of rooted cosmopolitanism. Like all forms of cosmopolitanism, rooted cosmopolitanism appeals to the moral worth of all human beings, including those far away from us. But it takes seriously the political power of nation-states and of national identities in the modern world, as well as the weakness of global political institutions, and attempts to make both moral sense of these facts and moral use of them, placing them at the service of cosmopolitan goals.

Rooting Cosmopolitanism in State, Nation, and Community

The various versions of rooted cosmopolitanism differ not only in their account of the roles that roots play – philosophical, political, epistemological, motivational – but also in their account of what these roots consist in. Which kinds of particularistic attachments and loyalties serve as appropriate roots for cosmopolitan values? An almost infinite list of such attachments can be (and have been) invoked in the literature, but for our purposes it may be worth distinguishing three broad (but also overlapping) accounts of how and where cosmopolitanism should be rooted.

First, some theorists explore how attachment to a particular(ist) *state* is compatible with, or necessary to, cosmopolitanism. The focus here is on the importance of bounded political communities, without necessarily assuming or hoping that these boundaries of the state coincide with those of a "nation." This statist approach is evident in Lea Ypi's "Statist Cosmopolitanism" (2008) and James Bohman's "Republican Cosmopolitanism" (2004), both of which argue that moral cosmopolitanism, even though it involves a moral commitment to others transcending state boundaries, requires the bounded political community of the state. For example, Ypi (2008, 48) argues that if we accept that every needy individual in the world has a justified claim to certain primary goods (moral cosmopolitanism), and if the nature of the claim is such that it requires the transformations of political institutions, then political communities provide the "unique associative sphere in which cosmopolitanism obtains political agency, may be legitimately enforced and cohesively maintained." Similar arguments are advanced by Bohman (2004), Fred Dallmayr (2003, 438), and Philip Pettit (2010).

The idea shared by all of these theories is that state-based political communities offer necessary motivation, legitimacy, agency, cohesion, and accountability. Yet these theorists often insist that relying in this way on bounded political communities does not require appealing to distinctly nationalist identities or ideologies, and that citizens of bounded political communities need not (and indeed should not) be assumed to share national identities. Ryoa Chung (2003), for example, argues that the conditions of globalization require a new non-nationalistic conceptualization of republicanism, one that challenges the belief that republican citizenship must be tied to a specific nation,[3] therefore making the cosmopolitan extension of citizenship viable (see also Benhabib 2006). A republican cosmopolitanism, in this view, can and should be "postnational."

A second approach contests this attempt to divorce state from nation, and argues that cosmopolitanism must be rooted in particular(ist) *nations*, not just in (denationalized or postnational) states. Kai Nielsen (2005, 284), for example, argues that it is distinctly national political units that serve to root cosmopolitanism: "One can, as a rooted cosmopolitan, be a good Dane and a loyal European as one can be a good Icelander and a loyal citizen of the world." Similarly, Kok-Chor Tan (2006) defends the reciprocal consistency, and indeed interdependence, of "liberal cosmopolitanism" and "liberal nationalism." Both theorists argue that when properly understood, cosmopolitanism does not oppose national commitments; on the contrary, a correct conception of cosmopolitanism *includes* the understanding that national attachments are critical to our moral and political lives, and to the very possibility of cosmopolitanism itself. One of the requirements of global justice – one of the things we owe to those outside our nation – is precisely respect for their national identities and national autonomy, even if (and indeed especially if) those nations lack their own state. David Miller's account (2002, 2008) makes similar claims. In this book, Patti Lenard, Margaret Moore, and Joseph-Yvon Thériault argue that properly (liberally) conceived, nationalism includes a commitment to universal ideals and values, including ideas of respect for other nations and peoples; in other words, a correct nationalism is already a form of cosmopolitanism.

A third approach seeks to broaden our options, looking beyond either state or nation to locate other possible ways of "rooting" cosmopolitanism. Toni Erskine (2008), for example, has recently defended an account of "Embedded Cosmopolitanism." Drawing on Marilyn Friedman's idea that the socially situated self is constituted by multiple and diverse communities, Erskine holds that moral reasoning needs to take into account the specific sites of moral concern, and as a consequence the abstract universalism of traditional cosmopolitanism should be jettisoned. For Erskine, however – and this is the distinguishing feature of her account – the requisite moral particularism is not and should not be confined to state borders or to national spheres of obligation. The sites of moral concern are diverse, multiple, national, *and* transnational; critically, they are detached from the nation and the state. Thus Erskine raises the possibility that the rooting of cosmopolitanism can, and should, function beyond both the state and the nation.

In some cases, this third account is seen as supplementing either state- or nation-based versions of rooted cosmopolitanism, offering further potential sites for the rooting of cosmopolitan values.[4] In other cases, however, the demand to look beyond the state and nation is driven by hostility to both state and nation, or at least hostility to the high modernist ideologies of statehood and nationhood advanced by hegemonic political elites, and to the kinds of governmentality they have pursued. Among various postcolonialist and Foucaultian theorists, the prospects for a truly emancipatory cosmopolitanism lie with coalitions and alliances among precisely those left outside state- and nation-based projects, such as indigenous peoples or migrant workers. A successful rooted cosmopolitanism will therefore be a "minoritarian" or "indigenous" cosmopolitanism – "a cosmopolitan community envisaged in marginality," as Homi Bhabha (1996) puts it.[5] These sorts of "new radical cosmopolitanisms from below" are still rooted in particularistic solidarities, not in an unrooted and impartial humanitarianism, but these solidarities are beyond, and to some extent against, the state and nation (Cheah 2006, 491).[6] In the words of Sheldon Pollack and his co-authors (2002, 6):

> The cosmopolitanism of our times does not spring from the capitalized "virtues" of Rationality, Universality and Progress; nor is it embodied in the myth of the nation writ large in the figure of the citizen of the world. Cosmopolitans today are often the victims of modernity, failed by capitalism's upward mobility, and bereft of those comforts and customs of national belonging. Refugees, peoples of the diaspora, and migrants and exiles represent the spirit of the cosmopolitical community.

Critical Perspective on Rooted Cosmopolitanism

Rooted cosmopolitanism is therefore not a single or simple doctrine, but rather a loose umbrella covering a range of different views both about *how* particularistic solidarities complement good global citizenship and about *which* particularistic solidarities do so. Despite this looseness, or perhaps because of it, rooted cosmopolitanism has quickly established itself as an exciting and attractive position within political theory. Indeed, one could argue that it now dominates the field. As Pnina Werbner (2006, 496) notes, we used to ask "whether the local, parochial, rooted, culturally specific and demotic may co-exist with the translocal, transnational, transcendent, elitist, enlightened, universalist and modernist." But today "the question is often reversed to ask whether there can be an enlightened normative cosmopolitanism which is not rooted, in the final analysis, in patriotic and culturally committed loyalties and understandings."

Nonetheless, rooted cosmopolitanism has also faced a number of objections. As with any attempt to negotiate and define a middle ground between traditional oppositions – in this case, cosmopolitanism and nationalism – there are worries about the intellectual coherence of the resulting position. Is the negotiation balanced, doing justice to both sides of the debate? To critics, some versions of rooted cosmopolitanism are really just old-fashioned cosmopolitanism, and pay only lip service to particularist values. For example, critics have argued that the particularities of nationalism and patriotism are given such a secondary status within Tan's Liberal Cosmopolitanism that his theory effectively undermines, deactivates, or problematically limits their significance (see Chapter 2 of this book). Conversely, some versions of rooted cosmopolitanism appear to be essentially an endorsement of nationalism, with only a window dressing of cosmopolitanism. Critics argue, for example, that David Miller's weak cosmopolitanism, with its minimalist account of global justice, does not deserve to be called a form of cosmopolitanism at all (see Chapter 9).

A further worry concerns the psychological or political stability of this compromise: can it ever really work as a basis for either individual commitment or political agendas? Perhaps our particular biases are too deeply engrained to be balanced with more universal concerns, such that our cosmopolitan aspirations will always be tainted by the roots that rooted cosmopolitanism requires and endorses. Or, conversely, perhaps the universalizing imperatives of cosmopolitanism will always run roughshod over respect for cultural difference and local autonomy, operating as a hegemonic and imperial force.

Yet others might argue, from a more metaethical perspective, that this search for a middle ground is inherently misguided. Perhaps universalism and particularism should remain irreconcilable opposites. On the one hand, neo-Kantians such as Onora O'Neill (1996, 39-44) argue that it is precisely the operation of universality that defines morality. Without the bracketing of our partial biases, including national partialities, we can never attain a truly moral position. On the other hand, a wide range of theorists – feminist theorists of an ethics of care (such as Virginia Held, Nel Noodings, Joan Tronto, and Carol Gilligan), communitarians (such as Alasdair MacIntyre, Michael Sandel, and Michael Walzer), and Nietzscheans or post-Nietzscheans[7] (such as Michel Foucault, Zygmunt Bauman, and Richard Rorty) – have argued that constraining or subordinating our partial commitments to impartialist norms of moral cosmopolitanism reflects a fundamental misunderstanding of the nature of moral reasoning, which is always partial and particularistic.

Even if we think that both partiality and universality play a legitimate role in moral reasoning, it does not follow that we should be seeking to unify them within a single theory. Thomas Nagel (2005), for example, insists on the necessary fragmentation of value. Questioning the "monism" of global justice, Nagel argues that there are multiple irreducible sources of value in human life, which cannot be subsumed within a single theoretical framework. Perhaps there are some problems that call for a purely cosmopolitan response; perhaps there are other problems that are best addressed from a purely statist or national position. Why the drive to theoretical univocality?

These and other concerns are addressed in several of the chapters in this book. It seems clear, however, that rooted cosmopolitanism has established itself as a serious position within the literature, worthy of more sustained exploration. Indeed, many of these worries are best addressed by exploring rooted cosmopolitanism in practice, to see how particularist attachments and universalist commitments interact in specific times and places, such as contemporary Canada.

Why Canada?

We believe that Canada provides a compelling test case for ideas of rooted cosmopolitanism. On the one hand, there can be no question of the enduring power of national identities and loyalties within Canada. Compared with other Western democracies, Canadians express above-average levels of national pride and national identity. We are not at all a postnational society that has renounced or transcended the identities and practices of nationhood. At the same time, however, it is often said that Canadian national identities have always been permeable to more cosmopolitan concerns. Indeed, much of the literature on Canada's role in the world seems to presuppose such a linkage between being Canadian and being "a good citizen of the world." Expressing a certain *zeitgeist* in Canada's self-understanding, this scholarship offers a vision of Canadian nationhood as a seedbed for global citizenship.

One can find countless expressions of this idea. For example, in the recent volume *What Is a Canadian?* Thomas Franck (2006, 37) claims that a Canadian is "humanity's best answer to the most complex puzzle of the twenty-first century: how to accommodate, within a functioning persona, the multiple identities layered on each person in an era in which responsibility to the global must coherently contend with loyalties to the nation and the local." Following suit, Jennifer Welsh (2004, 189) proposes "a simple but ambitious vision for Canada's global role: as Model Citizen." In her study of countries that are "global good Samaritans," Brysk (2009, 93) argues that Canada's commitment to global justice is rooted in its "benign form of liberal nationalism."

In short, the idea that Canada is a potential model or prototype of rooted cosmopolitanism is "in the air." It is has never, however, been subjected to a serious critical analysis. In what ways, precisely, does being Canadian facilitate or impede being a "citizen of the world"? In what ways does being rooted in Canada help to enable and inform cosmopolitan commitments?

A quick survey of the "Canada in the World" literature suggests a range of factors that make Canadian nationhood potentially more amenable to rooted cosmopolitanism. The first is Canada's ethnic and linguistic diversity. As a country built on treaties and political agreements among Aboriginal peoples, French, British, and immigrant groups, Canada has never had the dream or delusion of sharing a common language or ethnic culture. As a result, we have always needed to build bonds of solidarity and political dialogue across ethnic and linguistic lines. The idea that we have moral obligations to or political relations with only those who are "like us" has made little sense in Canada. In that sense, citizenship and solidarity within Canada has a more "cosmopolitan" potential, and may therefore be easier to extend to those beyond our borders.

It is not just the sheer level of diversity that matters, but also the way this diversity connects different groups of Canadians to different parts of the world. For example, the origin of Canada as a pact between British and French settlers has ensured that Canada plays a central role in both the Commonwealth and La Francophonie, linking Canada to many countries around the world. And as successive waves of immigrants have come to Canada, they have helped create new linkages to yet other countries. Foreign-born citizens often retain strong links to the "old country" – an identification that is legitimated by Canada's multiculturalism policy, which affirms the legitimacy of ethnic identities and which encourages the self-organization of ethnic groups on the basis of their national origin. While these ethnic groups lobby primarily to improve their own treatment within Canada, they also, naturally, seek to influence Canada's foreign policy toward their country of origin.[8] Aboriginal peoples have also engaged in their own forms of transnational linkages, uniting with indigenous peoples from the rest of the world as part of the international indigenous movement (Henderson 2008).

In all of these ways, the politics of diversity within Canada connects Canadians to those beyond our borders, yet without threatening the integrity of the state. Even as the Canadian state seeks to inculcate a shared sense of nationhood, it has not typically seen this as requiring the repudiation of transnational ties and loyalties, whether the identification of the Québécois with La Francophonie, or of immigrants with their country of origin, or of English Canadians with the Commonwealth. This has given Canada a special interest – indeed, expertise – in the global challenge of living with diversity and with multiple identities.

A second factor is Canada's ambiguous status as a "middle power" country. We are not strong enough to impose our views on other peoples, and indeed not even strong enough to defend ourselves militarily. So fantasies of imperial conquest or unlimited sovereignty have little resonance in Canada, and we are dependent on international rules and alliances for our security and prosperity. Yet as a wealthy state with powerful allies, we can nonetheless play an important role in shaping these international rules. In short, being a good citizen of the world, and encouraging the good citizenship of other countries, is in our interest. This is reflected in a long history of Canadian commitments to cosmopolitan ideals. For example, Canada was instrumental in the development of United Nations peacekeeping forces: in the heat of the Suez Crisis in 1956, Foreign Affairs Minister Lester B. Pearson proposed a UN peacekeeping force composed of soldiers from non-combatant countries to separate the warring armies and supervise a ceasefire. Other examples include Canadian leadership in the global fight against AIDS (Stephen Lewis), in the human rights movement (Louise Arbour), in banning landmines (Lloyd Axworthy), among many others. Although often described as examples of altruism, this sort of multilateralism is very much in the self-interest of middle powers like Canada, who depend on international law and international institutions and alliances to contain threats to their security and prosperity.[9]

For reasons stemming from both our internal diversity and our geopolitical status, therefore, Canada may be well placed to serve as a laboratory for practices of rooted cosmopolitanism.[10] And indeed in her study of "global good Samaritans," Brysk suggests that Canada has many of the preconditions that are optimal for developing practices of good global citizenship.

But of course this is only one-half of the story. As Brysk (2009, 40) notes, even under optimal conditions, practices of good global citizenship need to struggle against countervailing forces, including "alternative discourses of security threat, parochial nationalism, and narrowly material, short-term calculation," as well pressures of "fundamentalisms, neoliberal atomization, and postliberal complacency." And even a cursory glance at Canadian history reveals many ways in which Canadians have utterly failed to be good citizens of the world. If we have an honourable history of participating in, or indeed initiating, certain projects of multilateralist humanitarianism, we also have a long and dishonourable history of eager participation in the imperialist adventures of our British allies. Indeed, there have been times when "imperialism was one form of Canadian nationalism" (Berger 1970, 259). As dissension grew in the British Empire at the turn of the twentieth century, Canada stood by the imperial power, sending troops to the Sudan campaign (1896-99) and the Second Boer War (1899-1902), acting as "an enthusiastic junior partner in British imperialism in Africa" (Thakkar 2008, 138). Commemorating this, the memorial arch at the Royal Military College in Kingston, Ontario, is inscribed with words in memory of the graduates who "gave their lives for the Empire."

Similarly, if we have an honourable history of respecting the diversity of peoples and cultures, we also have a dishonourable history of discrimination at home and abroad. After all, Canada is built on the original sin of the European dispossession of Aboriginal peoples, and this initial act of racism has been compounded by many others, including the residential schools policy (from the 1840s to 1996), with its mandate to "civilize" and Christianize Aboriginal children. Similar racist attitudes characterized our immigration policy, including the 1914 turning back of the *Komagata Maru,* the 1923 Chinese Immigration Act, the 1939 refusal to admit Jewish refugees on board the SS *St. Louis,* and the 1942 detention of 22,000 Japanese Canadians.

Sadly, these shortcomings in Canada's global citizenship are not solely things of the past, they also characterize current policies. A particularly striking example, discussed in Chapter 10, concerns Canada's record on pollution and climate change. Canada is one of the greatest consumers of energy per capita (roughly fifty times the consumption rate of Bangladesh), our energy consumption surpasses that of all of Africa's 760 million inhabitants, and although Canada makes up less than one-half of 1 percent of the world's population, it is the world's eighth-largest producer of carbon dioxide (Ostling 2009). This is a paradigm case where countries must learn to place cosmopolitan values above short-term national self-interest, yet Canada's efforts to do so have been meagre. Despite having been an early supporter of the Kyoto Protocol, Canadian initiatives to meet its protocol obligations have simply not lived up to the Kyoto commitment. It is expected that Canada will be in default of its Kyoto obligations by some billion tonnes of carbon dioxide equivalent, by far the worst breach of any nation (Flannery 2009). Moreover, according to the Sierra Club (2008), Canada's failure to meet its Kyoto obligations means that the country is now in contravention of international and domestic law. In this respect, Canada has been rightly described as a "rogue state" (Broadhead 2001). An impartial review of other policy fields – including global trade agreements – would suggest that Canada not only operates in a very self-interested manner but is more than happy to exercise its power to bully states that are poorer and weaker.

These are not just minor blemishes on the Canadian record but rather raise deep and difficult questions about the very possibility of rooted cosmopolitanism. We might like to think that there is something "un-Canadian" about these cases where we have failed to live up to ideals of good global citizenship, or that they are temporary bumps on our road to truly cosmopolitan nationhood. But we need to take seriously the prospect that such failures are endemic to our identities and practices of Canadian nationhood. Perhaps there are limits on the extent to which ideas of nationhood, including Canadian nationhood, can be transformed in a truly cosmopolitan direction. Perhaps national identities are invariably prone to both national egoism and national exclusion, which are simply hidden rather than actually addressed by Canada's self-image as a model of diversity and global citizenship.

Indeed, even the cases where Canada is said to be acting as a global good Samaritan may not be as they appear. Consider the case of peacekeeping, which Brysk and others cite as the quintessential expression of Canadian rooted cosmopolitanism. Some commentators, such as Sherene Razack (2004) and Sunera Thobani (2007), argue that Canadian peacekeeping is essentially a projection of racism, and deeply informed by ideologies of white supremacy rooted in the national imaginary of Canada as a white settler state. For example, according to Razack (2004, 17, 156):

> Peacekeeping today is a kind of war, a race war waged by those who constitute themselves as civilized, modern and democratic against those who are constituted as savage, tribal and immoral ... [Canadian] peacekeepers imagine themselves as going to the Third World to sort out the tribalisms, ethnic hatreds, and warring tribes that now characterize so much of Africa and Eastern Europe. They go as members of a family of civilized nations, nations that understand themselves to be carrying the traditional white man's burden of instructing and civilizing the natives.

Similarly, Thobani argues that the apparent openness to Others said to characterize Canadian multiculturalism is in fact a way of maintaining a sense of racial privilege. White Canadians have adopted the self-identity of being tolerant and open cosmopolitans precisely to preserve their sense of superiority over the racialized Other:

> With whiteness coming to signify tolerance, a willingness to change and a cosmopolitan sensibility, people of colour could be tied all the more readily to cultural parochialism, authoritarianism, essentialism and intolerance. Multiculturalism as a specific policy and socio-political racial ideology has thus come to attest to the enduring superiority of whiteness, of its ability to transform and accommodate itself to changing times and new opportunities. It became a framework that assumed a certain rigidity in the cultures of racial others, of their enduring inferiority, immaturity, and the need for their reformulation under the tutelage of progressive – always modernizing – western superiority. (Thobani 2007, 155)[11]

In short, the self-identity of Canadians as rooted cosmopolitans is not a reflection of a "constructive" and "benign" liberal nationalism that reaches out to Others as moral equals, but rather is a form of "exaltation" that "constitutes that national subject as belonging to a higher order of humanity" (Thobani 2007, 248).[12]

Although they themselves do not put it in quite these terms, Razack and Thobani can be seen as acknowledging the reality and power of rooted cosmopolitanism. That is, they agree with Brysk that Canada's global citizenship is rooted in and motivated by our national identity, and that Canadians take national pride in being citizens of the world. They argue, however, that this link between national identity and global citizenship is itself a product of ideologies of racial supremacy, and operates to reproduce that ideology, both domestically and internationally.

It is precisely this sort of clash of perceptions and interpretations that makes Canada such an interesting test case for ideas of rooted cosmopolitanism. The Canadian experience can be invoked both to show why rooted cosmopolitanism is a feasible and compelling project and to show why it is a dangerous delusion. The chapters in this volume explore these competing views about the potential for, and limits to, rooted cosmopolitanism in Canada. As we will see, there are no simple answers to this question. Norms and practices of nationhood in Canada are related in complex ways to norms and practices of global citizenship, and our aim in this book is to try to identify some of the factors that mediate this relationship, pushing it in one direction or another, in different times and places, on different issues.

Overview of this Book

This book is divided into two broad parts. Part 1 explores the theory of rooted cosmopolitanism itself; Part 2 examines the practice of rooted cosmopolitanism in a variety of settings in Canadian social and political life.

Part 1 contains five chapters by Kok-Chor Tan, Patti Lenard and Margaret Moore, Joseph-Yvon Thériault, Daniel Weinstock, and Charles Blattberg. Each explores the meaning of rooted cosmopolitanism, contrasting it with other forms of cosmopolitanism, considering its relationship to nationalism, and examining its nature and scope.

The first three chapters – by Tan, Lenard and Moore, and Thériault – all seek to defend some version of the rooted cosmopolitan thesis by showing how national attachments need not conflict with cosmopolitan principles and values, and may indeed help to advance them. Tan focuses on the relationship between cosmopolitanism and national patriotism. He begins by distinguishing moral cosmopolitanism as a theory regarding the scope of justice from both political and cultural cosmopolitanism, and argues that once we make this distinction, cosmopolitanism need not conflict with patriotism. When we understand cosmopolitanism as a desire to be a just citizen of the world, and not as a call for a world state or cultural homogenization, then cosmopolitanism need not contradict the common features of patriotism, such as a strong identification with a particular state, a strong sense of solidarity with fellow citizens, and a belief that there is something intrinsically valuable in patriotic relations. As we noted earlier, some critics worry that his account makes room for only a very attenuated sense of patriotism, entirely subordinated to cosmopolitan principles. Tan responds directly to this critique, noting that the task of reconciling partial attachments with impartial obligations is one that arises at multiple levels, and that we have successful models in both theory and practice for addressing this challenge.

Lenard and Moore also defend the potential consistency of cosmopolitanism and nationalism, but they note that this reconciliation depends on how precisely we spell out the requirements of global distributive justice. In particular, they argue that the prospects for rooted cosmopolitanism depend on rejecting the "global luck egalitarian" form of cosmopolitanism of the sort defended by Tan. According to Lenard and Moore, if cosmopolitanism is to make room for liberal nationalism (and vice versa), our conception of global justice must incorporate a meaningful role for collective national responsibility, and must acknowledge the legitimacy of national claims to territory – both of which, they argue, are incompatible with a strict version of global luck egalitarianism. They conclude by considering how these ideas of national responsibility and national territory can be affirmed while still preserving a meaningful sense of global justice.

Joseph-Yvon Thériault defends perhaps the strongest form of rooted cosmopolitanism, emphasizing that nationhood is not only consistent with, but is in fact a vehicle for, cosmopolitan values. He argues that the tension between "the claims of the tribe" and the "claims of the human" is an essential feature of modern politics, and that the task of liberal-democratic nationalism is precisely to reconcile them, by combining cultural particularity and territorial boundaries with universal values. Thériault argues that although all modern democracies are instantiations of a rooted cosmopolitanism by which universal democratic values are situated within particular cultures and places, the rooted cosmopolitan nature of the modern nation is most visible in small societies such as Quebec because their cultural vulnerability requires more conscious and careful attention to their "rootedness." Drawing on two examples from Quebec history, Thériault illustrates how this modern democratic nationalism can serve as a vehicle of both cultural rootedness and universal values.

In their different ways, therefore, Tan, Lenard and Moore, and Thériault all affirm the basic cogency and desirability of reconciling cosmopolitanism and liberal nationalism. The final two chapters in Part 1 offer a more dissenting note. Weinstock engages in a careful analysis of a range of arguments for rooted cosmopolitanism, all of which he views as essentially efforts to water down the demands of cosmopolitanism in order to leave more room for national partiality or favouritism. He finds all of these arguments wanting, and concludes that, at least from a philosophical perspective, cosmopolitanism should be seen as prior to, and setting the limits of, national attachments.

Charles Blattberg, by contrast, attacks rooted cosmopolitanism from the other direction. In his view, influential accounts of rooted cosmopolitanism remain too wedded to "abstract" forms of impartial moral reasoning that are incapable of engaging people's moral sympathies. An effective moral practice must be rooted in everyday forms of conversation, through which particular forms of patriotism will emerge. These forms of conversation-based patriotism will inevitably have a local flavour, but Blattberg argues that they need not be indifferent to distant others, if those others can be seen as already part of "who we are." In the Canadian case, he argues that a concern for foreigners is part and parcel of the enactment of our national identity properly pursued, and that thinking of refugees in these terms – as part of who we are in Canada – is more effective than seeking to defend refugee claimants in the abstract language of human rights. In this way, Blattberg ends up with a position that is close to that sought by defenders of rooted cosmopolitanism, but he insists that developing a more expansive form of conversation-based patriotism is different from, and more realistic than, developing a more rooted form of abstract cosmopolitan principles.

Having explored a range of perspectives on the meaning of rooted cosmopolitanism, we turn in Part 2 to an exploration of rooted cosmopolitanism in practice in Canadian life. Four chapters – by Scott Schaffer, Yasmeen Abu-Laban, Howard Adelman and Robert Paehlke – consider issues of both domestic and foreign policy where cosmopolitan ideals might be at play.

Part 2 begins with two chapters on the connections between cosmopolitanism and multiculturalism and immigration in Canada. As we noted earlier, one of the core arguments for seeing Canada as a potential model of rooted cosmopolitanism is the extent to which Canadians have always had to build solidarity across ethnic and racial lines, to construct forms of national identity that include people from all over the world, and to respect and accommodate the diversity of people's ethnic and geographical attachments. This experience of accommodating "the world in Canada" is said to have lessons for, and to naturally encourage, an active engagement of "Canada in the world." Yet, as we also noted, many critics argue that this fabled openness of Canadian national identity involves a racialized denigration of other peoples and cultures, both at home and abroad. A crucial task, therefore, is to examine these links between domestic diversity and cosmopolitan commitments – a task taken up in these two chapters.

In Chapter 7, Schaffer argues that the recent debate on "reasonable accommodation" in Quebec offers a unique opportunity to explore how rooted cosmopolitanism is lived in Canada. Like Thobani and Razack, he notes that traditional forms of cosmopolitan tolerance tacitly rehearse a colonial world view in which the Other (of the postcolonial South) is viewed as a passive and silent recipient in its encounter with the well-meaning and enlightened cosmopolitan (of the colonial West and North). To overcome this dynamic, he defends a model of rooted cosmopolitanism predicated on an acknowledgment – by both native-born and immigrant – of our incompleteness, and hence the need for a fusion of horizons through "diatopical hermeneutics." He argues that this model, gestured at but not fully articulated in the Bouchard-Taylor Report, applies to our interactions with others at a local, national, and global level, since the duty of openness to the Other arises at all levels, and so applies to both domestic diversity and global relationships.

Abu-Laban uses the foreign domestic worker program in Canada as her test case for examining issues of rooted cosmopolitanism. She notes that the traditional debate about the relationship between the (national) "us" and the (distant) "other" has operated in a gender-blind way: neither the "us" nor the "other" has been conceptualized in gender-specific terms. The result, she argues, is a persistent failure in the cosmopolitanism literature to take into account issues of care, and the role of care in global migration. The Live-In Caregiver Program in Canada has been seen by some commentators as a form of racialized exclusion from the national body, and by other commentators as evidence of Canada's inclusive approach to immigration and citizenship. In Abu-Laban's account, we can resolve this debate only through an approach based on the values of "care ethics" – an approach that would attune immigration policy to gender and other markers of difference, would compel a way of seeing our interconnectedness at many levels, and would demand that attention be paid to the most vulnerable. Such an approach, she argues, would force us to link the local and the global, by forcing us to ask what sort of moral worth is attributed to care and caring relationships; moreover, it would do so not only at the domestic level but also in terms of the caring relationships that are either nurtured or inhibited in the societies from which caregivers are drawn. A rooted cosmopolitan approach to gendered migration, such as the caregiver program, would insist that we affirm the moral value of caring relationships at home and abroad.

In the final two chapters, we turn from domestic immigration policy to the international context, examining how Canada's global actions do or do not exhibit forms of rooted cosmopolitanism. In his chapter, Adelman examines Canada's role in the global "responsibility to protect" (R2P) debate. As we noted earlier, Canada's active championing of the R2P doctrine at the United Nations has often been cited as an example of this country's rooted cosmopolitanism. Adelman argues, however, that cosmopolitan ideologies distort rather than illuminate our moral thinking about humanitarian interventions. Like Blattberg, he argues that cosmopolitanism has proven morally and politically ineffective. Indeed, he traces a precipitous long-term decline in cosmopolitan aspirations along all of its various cultural, political, legal, and moral dimensions, to the point that the currently fashionable forms of "rooted moral cosmopolitanism" are so weak as to be essentially morally bankrupt. Rather than trying to resuscitate this failed cosmopolitan project, Adelman argues that a better approach lies in what he calls "Scottish communitarianism," which avoids the high-minded but ultimately vacuous pronouncements of rooted moral cosmopolitanism and focuses instead on more practical issues of accommodating conflicting interests and identities. He demonstrates the difference between these approaches by contrasting the failure of R2P (reflective of rooted moral cosmopolitanism) with the partial effectiveness of Canadian engagement with Darfur (reflective of Scottish communitarianism).

In the final chapter, Paehlke explores the challenge of climate change, noting that it is a paradigm case of the sort of issue that requires a rooted cosmopolitan approach. It is a decisively global problem – no country can solve the problem on its own – but one that requires effective action to be taken at a national level, through national-level debates and consensus. Given Canada's cosmopolitan self-image, one might have expected Canada to be a world leader on this issue. And indeed public opinion seems to strongly support such action. Yet, as we noted earlier, Canada has been one of the world's worst laggards on climate change. What explains this? Paehlke suggests that the problem is not that Canadians' expressed cosmopolitan values are illusory, but rather that they have been undermined by a range of political and institutional factors, such as federalism. Although optimistic that these barriers can be overcome, his chapter is a sober reminder of the vast gulf that can separate expressed cosmopolitan values and effective political action. As we have seen, rooted cosmopolitanism was intended to help reduce that gulf by drawing on the legitimacy and loyalty of nation-states as vehicles for cosmopolitan projects. But as Paehlke shows, the "nation-state" is not always the coherent and effective collective agent that rooted cosmopolitans would like it to be, at least in the Canadian case. Indeed, the fragmented nature of the Canadian federal system raises important questions about the appropriate unit or level for rooted cosmopolitan projects – perhaps municipal or provincial governments, rather than centralized national governments, are the best bet for leveraging particular attachments in the service of cosmopolitan goals.

Conclusion

We began this introductory chapter by saying that while current developments at the global level make some form of cosmopolitan ethics inevitable, they also discredit those traditional forms of cosmopolitanism that have been associated with cultural homogenization and unified global governance. This is the challenge to which rooted cosmopolitanism seeks to respond, offering a new image of how the irreducible plurality of culturally distinct and politically bounded communities can nonetheless respect and advance universal cosmopolitan values. This has been an exciting idea, not least for Canadians, given the deep diversity and plurality of our cultures and communities.

But is it a coherent and realistic idea? The chapters in this book obviously represent just a first step in the investigation of the prospects for rooted cosmopolitanism, and it would be premature to draw any firm conclusions. As we have seen, the various authors defend a wide range of views about both the conceptual coherence and political feasibility of projects of rooted cosmopolitanism. Yet they all affirm the urgency of the challenge to which rooted cosmopolitanism is a response. There is no reason whatsoever to think that the salience of either our local attachments or our global responsibilities will fade in the foreseeable future. We will continue to live in a world where powerful local loyalties and solidarities coexist with the increasingly urgent moral claims of distinct and distant others. We hope that the essays found in this book will enrich our understanding of the universe of possibilities for addressing this challenge, and that they will stimulate further research into the theory and practice of rooted cosmopolitanism.

Notes

1 This version of the rooted cosmopolitanism thesis is closely related to the debate in sociology about "enlightened localism." See Gregg 2003 and the 2010 symposium on enlightened localism in *Comparative Sociology.* Indeed, in a sense, rooted cosmopolitanism can be seen as the flip side of enlightened localism. Rooted cosmopolitanism seeks to overcome the limitations of traditional forms of cosmopolitanism by highlighting the significance of local autonomy and cultural difference; enlightened localism seeks to overcome the limitations of traditional forms of "parochial localism" by highlighting how the claims of outsiders can "enlighten" local practices and make them more encompassing. The desire to "root" cosmopolitanism and the desire to "enlighten" localism arguably reflect the same constellation of factors: i.e., the need to find a way of thinking and acting morally that acknowledges the increasingly global nature of our interactions while avoiding the dangers and impossibilities of traditional cultural and political cosmopolitanism.

2 It is not always easy to determine which authors are advancing which version of the rooted cosmopolitan thesis: defenders often invoke a mix of arguments about philosophical consistency, political functionality, epistemological preconditions, and moral motivation without distinguishing them. For a clear statement of both the political functionality and moral motivation arguments, see Ypi 2010.

3   Similar arguments are made by Lena Halldenius (2010) and Cécile Laborde (2010).
4   For example, Keeble (2007, 123) argues that transnational non-governmental organizations are the most viable path through which human security can be pursued globally, concretizing the idea that cosmopolitanism can be rooted in affiliations that are neither national nor state-based. She also emphasizes, however, that this empowering of civil society organizations is intimately tied up with state-based foreign policy, itself predicated on particular national identities. One way to enact a cosmopolitan national identity is to empower transnational civil society organizations.
5   For a similar view, see Appadurai 1993 and 2000. On "indigenous cosmopolitanism," see Biolsi 2005. On minoritarian cosmopolitanism, see Pollack et al. 2002, 6.
6   Cheah himself is skeptical of these postnational, transnational, or supranational accounts of rooted cosmopolitanism, and argues that national forms of solidarity remain normatively significant.
7   On the use of these terms, see Dallmayr 2003, 430.
8   On how immigration/multiculturalism generates a "predisposition to international activism," see Gwyn 1999, 15, and Brysk 2009, 89-90.
9   Welsh (2004, 165) argues that "internationalism has also become a defining feature of the new Canadian identity," but as Mackenzie (2009, 331-32) notes, "these engagements were firmly rooted in Canada's international alignment and alliances," and neglect of this fact has led people to exaggerate how disinterested our behaviour has been. Multilateralism is presented as a Canadian virtue, but in fact is a necessity given our limited power.
10 One can think of other factors, such as Canada's unique geography. The largest country in the world, Canada spans 9,093,507 square kilometres, 20 terrestrial and marine ecozones (as classified by Environment Canada), and 52 of the world's 825 terrestrial ecoregions (as classified by the World Wildlife Foundation). Consequently, Canada has grappled with the demands of disparate ecological systems and concerns; in this expanse of climatic and vegetative conditions, flood and drought, heat and cold, feast and famine are contemporaneous. Canada's broad and complex ecological horizon has required that the nation develop an equally broad and equally complex environmental understanding. Our geographic diversity may play a role in positioning Canada as uniquely cosmopolitan by forcing Canadians to develop bonds of solidarity that transcend the very different physical landscapes and regional economies we inhabit.
11 This is not unique to Canada. Melamed (2006) makes a similar argument about how official anti-racism in the United States serves to "renew white privilege" by presenting white liberals as the heroic protagonists or "saviours" of American ideals, both domestically and internationally.
12 As Bell (2010) notes, the idea of being hospitable to and welcoming of Others is also a way in which the native-born reassert their legitimate sovereignty and ownership of the state. To open up one's house to strangers implies that this is indeed one's house to begin with, which is not obvious in the case of settler states like Canada, since the land originally belonged to indigenous peoples. Extending an invitation to guests is a way in which settler societies can shore up their sense that they are "at home" in lands they have usurped from others.

Here again, what looks at first glance like an expansive and inclusive evolution of national identity can operate to reaffirm and entrench an old power dynamic of dispossession.

References

Appadurai, Arjun. 1993. "Patriotism and Its Futures." *Public Culture* 5 (3): 411-29.

–. 2000. "Grassroots Globalization and the Research Imagination." *Public Culture* 12 (1): 1-19.

Appiah, Kwame Anthony. 1996. "Cosmopolitan Patriots." In *For Love of Country,* ed. by Joshua Cohen, 21-29. Boston: Beacon Press.

–. 2006. *Cosmopolitanism: Ethics in a World of Strangers.* New York: W.W. Norton.

Baynes, Kenneth. 2007. "The Hermeneutics of 'Situated Cosmopolitanism.'" *Philosophy and Social Criticism* 33 (3): 301-8.

Beck, Ulrich. 2006. *The Cosmopolitan Vision.* Trans. by Ciaran Cronin. Cambridge: Polity Press.

Bell, Avril. 2010. "Being 'at Home' in the Nation: Hospitality and Sovereignty in Talk about Immigration." *Ethnicities* 10 (2): 236-56.

Benhabib, Seyla. 2006. *Another Cosmopolitanism.* Oxford: Oxford University Press.

Berger, Carl. 1970. *Sense of Power: Studies in the Ideas of Canadian Imperialism: 1867-1914.* Toronto: University of Toronto Press.

Bhabha, Homi. 1996. "Unsatisfied: Notes on Vernacular Cosmopolitanism." In *Text and Nation,* ed. by Laura Garcia-Morena and Peter Pfeifer, 191-207. London: Camden House.

Biolsi, Thomas. 2005. "Imagined Geographies: Sovereignty, Indigenous Space, and American Indian Struggle." *American Ethnologist* 32 (2): 239-59.

Bohman, James. 2004. "Republican Cosmopolitanism." *Journal of Political Philosophy* 12 (3): 336-53.

Brighouse, Harry, and Gillian Brock. 2005. "Introduction." In *The Political Philosophy of Cosmopolitanism,* ed. by Harry Brighouse and Gillian Brock, 1-9. Cambridge: Cambridge University Press.

Broadhead, Lee Ann. 2001. "Canada as a Rogue State: Its Shameful Performance on Climate Change." *International Journal* 56 (3): 461-80.

Brysk, Alison. 2009. *Global Good Samaritans: Human Rights as Foreign Policy.* New York: Oxford University Press.

Cabrera, Luis. 2004. *Political Theory of Global Justice: A Cosmopolitan Case for the World State.* New York: Routledge.

Calhoun, Craig. 2002. "The Class Consciousness of Frequent Travelers: Toward a Critique of Actually Existing Cosmopolitanism." *South Atlantic Quarterly* 101 (4): 869-97.

Cheah, Pheng. 2006. "Cosmopolitanism." *Theory, Culture and Society* 23 (2): 486-96.

Chung, Ryoa. 2003. "The Cosmopolitan Scope of Republican Citizenship." *Critical Review of International Social and Political Philosophy* 6 (1): 135-54.

Dallmayr, Fred. 2003. "Cosmopolitanism." *Political Theory* 31 (3): 421-42.

Erskine, Toni. 2008. *Embedded Cosmopolitanism: Duties to Strangers and Enemies in a World of "Dislocated Communities."* Oxford: Oxford University Press.

Flannery, Tim. 2009. "Why Canada Failed on Kyoto and How to Make Amends." *The Star,* 22 November. http://pqasb.pqarchiver.com/thestar/search.html.

Franck, Thomas. 2006. "A Canadian Is ..." In *What Is a Canadian?* ed. by Irvin Studin, 37-40. Toronto: McClelland and Stewart.

Gregg, Benjamin. 2003. *Coping in Politics with Indeterminate Norms: A Theory of Enlightened Localism.* Albany: State University of New York Press.

–. 2010. Symposium on Enlightened Localism. *Comparative Sociology* 9 (5).

Gwyn, Richard. 1999. "Lloyd Axworthy Makes Pearsonianism Permanent." *Policy Options* (December): 13-16.

Habermas, Jürgen. 1998. *The Inclusion of the Other.* Boston: MIT Press.

Halldenius, Lena. 2010. "Building Blocks of a Republican Cosmopolitanism: The Modality of Being Free." *European Journal of Political Theory* 9 (1): 12-30.

Held, David. 2002. "Globalization, Corporate Practice and Cosmopolitan Social Standards." *Contemporary Political Theory* 1 (1): 59-78.

–. 2005. "Principles of Cosmopolitan Order." In *The Political Philosophy of Cosmopolitanism,* ed. by Harry Brighouse and Gillian Brock, 10-27. Cambridge: Cambridge University Press.

Henderson, James Youngblood. 2008. *Indigenous Diplomacy and the Rights of Indigenous Peoples: Achieving UN Recognition.* Saskatoon: Purich.

Keeble, Edna. 2007. "Canadian and Global Beneficence: Human Security Revisited." In *Engaged Philosophy: Essays in Honour of David Braybrooke,* ed. by Susan Sherwin and Peter Schotch, 102-25. Toronto: University of Toronto Press.

Laborde, Cécile. 2010. "Republicanism and Global Justice: A Sketch." *European Journal of Political Theory* 9 (1): 48-69.

Mackenzie, Hector. 2009. "At Home in North America? Canada in World Affairs." In *Beyond National Dreams: Essays in Canadian Citizenship and Nationalism,* ed. by Andrew Nurse and Raymond Blake, 319-43. Markham, ON: Fitzhenry and Whiteside.

Melamed, Jodi. 2006. "The Spirit of Neoliberalism: Racial Liberalism to Neoliberal Multiculturalism." *Social Text* 24 (4): 1-24.

Miller, David. 2002. "Cosmopolitanism: A Critique." *Critical Review of International Social and Political Philosophy* 5 (1): 80-85.

–. 2008. *National Responsibility and Global Justice.* Oxford: Oxford University Press.

Moellendorf, Darrel. 2005. "Person's Interests, State's Duties and Global Governance." In *The Political Philosophy of Cosmopolitanism,* ed. by Harry Brighouse and Gillian Brock, 148-63. Cambridge: Cambridge University Press.

Nagel, Thomas. 2005. "The Problem of Global Justice." *Philosophy and Public Affairs* 33 (2): 113-47.

Nielsen, Kai. 2005. "Cosmopolitanism." *South African Journal of Philosophy* 24 (4): 273-88.

Nussbaum, Martha. 1996. "Patriotism and Cosmopolitanism." In *For Love of Country,* ed. by Joshua Cohen, 3-20. Boston: Beacon Press.

O'Neill, Onora. 1996. *Towards Justice and Virtue: A Constructive Account of Practical Reasoning.* Cambridge: Cambridge University Press.

Ostling, Kristen. 2009. "Countdown to Copenhagen." *Finding Solutions* (Fall): 6-7 (Vancouver: David Suzuki Foundation). http://www.davidsuzuki.org/publications/downloads/2009/FS_Fall09_web.pdf.

Pettit, Philip. 2010. "A Republican Law of Peoples." *European Journal of Political Theory* 9 (1): 70-94.

Pollack, Sheldon, Homi Bhabha, Carol Breckenridge, and Dipesh Chakrabarty. 2002. "Cosmopolitanisms." In *Cosmopolitanism,* ed. by Carole Breckenridge et al., 1-14. Durham, NC: Duke University Press.

Razack, Sherene. 2004. *Dark Threats and White Knights: The Somalia Affair, Peacekeeping and the New Imperialism.* Toronto: University of Toronto Press.

Sierra Club. 2008. "Kyoto Report Card 2008: Executive Summary." http://www.sierraclub.ca/national/kyoto/executive-summary-2008.html.

Sullivan, William, and Will Kymlicka, eds. 2007. *The Globalization of Ethics: Religious and Secular Perspectives.* Cambridge: Cambridge University Press.

Tan, Kok-Chor. 2004. *Justice without Borders: Cosmopolitanism, Nationalism, and Patriotism.* Cambridge: Cambridge University Press.

–. 2006. "Priority for Compatriots: Commentary on Globalization and Justice." *Economics and Philosophy* 22: 115-23.

Thakkar, Sonali. 2008. "Under Western Eyes: *Into the Heart of Africa,* Colonial Ethnographic Display, and the Politics of Multiculturalism." In *The Politics of Reconciliation in Multicultural Societies,* ed. by Will Kymlicka and Bashir Bashir, 136-64. Oxford: Oxford University Press.

Thobani, Sunera. 2007. *Exalted Subjects: Studies in the Making of Race and Nation in Canada.* Toronto: University of Toronto Press.

Welsh, Jennifer. 2004. *At Home in the World.* Toronto: HarperCollins.

Werbner, Pnina. 2006. "Vernacular Cosmopolitanism." *Theory, Culture and Society* 23 (2-3): 496-98.

Ypi, Lea. 2008. "Statist Cosmopolitanism." *Journal of Political Philosophy* 16 (1): 48-71.

–. 2010. "Basic Rights and Cosmopolitan Justice from an Enlightened Localist Perspective." *Comparative Sociology* 9 (5): 594-610.

Part 1
The Theory of Rooted Cosmopolitanism

2
Cosmopolitanism and Patriotism
Kok-Chor Tan

Cosmopolitan Patriotism

The quintessentially Canadian aspiration of both "being a Canadian" and "being a good citizen of the world" encapsulates the ideal of rooted cosmopolitanism or cosmopolitan patriotism.[1] This ideal is crisply articulated in Jennifer Welsh's vision of the Canadian as a "Model Citizen for the 21st Century" (2004, 189), an internationalist committed to democracy, rule of law, and human rights but grounded in a "unique national identity." "The cosmopolitan patriot," Kwame Anthony Appiah (1996, 22) notes, "can entertain the possibility of a world in which everyone is a rooted cosmopolitan, attached to a home of his or her own, with its own cultural particularities, but taking pleasure from the presence of other, different, places that are home to other, different, people." More significantly from the perspective of social justice, the cosmopolitan patriot understands that her responsibilities of justice to her fellow human beings do not cease at the borders of her own country but extend also to strangers beyond (Appiah 2006, ch. 10; cf. Beitz 1979 [1999]; Pogge 2001).

Yet the notion of rooted cosmopolitanism or cosmopolitan patriotism can appear to skeptics to be inherently at odds with each other, for each conjunct of the ideal seems to express fundamentally contradictory moral commitments, forms of identification, political institutional commitments, ways of valuing, and competing spheres of responsibilities. But there are different ways of being a patriot or a cosmopolitan, and if being both a Canadian and a citizen of the world is to be a coherent aspiration, it is important to clarify and identify the specific forms of patriotism and cosmopolitanism that are presumed under that aspiration.

Forms of Cosmopolitanism

From the contemporary literature on cosmopolitanism, we can note the following different categories of cosmopolitanism.[2] It is perhaps helpful to present these categories by way of sets of distinctions. Adopting some common labels, first, there is "institutional cosmopolitanism" versus "moral cosmopolitanism." Second, there is cosmopolitanism as a claim about personal identity versus cosmopolitan as a claim about justice and attendant individual responsibility. Third, there is the distinction between "moderate" and "extreme" cosmopolitanism; finally, there is "weak" versus "strong" cosmopolitanism.

On the first distinction, between institutional and moral cosmopolitanism (Beitz 1999), institutional cosmopolitanism is a claim about forms of political institutions to support; specifically, it is a call for the creation of a world state. Moral cosmopolitanism, on the other hand, is an expression of a moral outlook or aspiration. It urges the ideal that all persons be given equal consideration and respect. To contrast it most vividly with institutional cosmopolitanism, moral cosmopolitanism does not endorse a specific institutional form (such as a world state) but requires that any institutions that we design be justified impartially to persons who would be affected (Beitz 1999, 287). To be sure, one might think that taking the cosmopolitan moral ideal seriously would require the creation of a world state, perhaps because any global institutional order short of a world state would fail to treat individuals as the ultimate units of equal moral worth irrespective of their particular nationality or citizenship. But this must be argued for, and most cosmopolitans in fact reject the ideal of a world state for the typically Kantian reasons, such as that such a world state would be unattainable or, if attainable, would take the form of a global despot. The key point to note is that the cosmopolitan aspiration is not necessarily a call to replace sovereign states with a world government, and to replace local patriotic ties with a global common patriotic ideal. It is most commonly understood as the call to adopt a particular moral point of view.

Regarding the second set of distinctions, cosmopolitanism as a claim about culture or identity denies that membership in a particular cultural community is constitutive of a person's social identity and is a condition of her individual autonomy. Cosmopolitanism about justice, however, is concerned with quite a different subject matter, namely, that of the scope of justice. Cosmopolitanism about justice holds that social boundaries (for example, that of nationality) do not impose "principled restrictions on the scope of an adequate conception of justice" (Scheffler 2001,

112). It rejects the view that principles of justice may be fundamentally limited by boundaries such as those defined by nationality or citizenship. In short, cosmopolitanism about culture is a thesis about the irrelevance of membership in particular cultures for personal identity formation and individual autonomy, whereas cosmopolitanism about justice is a thesis about the irrelevance of boundaries for the scope of justice considered at the fundamental level.

The third distinction is that between "extreme" cosmopolitanism and "moderate" cosmopolitanism (Scheffler 2001, 115-19). Extreme cosmopolitanism takes cosmopolitan morality to be the sole and unifying source of value in the sense that all other moral commitments must be justified by reference to cosmopolitan principles or goals. Thus, special concern, say, between compatriots is justified, in the extreme cosmopolitan account, on the ground that this special concern offers a useful division of moral labour for realizing cosmopolitan goals, or that this special concern is derived from certain fundamentally cosmopolitan commitments (for example, the principle of universal reciprocity or fair play). In either explanation, however – whether patriotic concern is taken to be derivative or instrumental – extreme cosmopolitanism denies that patriotic concern has any independent moral worth; that is, it holds that its value cannot be fully accounted for without appeal to cosmopolitan principles. Extreme cosmopolitanism thus holds a reductive view of special concern and obligations. Moderate cosmopolitanism, on the other hand, acknowledges the normative independence of certain special obligations, and does not insist that cosmopolitan values are the only fundamental values by reference to which all other values must be justified. Thus, moderate cosmopolitanism does not take a reductive view of special obligations, accepting that there may be moral reasons for certain kinds of special obligations that are not ultimately explainable in cosmopolitan terms. It recognizes that treating all special obligations to be worthy only because they promote, or are derived from, cosmopolitan principles, misrepresents and devalues some of the special ties and commitments that matter to people. Simply put, moderate cosmopolitanism affirms the plurality of values, or value pluralism, whereas extreme cosmopolitanism takes cosmopolitan principles to represent the dominant single unifying ideal.

Finally, there is the distinction between "weak" cosmopolitanism and "strong" cosmopolitanism. This category is less directly relevant to the present discussion (although I will come back to it at the end of the chapter), but it is worth noting now in order to better clarify the earlier distinction between moderate and extreme cosmopolitanism. Following David Miller (2000, 174), this distinction captures the contrast between a conception of global justice that "respects the conditions that are universally necessary for human beings to lead minimally adequate lives" on the one hand, and a conception of global justice that takes inequalities between persons across borders in themselves to be a concern of justice. Weak cosmopolitanism is still a form of cosmopolitanism because it recognizes the equal moral worth of individuals, but it is a weak form of cosmopolitanism because it considers respect for the equal moral standing of individuals as something to be demonstrated by ensuring that individuals are able to live minimally adequate lives (however this may be defined). Once this goal of ensuring minimal adequacy is achieved, any remaining inequality between persons is not a concern of cosmopolitan justice. Strong cosmopolitanism, in contrast, considers that equal concern for persons entails a commitment to some form of global distributive equality, and will aim to regulate inequalities between persons, even above the threshold of minimal adequacy, against some appropriate distributive principle.

The difference between moderate and extreme cosmopolitanism on the one hand, and that between weak and strong cosmopolitanism on the other, may appear synonymous given their labels, but it is worth recognizing these as separate categories in the way I have described. The latter refers to the content of the principles required by cosmopolitan justice and hence its strength (whether it is weak or strong); the former, on the other hand, is a claim about how these principles stand in relation to other, non-cosmopolitan commitments. That is, one concerns the normative requirements of cosmopolitanism, whereas the other concerns the moral conceptualization of these requirements. The difference is important: weak or strong cosmopolitanism speaks to the scope and content of our duties of global justice; moderate or extreme cosmopolitanism is an account of how we should understand the structure of values (whether value pluralism is true or false), especially with regard to our understanding of the moral bases of our special commitments in relation to more general cosmopolitan principles. Thus understood, a "weak moderate" cosmopolitan is not a redundancy; nor is a "strong moderate" cosmopolitan a contradiction.

With these variants of cosmopolitanism in mind, it seems to me that the idea of being a good citizen of the world as commonly articulated captures the following aspects of cosmopolitanism: it expresses the moral claim that all persons are of equal worth and that individual duties and responsibilities extend to all strangers. The call for world citizenship is not usually, if at all, understood literally as a demand for a world state. Neither does the notion of world citizenship as a moral ideal deny that persons can identify primarily with their specific national community, nor does it presume the extreme moral doctrine that the only values that matter are cosmopolitan ones. So understood, then, the idea of a good "world citizen" is not in conflict with many of the common features of patriotism, such as strong identification with a particular state, a strong sense of solidarity with fellow citizens, and the notion that there is something intrinsically valuable in patriotic relations with others. In sum, there are significant and important ways of understanding cosmopolitanism, primarily as a doctrine of justice based on a universalistic moral perspective; this understanding gives coherence to the ideal of cosmopolitan patriotism.

Identity and Responsibility

Thus, cosmopolitanism understood primarily as a statement about the scope of justice need not contradict the common features of patriotism, such as strong identification with a national political culture, special attachment to co-nationals, and the sense of belonging to a distinct political community. That is, by treating cosmopolitanism mainly as an account of justice, and patriotism as an account of identity, the tension between the two ideals is mitigated.

But this conceptual ground clearing does not go far enough toward reconciling patriotism and cosmopolitanism fully, for it should be pointed out that although identity and responsibility are distinct moral notions, they are tightly interdependent. One's sense, and even one's correct understanding, of one's responsibility toward others is normally contingent on how one stands in relation to others and hence how one identifies with them. Indeed, some communitarian theorists suggest that shared identity must precede shared responsibility, that a joint commitment to social justice in a society must presuppose a prior sense of mutuality and solidarity among persons (Sandel 1992; Walzer 1983). Individuals will undertake substantial responsibilities toward each other only if they see themselves as members of a relevant type of society to begin with. Hence, Michael Walzer (1983, 31) famously notes that membership in a group is the first thing that has to be distributed before anything else can be.

Thus, to the extent that the patriot identifies most strongly and most closely with her compatriots, her duties and responsibilities toward others are also possibly weaker. If this is right, cosmopolitan patriotism is a compromised cosmopolitanism. True enough, it can continue to encourage toleration of differences and appreciation of other ways of life from within a specific national cultural standpoint, but the strong identification with a particular group risks undermining what is most significant about cosmopolitanism as a claim about justice, namely, its thesis that one's responsibilities extend beyond the boundaries of one's national community.

Cosmopolitan justice is potentially without force, then, if it cannot offer a corresponding account of identity and affinity that exceeds that of patriotism. This may be called the problem of cosmopolitan *affinity* in cosmopolitan patriotism. Moreover, it might be further pointed out that strong patriotic identification means that persons will and should prioritize the needs of compatriots over those of strangers, quite independently of the relative urgency of these needs. This form of favouritism is, in fact, part of what it means to take patriotism seriously. Thus patriotism seems to run against the very goal of cosmopolitan justice – the partiality (toward compatriots) it encourages and even demands seems to conflict with the impartiality (with respect to nationality) central to the cosmopolitan ideal. We can call this problem for cosmopolitan patriotism the problem of *patriotic favouritism*. I will examine each of these challenges of patriotism in turn.

Problem of Affinity

It is a plausible thesis that patriotism promotes justice within a society by instilling in the minds of persons the image of their union (Anderson 1993) and a sense of responsibility for each other. Common patriotism moves persons to see themselves as being mutually indebted and obliged to the fellow members of their society who are, in the context of the modern state, necessarily strangers to them. In a sense, one can say that nationalism provides the solution to what we may refer to as Rousseau's problem, namely, that democratic membership cannot properly exceed the boundaries of intimate and personal relations. Nationalism offers a solution to this problem by substituting the intimacy and personal closeness that Rousseau took to be preconditions for democracy with the image in the minds of individuals – the idea that they belong to a significant historic community and share a common destiny. Even if they are not intimately connected with everyone, nationalism inculcates in persons the belief that they nonetheless share a common and rich kinship of sorts as defined by the nation. The issue for the rooted cosmopolitan is this: do the sentiments of patriotism, argued to be essential to democratic deliberation and social justice within the state, tell against the cosmopolitan aspiration of justice? The affinity problem assumes that the kinds of affiliation and ties necessary for responsibilities of justice are achievable at the national level but are apparently not obtainable beyond the boundaries of nations.

This affinity argument is mainly about the basis of the moral motivation among persons to engage in distributive commitments. Before addressing this argument, however, it is worth noting another aspect of the identity and affinity argument. What shared identity and affinity make possible is an agreement on the sorts of goods that ought to be distributed fairly according to some distributive ideal. Absent this affinity, according to this argument, there is not any shared understanding or consensus as to the things whose distribution a social order ought to regulate. As Walzer (1983, 31) has put it, "the idea of distributive justice presupposes a bounded world within which distribution takes place." It is only within such a bounded world that individuals can agree on the kinds of goods that they need to share and distribute, and some theorists have argued that such shared meanings and common understandings are not available outside the context of a national community (Walzer 1983; also Miller 1995, 75, 105-6; 2007). One might say that there is a global "equality of what?" problem, a problem that we cannot even begin to tackle (as we can in the domestic setting) due to the lack of a common global view on the goods that matter to persons.

This claim that there is not any shared understanding of the things that are valued by people across national or citizenship boundaries is an empirical claim, and the way to respond to it is to present actual counter-examples. In this regard, one might venture to say that the set of indices currently deployed by development economics for the purpose of interstate evaluation of quality of life does provide one counter-example. Factors such as average lifespan, literacy rates, access to health care, infant mortality levels, and so on appear to provide a common benchmark for evaluating and comparing quality of life across societies, and indeed the United Nations Development Programme (UNDP) has been relying on these indicators in their regular cross-societal assessments.[3] To use John Rawls's way of speaking, it does seem that whatever else individuals may want (and that may be determined by their specific national understandings and values), they want longer lifespans, better education, more income, better health. Like Rawls's primary goods, these developmental indices are neutral with respect to culture or individual conceptions of values, but are, it seems, universally and objectively valued by all persons as means to whatever ends they wish to pursue (Nussbaum 2000, ch. 1; Rawls 1971).[4]

Let me turn now to the motivation challenge. This argument holds that there is the need for a sense of common belonging, in particular a moral community (the "bounded world") shared by individuals, before we can reasonably (and possibly) expect their compliance with the demands of justice. As Michael Sandel (1992, 22) writes, a distributive principle "must presuppose some prior moral tie among those whose assets it would deploy and those whose efforts it would enlist in a common endeavor." But unlike nations that are "historic communities" embodying a common history, language, culture, and way of life, and hence embodying a viable moral community, the global society exhibits none of these shared common ideals, and hence, unlike the nation, cannot be a moral community (Walzer 1980, 1983). Thus, Sandel (1996, 339) concludes that "political associations more expansive than nations, and with fewer cultural traditions and historical memories to draw upon, may find the task of cultivating commonality more difficult still."

Cosmopolitan patriots can endorse the major premise of the argument that national affinity provides an important precondition for social justice, but there is no reason why they are forced to accept the minor premise that shared nationality is the only feasible grounding for the realization of social justice. As noted above, nationalist theorists have stressed the importance of shared nationality for the purpose of creating a community in the minds of persons for, among other things, the sake of motivating the ends of social justice. But this cultivation of common nationality for the end of justice has to be read as an expansionary rather than constricting moral aspiration and project with respect to justice. That is, the purpose of a common nationality, one could argue, is to move citizens to transcend the local and parochial bonds and ties of family, kin, and tribe, and to expand the scope of their moral universe to also encompass strangers (who are fellow citizens). Shared nationality and patriotism, therefore, motivate citizens to tend to the needs of compatriots who are otherwise strangers by making all of them fellow members of a shared "imagined community." This reason for cultivating a shared nationality operates as an equally compelling reason for "cultivating humanity," to borrow Martha Nussbaum's inspiring phrase (1997). Patriotism and nationalism, seen as a response to Rousseau's problem, as I have suggested, seek to enlarge our moral sentiments, not to constrict them.

Understood as an expansionary moral project, there is nothing in the liberal nationalist idea of affinity to suggest that our moral world has to end suddenly at our national borders. As Charles Jones (1999, 160) asks, why not capitalize on this "expansionary momentum" to expand the scope of our moral concern beyond co-nationals to include also foreigners? To the extent that liberal nationalism does succeed (and to a not inconsiderable extent) in enabling individuals to extend their moral spheres to include fellow strangers within a given state, there is no reason offhand to think that this expansionary project cannot be pursued beyond the borders of the state. To assume that this development of our moral world has to be arrested at our national borders seems grossly arbitrary (Nussbaum 1996, 14-15). To be sure, different forms of individual affinity must be identified and forged (other than those based on shared nationality) in the global context to support the possibility of a global moral community,[5] but one should not pre-empt such a possibility by assuming, offhand, that national boundaries are morally impermeable, that they fix once and for all the outermost limits of the scope of people's moral concern.

The argument from national affinity tells us that it is important that the liberal nation-state cultivate some sort of shared nationality among its citizens for the purpose of promoting social justice. But this alone does not mean that considerations of social justice are important only within a national community, nor does it tell us that such considerations have no prospect outside the national community. Indeed, the achievements of liberal nationalism in fostering shared sentiments and affinity could serve as the basis for extending people's commitments toward global justice (Kymlicka 2001a, 270). The search for some form of global affinity to ground global justice may be an ongoing quest, but this does not mean that such searches are in principle futile or irrelevant, as the affinity argument claims. If anything, patriotism and nationalism show us that it is possible for individuals to overcome the near and the familiar and to include strangers in our moral world. The trick is not to curtail this expansionary quest at the national level, "not to lose steam when [we] get to the borders of the nation" (Nussbaum 1996, 14). As Rawls (1999, 112-13) writes, it is "the task of the statesman to struggle against the potential lack of affinity among different peoples ... What encourages the statesman's work is that relations of affinity are not a fixed thing, but may continually grow stronger over time as peoples come to work together in cooperative institutions they have developed."[6]

Rather than being parochial, democratic education for patriotism can in fact go hand in hand with cosmopolitan aspirations. Amy Gutmann (1996, 70) introduces the ideal of "democratic humanism" that "supports an education that encourages citizens to deliberate about justice as part of their political culture – justice for their fellow citizens as well as for their fellow human beings, who are citizens of other societies" (see also Kymlicka 2001b, ch. 16). Truly democratic citizens would be interested in dealing justly and fairly with other nations, and this would involve at a minimum the requirement that their representatives deal with other representatives on fair and democratic terms in the global plane. Education for patriotic membership can go together with the inculcation of cosmopolitan responsibilities. A good democratic patriot is not so limited in her moral sights as to hold the ideal of democratic respect to be exclusive to compatriots and not applicable to non-nationals. Good patriots are able to transcend their limited national interests to take into account the interests of others.

Patriotic Favouritism

The second patriotic challenge for cosmopolitanism is that patriotism includes the ideal that individuals may, or even have the obligation to, privilege the interests of compatriots over those of strangers. If there is an obligation to improve the standard of living of fellow members, this demand of justice may run counter to the cosmopolitan demands with respect to outsiders. Various reasons may be offered for this special obligation to compatriots. One thesis is that membership in a shared political society is a mutually beneficial one, and, in order not to be a free rider, a member of this society has to take on special duties vis-à-vis others since she accepts the benefits of her common membership. Call this the *mutual-benefit argument* for patriotic favouritism. Another thesis may be called the *associative-ties argument* for patriotic favouritism. The associative-ties argument emphasizes simply the fact of a valued association (whether or not it is actually mutually beneficial) as the basis for special duties among fellow members. Unlike the mutual-benefit argument, which suggests a form of voluntarism, the associative-ties argument holds that persons can accrue special duties by virtue of their relationship to others, even when these relationships are non-voluntary in any meaningful sense of the term (and where there is no material mutual benefit). Paradigmatic examples of non-voluntary associative ties that generate special duties are those of kinship (such as child-parent relationships) and many forms of friendship. For some nationalist theorists, membership in a nation-state is, like kinship, a form of non-voluntary but valued affiliation, and part of what it means to be a member of a nation-state is to accept special obligations toward one's country and fellow members.

I will not examine the specific arguments of patriotic favouritism here. Rather, granting the truth of the claim that compatriots have special obligations toward fellow members (on either of the grounds described above), my purpose is to see how much stress this ideal of patriotism really places on cosmopolitanism as a claim about global justice.

The first response to this challenge has to be that the problem of justice versus partial or special concern is neither unique to the global versus national context nor fundamentally an insurmountable dilemma. This problem of justice and partial or personal pursuits occurs of course in the domestic context. And in the domestic context, we accept that the requirements of social justice place constraints on the kinds of special commitments and pursuits that individuals may have, be these self-interested, familial, or cultural pursuits. That is, personal projects or cultural claims that are at odds with the fundamental ideals of social justice within a society are not admissible. And how persons may pursue the already constrained ends that they have is also restricted by the requirements of justice. That is, strategies and means of meeting otherwise admissible personal ends that transgress the accepted principles of justice within society are not acceptable. In short, from the perspective of liberal social justice, persons can have any commitments and special concerns so long as these ends and commitments do not violate the fundaments of liberal social justice, and their pursuit of these ends must be within the parameters established by liberal principles. This priority of justice over personal ends holds independently of the bases of the value of these personal ties and projects. Justice need not make any judgment about the intrinsic value of genuinely personal ends and pursuits and their moral groundings, but the priority of justice sets limits on the kinds of ends that may be adopted and how these ends may be pursued.

To illustrate all of this: in a liberal society, persons can have life-encompassing commitments based on, say, their religious beliefs. Liberal justice does not question the grounding of these beliefs and their entailed commitments. What it does require is that these commitments, to be admissible, must not violate basic liberal standards, such as the ideal of tolerance. Thus, religious goals premised on the destruction of other religious doctrines are immediately ruled out. And the pursuit of otherwise admissible religious ends must not violate the requirements of justice. An organization must not utilize more than its fair share of social resources as defined by liberal principles in the pursuit of its objectives.

Hence, just as in domestic justice we can permit personal pursuits and commitments only within the terms of domestic social justice, so too at the global level patriotic favouritism is permissible only within the terms of global justice. Accordingly, the patriotic claim that persons have special obligations and concern toward fellow members, rather than putting pressure on the cosmopolitan ideal of justice, can be fully demarcated only against the terms of cosmopolitan justice. There is no tension between the competing special claims of patriotism and universal claims of cosmopolitanism because the claims of cosmopolitanism take precedence. They define the admissible bounds of patriotic concern and favouritism. Structurally, this thesis of the priority of cosmopolitan justice over patriotism is uncontroversial. For instance, we do not say that in the name of national security, any global concern for strangers may be overridden. Nor do we say that in the name of national economic advancement, we may disrespect the rights of strangers and choose to wage wars of conquest against them. On the contrary, respecting cosmopolitan ideals is how we can specify and determine the bounds of admissible patriotic favouritism.

Notice that this claim of the priority of cosmopolitanism does not make the extreme, and harder to defend, claim that the worth of patriotism and patriotic commitments is justified only with reference to cosmopolitan ends. It does not say, for example, that patriotic favouritism is permissible because this is how some overall cosmopolitan good such as global well-being can be maximized (as in Goodin 1988). Cosmopolitan justice can accept the associative-ties thesis that some relationships may be intrinsically valuable and non-reducible for individuals. What it holds is that, whatever the basis and justification of the value of special ties and commitments, the demands of global justice set limiting conditions for the content and pursuit of these ends.

It is also important to note that this priority of global justice does not lead to the implausible thesis that, in the case of emergencies, foreigners get preference whenever there are conflicting demands. Miller (2007, 45), for instances, sketches the scenario of a government having a limited amount of vaccine in the face of a global flu pandemic to illustrate the implausibility of the priority doctrine; he says that the priority of global justice holds that compatriots cannot have first claim on this scarce vaccine, yet this seems unacceptable. In response, however, one has to note that the priority-of-justice claim presumes that justice considerations are relevant. In the case of abject scarcity and stark tragic conflict that results from it, as in the scenario offered by Miller, justice is irrelevant and so the priority claim does not take effect. Social justice presupposes, among other things, *moderate scarcity* of the goods of distribution. In a desert island situation, social justice considerations do not kick in. This recalls Hume's remarks on the objective circumstances of justice. Put another way, when a given good is absolutely scarce and very urgently needed by many, we find ourselves in a special situation where it could be inappropriate to determine the distribution of this good via a distributive principle designed for conditions where the basic circumstances of justice obtain.[7] A distributive principle such as, say, Rawls's difference principle, although plausible as a distributive principle under conditions of moderate scarcity, seems out of place in desert island cases, where the problem before us is that of determining which lives to save and which to abandon through our resource allocation. Just as the difference principle does not tell a doctor what to do when there are three patients and only two organs, so the difference principle, even if adopted as the global distributive principle, says nothing about how to proceed in special situations where real moral trade-offs have to be made between compatriots and non-compatriots. It is entirely consistent with the priority thesis, following Miller's sound intuition, that a government gives preference to its citizens when it comes down to a question of saving the lives of its own or those of outsiders in a global emergency.

To clarify, the priority of global justice means simply, and plausibly, that we can do things for our own people only on the condition that we do right by others – that others are treated justly in the process. It does not mean that we can do things for our own people only when we have done all we can for others.[8]

In sum, patriotic affinity, although recognized by the patriot to be important for domestic social justice, need not be assumed to be the only possible motivational basis of social justice; and while patriots are permitted, if not also required, to show special concern for their fellow members, this does not preclude cosmopolitan responsibility. Rather, patriotic concern gets its form and limits by reference to the demands of cosmopolitan justice. The rooted cosmopolitan takes patriotism to be an important means of social justice at home, but at the same time realizes that the promotion of social justice at home cannot be at the expense of justice abroad.

Conclusion

So far I have left the content of cosmopolitan justice undefined. My argument has been primarily structural only – that there is no fundamental conflict between patriotism and cosmopolitanism, and so the ideal of rooted cosmopolitanism is not basically oxymoronic. The main point is that once cosmopolitanism is understood as a claim about responsibility and contrasted "with its real enemies – xenophobia, intolerance, injustice, chauvinism, militarism, colonialism, etc." (Kymlicka 2001b, 220), the philosophical tension within cosmopolitan patriotism will appear less stark. Whether cosmopolitanism as a claim about responsibility should ultimately take on the weak or the strong form is not something I can argue for here. I would suggest, however, that the strong cosmopolitan ideal is more consistent with the liberal democratic principles of justice that countries such as Canada openly affirm.[9] The content of cosmopolitanism derives from the principles of justice that persons openly accept, and I believe that the liberal egalitarianism that Canadians endorse commits them to a form of patriotic cosmopolitanism that accepts global egalitarianism. The priority of global justice means, then, that Canadian patriotism has to be tempered by this strong egalitarian commitment. Be that as it may, even "weak" cosmopolitan patriotism will go a long way toward meeting Welsh's ideal of the Canadian as a "model citizen" of the world.

Patriots have good reasons to be cosmopolitans. A Canadian patriot is one who takes pride in her Canadian national identity and accepts her responsibilities of social justice toward fellow Canadians, but who also understands that these patriotic commitments, in order to be legitimate, must be situated within a more just global order, lest her patriotism stand in violation of the principles of justice that she openly affirms. The ends of patriotism and cosmopolitanism come together, therefore, in this way: the genuine Canadian patriot has a very fundamental personal interest in pursuing cosmopolitan ends, for it is only against the backdrop of global justice that her patriotic concerns are fully legitimate from her own standpoint of justice.

Notes

1 See Chapter 1 of this book.
2 I repeat in this section, with some revisions, an earlier presentation (Tan 2004, 10-12).
3 To be fair, one has to note that Walzer and Miller are arguing that there is no shared agreement on the goods to be distributed along some egalitarian principle. They could well agree with the UNDP use of these indices to respond to the problem of poverty (as opposed to inequality as such). But it does seem to me that the UNDP indices can equally serve the purpose of Rawlsian primary goods; that, all else being equal, people will want more of these goods regardless of their ends and cultural and national backgrounds.
4 Indeed, if the national affinity argument allows for (as it seems to presuppose) agreement within multicultural countries over shared goods and meanings in

spite of the great diversity within such groups, its conclusion that the global society is culturally too diverse and deeply divided to constitute a common moral community needs to be reassessed. If citizens of multicultural states can come to an agreement concerning shared goods, it is not too much of a stretch to think that perhaps individuals of the world too can have some shared understandings about basic goods. At the very least, this shows that national affinity does not present an insurmountable obstacle for cosmopolitan justice.

5 There is reasonable hope that this can be done. See, for example, the substantial cross-regional and transnational resource redistribution that member nation-states of the European Union support.

6 Rawls (1999, 112-13), it should be pointed out, recognizes this need for affinity between peoples not to ground global distributive schemes but to ground modest duties of assistance among peoples. Yet his comments "that the narrow circle of mutually caring peoples in the world today may expand over time and must never be viewed as fixed" express the expansionary ideal I noted above, and there is no reason within Rawls's thesis why global mutual concern could not cement a strong commitment to global distributive justice. His arguments against global distributive justice have less to do with the absence of global affinity than with the beliefs that there are no appropriate institutional structures and that there is no common global conception of justice to ground this commitment. I discuss this in an earlier work (Tan 2004, ch. 4).

7 Would "contested" goods due to disagreements among societies as to what is valuable not reintroduce a similar problem? See Chapter 3 of this book. This is an important question, owed to an anonymous reader, that I will not be able to fully address here. As a start, however, my reference to the relative success of the UNDP indices is an attempt to suggest that such contestations can be minimized.

8 Suppose Canada can choose to either improve health care at home or support the provision of basic health care that is completely lacking in an impoverished country. How does "the priority of global justice" settle this question? The response will be that so long as there is a lack of confidence that Canada is legitimately entitled to all the resources it is deciding how to utilize in this case – for example, if there is some concern that potentially a portion of these resources has been unjustly acquired in the past or acquired because of prevailing failures of global justice – then a decision to devote these resources entirely to the improvement of health care at home will be tainted from the perspective of justice. Under this assumption, the practical response is that Canada may attend to health care needs at home if it also devotes some of these resources to meet global needs.

9 I try to argue for this elsewhere (Tan 2004, part II).

References

Anderson, Benedict. 1993. *Imagined Communities*. New York: Verso.

Appiah, Kwame Anthony. 1996. "Cosmopolitan Patriots." In *For Love of Country*, ed. by Joshua Cohen, 21-29. Boston: Beacon Press.

–. 2006. *Cosmopolitanism: Ethics in a World of Strangers*. New York: Norton.

Beitz, Charles. 1979 [1999 2nd ed]. *Political Theory and International Relations*. Princeton, NJ: Princeton University Press.

–. 1999. "International Liberalism and Distributive Justice: A Survey of Recent Thought." *World Politics* 51: 269-96.

Goodin, Robert. 1988. "What Is So Special about Our Fellow Countryman?" *Ethics* 98 (4): 663-86.

Gutmann, Amy. 1996. "Democratic Citizenship." In *For Love of Country,* ed. by Joshua Cohen, 66-71. Boston: Beacon Press.

Jones, Charles. 1999. "Patriotism, Morality, and Global Justice." In *Global Justice,* ed. by Ian Shapiro and Lea Brilmayer, 125-70. New York: New York University Press.

Kymlicka, Will. 2001a. "Territorial Boundaries: A Liberal Egalitarian Perspective." In *Boundaries and Justice,* ed. by David Miller and Sohail Hashmi, 249-75. Princeton, NJ: Princeton University Press.

–. 2001b. *Politics in the Vernacular.* Oxford: Oxford University Press.

Miller, David. 1995. *On Nationality.* Oxford: Oxford University Press.

–. 2000. *Citizenship and National Identity.* Cambridge: Polity Press.

–. 2007. *National Responsibility and Global Justice.* Oxford: Oxford University Press.

Nussbaum, Martha. 1996. "Patriotism and Cosmopolitanism." In *For Love of Country,* ed. by Joshua Cohen, 3-17. Boston: Beacon Press.

–. 1997. *Cultivating Humanity.* Cambridge, MA: Harvard University Press.

–. 2000. *Women and Human Development.* Cambridge: Cambridge University Press.

Pogge, Thomas. 2001. *World Poverty and Human Rights.* Cambridge: Polity Press.

Rawls, John. 1971. *A Theory of Justice.* Cambridge, MA: Harvard University Press.

–. 1999. *The Law of Peoples.* Cambridge, MA: Harvard University Press.

Sandel, Michael. 1992. "The Procedural Republic and the Unencumbered Self." In *Communitarianism and Individualism,* ed. by Shlomo Avineri and Avner de-Shalit, 12-28. Oxford: Oxford University Press.

–. 1996. *Democracy's Discontent.* Cambridge, MA: Harvard University Press.

Scheffler, Samuel. 2001. *Boundaries and Allegiances.* New York: Oxford University Press.

Tan, Kok-Chor. 2004. *Justice without Borders.* Cambridge: Cambridge University Press.

Walzer, Michael. 1980. "The Moral Standing of States." *Philosophy and Public Affairs* 9 (3): 209-29.

–. 1983. *Spheres of Justice.* New York: Basic Books.

Welsh, Jennifer. 2004. *At Home in the World.* Toronto: HarperCollins.

3
A Defence of Moderate Cosmopolitanism and/or Moderate Liberal Nationalism

Patti Tamara Lenard and Margaret Moore

This chapter explores the idea of rooted cosmopolitanism. Although both elements of this term have a number of different meanings or interpretations, the adjective "rooted" suggests that there are normative claims that attach to people's particularist commitments and attachments, especially attachments to particular places and communities that are spatially limited. Cosmopolitanism, at the minimum, suggests universalist commitments or duties.

It used to be said that cosmopolitanism and liberal nationalism were inherently incompatible, on the grounds that cosmopolitanism is ideologically opposed to attaching normative significance to groups, and nationalism is ideologically opposed to universal values. This is wrong on both counts, however. On the one hand, we will argue that liberal nationalists have always recognized certain universal values and defended nationalism precisely by reference to its universal values. On the other hand, cosmopolitan theorists have increasingly recognized that any cosmopolitanism that denies moral significance to group membership is a *reductio ad absurdum*. We therefore find an increasing number of "reconciliation" strategies, mainly among cosmopolitan theorists, that take three forms (discussed in this chapter): (1) an instrumental strategy; (2) one constraining strategy, where local duties are constrained by cosmopolitan commitments; and (3) another constraining strategy, where both particularist values and universal values are acknowledged, and a successful cosmopolitanism is said to find "room" for particularist attachments and the duties to which they give rise.[1] Although we suggest that all three attempts at reconciliation are problematic in different ways, we agree with the general idea of rooted cosmopolitanism, which suggests that particularist and general duties are not in fundamental tension. While this chapter suggests reasons for thinking that the precise form that this relationship takes among current cosmopolitan thinkers is problematic, it agrees that the only plausible kind of cosmopolitanism is one that accepts the justice of people's more particularist commitments and attachments, including their attachment to particular (bits of) land. This chapter suggests by way of example, however, that there are cases where the tension between cosmopolitanism and non-cosmopolitanism cannot be bridged, or where the priority relations are unclear. Seth Lazar (2009) argues that this is true of killing in war; we argue here that it may also be true of group attachment to particular lands. It may be unsatisfactory to conclude by referring to the need for contextual political and moral judgment, but we think that this is better than a more determinate, but false, account of the relations between the cosmopolitan and nationalist principles.

Universalism and Non-Cosmopolitanism

As the foregoing suggests, philosophical non-cosmopolitans have always incorporated – indeed, relied on – universal moral components in their theory,[2] for example, in terms of the endorsement of basic rights[3] or a principle of non-exploitation in their account of transactional justice.[4] Indeed, liberal nationalism, which is a type of non-cosmopolitan theory, is premised on an equality principle, in particular the idea of equal respect for different national groups – that is, self-determination for all similarly situated national groups – and this has important consequences for global redistributive justice between national groups. The requirement of equal nations implies, at minimum, that there should be some sort of threshold level of goods, resources, and powers for all minimally legitimate political communities so that they can enjoy self-determination. This is reflected in the theories of contemporary liberal nationalists. For example, David Miller, who is often derided for his anti-cosmopolitanism, argues that we should aim for a global environment in which all national communities have adequate opportunity to be self-determining. In his view, in order to be self-determining, nations must (1) have access to secure territory (2) not be subject to coercive conditions imposed by others, and (3) be able to command the material resources and other capacities to exercise real choices, both domestically and globally.[5] Miller's central concern here is the exploitability of inadequately self-determining nations, and the concern to protect nations from exploitation is unambiguously universal, even if it is not as fully egalitarian as some might like.

Perhaps the most common *criticism* of liberal nationalism is that it is too quick to approve of the cultural dimensions that are particularly associated with virulent forms of nationalism. For those who launch this criticism, the anxiety has to do with the marginalization and oppression of those who will not be able to, or will not desire to, live up to the supposed cultural ideal espoused by a given nation, and who will therefore be unjustly excluded or, even worse, persecuted. Yet even nineteenth-century nationalists, who spoke of the importance of defending the cultural life of the national community, typically thought that this defence was compatible with a range of universalist ideals. For example, although Giuseppe Mazzini appealed to the idea of Italianness, his account reveals an interpretation of Italian nationhood as porous, and therefore as capable of including people from a variety of religious, linguistic, ethnic, and cultural backgrounds. Similarly, most liberal nationalists today are anxious to account for the cultural dimension of the nationalist project in relatively thin terms: for example, the "societal culture" that Will Kymlicka suggests ought to underpin nation-states is culturally thin, and operates mainly to provide the basic opportunity sets within which individuals can exercise autonomy. Moreover, the objection – that liberal nationalists are too committed to cultural uniformity or cultural homogeneity – often blinds their critics to the strong components of universalism that define all defensible forms of nationalism.

In some cases, liberal nationalists defend the nation primarily for its contribution to individual well-being; in this view, nations are valuable because individuals' self-worth and self-respect are tied up with their membership in a given group, and thus the value of the national community rests ultimately on its contribution to the well-being or interests of individual people (for whom national relationships are themselves valuable) (Raz and Margalit 1990, 439-62). In others, liberal nationalists not only emphasize the connection between nationalism and individual well-being but also argue that the autonomy to which liberals are committed is intimately tied to the nation (see, for example, Kymlicka 1996; Tamir 1993). In particular, individuals require a stable and vital national culture, which generates an environment from which individuals can make genuinely autonomous choices. The importance of individual self-determination is emphasized equally by nationalists who defend the nation for its contribution to democratic self-determination; for those who defend the nation in democratic terms, the nation is essential for creating an environment in which individuals can participate meaningfully in democratic politics (see Tamir 1993).

Each of these defences of the nation is founded on a basic justificatory individualism, that is, a view that the value of the national community rests ultimately on its value to, or contribution to, the interests of individual people, who are conceived of as having important group relations. This of course is less true of the nineteenth-century nationalists, who sometimes adopted a strong (metaphysically problematic) language of organic communities, but it is certainly true of contemporary liberal nationalists, such as Kymlicka, Margalit and Raz, and Miller. This means that, for liberal nationalists, indeed for most non-cosmopolitans, there is not necessarily an antagonism between universalist values and nationalism, since some forms of nationalism are compatible with value-individualism and the universal values specified within it. In other words, rather than reject universalism, as cosmopolitans sometimes suggest, liberal nationalists have tended to adopt a split-level or pluralist theory, in which certain relatively demanding principles of justice and equality apply at the domestic level, while other, less demanding principles, such as securing a basic threshold for a "decent life" or ensuring that basic rights are respected, apply at the global level (Miller 2009, 23-37). Thus, while their arguments do not attempt a full-fledged reconciliation between liberal nationalist and cosmopolitan views, and while they do demarcate distinctive principles of justice for domestic and global spheres, they have never required or advocated the wholesale rejection of universalist principles. On the contrary, liberal nationalism is defended for its commitment to, and contribution toward realizing, most of the values to which cosmopolitans are committed.

Currently, the battle between cosmopolitanism and liberal nationalism is being fought not in the language of principle per se but rather in the language of *duties*, particularly with respect to the relative importance of general duties, which are those that everyone owes to everyone else by virtue of shared humanity alone, and special duties or responsibilities, which people owe to specific others by virtue of the relationships they share (Scheffler 2003). Cosmopolitan critics worry that liberal nationalists' recognition of the value of special duties, duties that derive from relationships among co-nationals, trumps the more general duties we owe to all people. This apparent privileging of insiders would not be objectionable, or at least it would not be as objectionable as it is now, if we lived in a more egalitarian world. Since we do not live in an egalitarian world, however, the ways in which liberal nationalists permit, and even advocate, privileging the needs, particularly the non-basic needs, of insiders, at the expense of meeting the basic needs of the global poor, are sufficient to undermine the moral plausibility of the liberal nationalist project.

This is not the whole story, however, as the next section suggests. Of late, cosmopolitans have recognized the essential role that special relationships play in individual lives, and in particular the moral importance of the duties to which these relationships give rise. As a result, they have increasingly attempted to find room, within cosmopolitanism, in which duties arising from special relationships can legitimately operate. Let us consider, next, three attempts to find room within cosmopolitan political theory for the special relationships to which liberal nationalists are committed, and for the duties to which these relationships give rise.

The Instrumental Strategy

One strategy employed by cosmopolitans suggests that we can ascribe an instrumental value to national communities. This strategy acknowledges the motivational efficacy of special relationships, and therefore lends its support to national communities insofar as they enable the meeting of cosmopolitan objections in an efficient way. To the extent that we have special duties to support co-nationals, they therefore derive from the more general duties we have toward mankind.

Robert Goodin's account is a case in point. In his discussion of the relationship between patriotism (non-cosmopolitanism) and cosmopolitanism, Goodin suggests that the two are reconcilable. Although he notes that "how this particularism of special duties fits with the universality and impartiality of the general moral law is problematical," and that there are many different theories about the relationship between the two, Goodin (2008, 269) suggests that special duties should ultimately be understood to derive from, or largely derive from, general duties. In this view, non-cosmopolitan principles are acceptable as long as they are instrumental to the achievement of global justice. Special relationships, he says, can serve to *magnify* our pre-existing duties, where having a special relationship assigns responsibility for discharging a duty to a particular person or particular institution, and therefore transforms imperfect duties into perfect duties; and they can serve to *multiply* our duties, by creating duties that we did not have before, as in the case of a contract that creates a duty where no general duty existed before. In many cases, it will not be clear who in particular should take it on themselves to discharge general duties; where this is left open, the existence of special relationships, and the duties to which these give rise, can specify who is responsible for discharging general duties with respect to specific others.

Goodin (2008, 272) applies this analysis of the relationship between particular and general duties to the case of (national) states:

> The duties that states (or, more precisely, their officials) have vis-à-vis their own citizens are not in any deep sense special. At root, they are merely the general duties that everyone has toward everyone else worldwide. National boundaries simply visit upon those particular state agents special responsibility for discharging those general obligations vis-à-vis those individuals who happen to be their own citizens.

In this view, dividing up our duties along the lines of our national affiliations is an efficient way to coordinate the fulfillment of our universal duties, that is, our duties to individuals at large. Local duties should be seen as mere instruments for discharging cosmopolitan duties, and although they may have moral weight of some rather limited kind, they do not have any *independent* moral weight.

The problem with this account is that its instrumental character appears to accommodate these duties by morally impoverishing them.[6] It treats the duties that arise in political associations, and, by extension, any kind of association, as merely instrumental to the achievement of the requirements of an impartial principle, not as themselves arising from morally valuable relationships; in so doing, the account appears to misdescribe the source of these duties. My duties to my mother, or to my friends, or to the state appear to be based on something about the nature of the relationship, on what it means to be one's daughter, or one's friend, or a co-citizen. As Samuel Scheffler suggests, some of our duties appear to stem from the relationships in which we find ourselves.[7] Thus, the instrumental account cannot serve as a genuine reconciliation, because although it recognizes the contribution that nation-states can make toward protecting and promoting cosmopolitan values, it ultimately fails to acknowledge the source of the value attributed to national associations and special relationships more generally. At the heart of nationalist theorizing is a deep commitment to the nation as a valuable association, in and of itself; yet, in the instrumental view, nationalism is tolerated only insofar as it is best placed to achieve cosmopolitan objectives. The attempt at reconciliation fails here because although it takes seriously individuals' perceptions, it does not take seriously the independent moral worth of nation-states.

One Constraining Strategy: Nationalism Constrained by Egalitarian Commitments

What we term the "constraining strategy" is at first glance a more plausible attempt at reconciling non-cosmopolitanism and cosmopolitanism, since those who adopt this strategy take seriously the significance of special relationships and the obligations these appear to entail for those involved in them. Constraining strategists are perfectly willing to acknowledge the importance of special duties, so long as they do not inhibit the meeting of cosmopolitanism goals. So, for example, Gillian Brock (2009, 282) writes that while she is "critical of the view that there are good arguments as to why we have stronger obligations to compatriots than non-compatriots," she acknowledges that any realistic account of cosmopolitanism must "accommodate" the fact that "in the real world" people believe they have duty-generating relationships to co-nationals. This accommodation takes the form, first, of delimiting the cosmopolitan obligations that must be met, and, second, of arguing that so long as these obligations are met, individuals can legitimately prioritize the needs of insiders. Brock (2009, 282) explains that "in the end the question is one about what limits should be placed on the attachments."

While Brock (2009, 290) suggests that our special duties are constrained simply by the requirement that we "contribute our fair share to the collective project of supporting just institutions," Kok-Chor Tan adopts a more ambitious account in his recent work. He suggests, first, that it would be foolish for cosmopolitans to argue that partiality toward co-nationals is not philosophically warranted, because it reduces the cosmopolitan position to a kind of *reductio ad absurdum*. A view that insists on undifferentiated global equality, no matter how we are related to others, ignores the moral relevance of people's genuine felt associations and attachments. Tan thus defends a form of reconciliation according to which particularist attachments and obligations are constrained by the obligations and requirements of universal justice, conceived of as a form of global luck egalitarianism.

Before we assess Tan's view further, let us distinguish between an ordinary-language view of what a constraining strategy might involve, and Tan's particular version of the strategy, which views luck-egalitarian global justice as a background condition for the achievement of justice and thus as defining the limits of special relationships and patriotic attachments. One interpretation of a "constraining strategy" simply appeals to a well-known positive/negative distinction among duties. This is the view that negative duties – duties not to harm others – are more stringent than positive duties – duties to help others. While we might have quite different intuitions about our duty to aid others, and there is much more disagreement on the content of our positive duties, many people can accept negative duties, including, for example, the duty not to kill, torture, or deliberately maim others. There are, of course, important questions about what counts as "harm," but there is general agreement on the basic idea that this is a fundamental moral requirement. For those who accept some version of the positive/negative distinction, the idea that our commitments to others, to our families, to co-nationals, and others should be constrained by the requirement that we do not harm others is not especially problematic. In David Miller's compelling example, we may love our child and should work toward his or her flourishing, but this does not entitle us to take a kidney from some other child if our child needs it. In this way, our positive duties are limited, or constrained, by the requirements of a no-harm principle.

This is not the kind of constraining strategy argued for by Tan, and we mention the above only to distinguish that account from his much more demanding account, according to which the rigorous positive and negative duties that derive from a commitment to global luck egalitarianism considerably constrain our more particularist duties. For Tan (2004, 54), it is essential to emphasize the fundamental individualism of justice theorizing – and especially that individuals are the basic units of moral concern – as a result of which individuals have a right to equal consideration that entails, among other things, a direct concern with distributive equality among persons. By "distributive equality among persons," he means "removing arbitrary and unchosen sources of disadvantage" and ensuring that people are situated equally, at least with respect to the background conditions of the choices that they make. Interestingly, especially since Tan aims to "reconcile" cosmopolitanism with group-based attachments such as nationalism and patriotism – and indeed, as we noted above, recognizes that it would be implausible to endorse an undifferentiated global equality and ignore people's felt attachments, aims, and projects – his conception of global justice is based on a luck-egalitarian reading of John Rawls, according to which all elements of contingency or moral arbitrariness are eliminated. He then argues that this luck-egalitarian ideal should define the background global rules. We will suggest that this does not augur well for his supposed "reconciliation" of cosmopolitanism with nationalism, patriotism, or other group-based attachments.

In some ways, Tan is appealing to one of our core intuitions, which is at the heart of the (cosmopolitan) luck-egalitarian ideal, namely, that it is unfair that some people are simply born into poorer societies than others and, through no fault of their own, fare worse than others. As Richard Arneson (2008, 80) has argued in defence of the luck-egalitarian distributive ideal: "The concern of distributive justice is to compensate individuals for misfortune. Some people are blessed with good luck, some are cursed with bad luck, and it is the responsibility of society – all of us regarded collectively – to alter the distribution of goods and evils that arise from the jumble of lotteries that constitutes human life as we know it." It is but a short step from a concern with the degree to which our lives are affected by good and bad luck to seeing the very society that one is born into as a matter of luck. As Thomas Nagel (2005, 126) has recognized, "the accident of being born in a poor rather than a rich country is as arbitrary a determinant of one's fate as the accident of being born into a poor rather than a rich family in the same country." Not surprisingly, luck egalitarian arguments are appealed to in many prominent versions of cosmopolitanism. For example, in addition to his emphasis on the extent of global interaction, and the concomitant argument that the globe constitutes a single "basic structure," Pogge (1989, 247) offers as a reason for extending Rawls's principles of justice globally that "nationality is just one further deep contingency (like genetic endowment, race, gender and social class) ... [It represents] one more potential basis of institutional inequalities that are inescapable and present from birth."

Running through all these cosmopolitan positions is the view that persons deserve equal treatment, as a result of which we cannot justifiably make arbitrary distinctions between individuals in allocating our moral responsibilities. This commitment is cosmopolitan in nature because it assumes that all persons *qua* persons have equal moral worth. What is striking about this view – from the point of view of this chapter – is that it is frequently interpreted as being hostile to nationalism, because luck-egalitarian cosmopolitanism typically views membership in one's nation and/or political community as among one's arbitrary features.

Tan draws on this luck-egalitarian account of cosmopolitan justice, according to which all elements of contingency or moral arbitrariness, including one's membership in a nation-state, are dismissed as without moral relevance. Patriotic attachments or political communities may well be valuable, but this does not affect the validity of the background framework, of luck-egalitarian global justice, which operates in a priority relationship to one's more particularist obligations. To see that this is indeed at the core of his argument, consider Tan's claim[8] that

> the "liberal" part of the liberal nationalist equation limits the ways in
> which national self-determination may be expressed. More precisely, if
> we begin from an egalitarian conception of liberalism and want to marry

that understanding of liberalism to nationalism, then the liberal nationalism we get has to be an *egalitarian* liberal nationalism. And as
egalitarian liberalism begins from the basic idea that there are no principled differences between individuals on the basis of contingencies or
what Rawls has called factors that are "arbitrary from a moral point of
view" (Rawls 1971, 15) so too must egalitarian liberal nationalism dis-
count morally arbitrary facts about persons when it comes to determining their just global entitlements. And one arbitrary factor here would
be people's national membership. (Tan 2004, 101)

Note that the "reconciliation" is here revealed as the view that national
partiality is only legitimate insofar as it is constrained by a fairly demanding luck-egalitarian conception of global justice. Tan recognizes the
problem with his "reconciliation" to some extent, at least noting that
it must be jarring to call "national membership" an "arbitrary feature."
He writes: "It may seem odd that liberal nationalists, if they are egalitarian liberals, must consider nationality a morally irrelevant factor when
determining the terms of global distributive justice. What does it mean
to be a nationalist in this case? But this oddity dissipates once we are
clear about the circumscribed place of nationality in liberal nationalist
theories" (Tan 2004, 101). In this passage, Tan's global luck egalitarianism commits him to describing nationality as arbitrary. Yet, although it
is true that particular political communities to which we are attached
are often descriptively arbitrary, in the sense that we can easily imagine
being born in one political community rather than another, it does not
follow that they are morally arbitrary. In other words, what is question-
able here is whether nationalists (even of the liberal variety), or indeed
any person who is trying to find some (ethical) room for these more
particularist relationships and attachments, would consider nationality
to be arbitrary from the moral point of view. Indeed, the point that
liberal nationalists have made is that national groups are *neither* morally
arbitrary nor morally irrelevant: they provide a framework in which
autonomy is exercised; they protect people's cultural options, both by
protecting the options themselves and by giving meaning to those options; and they tie people together into institutional relationships that
change their duties and relations with one another.

Ultimately, the problem with Tan's constraining strategy is that it gives
conceptual priority to a luck-egalitarian version of justice, which views
the attachments and communities that people have as morally arbitrary
or morally irrelevant *in defining the requirements of justice.* It does not
attempt to specify the duties that emanate from these relationships, ties,

or communities and then proceed to theorize global justice in accordance with them. It argues that political communities must be constrained, or, in his words (quoted above), "circumscribed," by this demanding luck-egalitarian conception, according to which the political communities are themselves viewed as morally arbitrary. The fact that Tan argues that nationalism has to be constrained, or made consistent with luck egalitarianism (rather than the other way round) indicates a clear priority relationship. The morally arbitrary status of one's nation or political community justifies a priority relationship between cosmopolitan and non-cosmopolitan principles such that cosmopolitan principles are more fundamental. And, although it may be true that nationalism or patriotism and luck egalitarianism are in tension, this could as well be resolved against Tan's version of cosmopolitanism as against nationalism.

In the end, Tan's strategy seems fairly close to Goodin's instrumental strategy, which Tan himself rejects, and is thus unstable for the same reasons. While Tan's view does appear to allow for forms of particularist attachments that are not instrumental to global justice, this acknowledgment is granted only as long as they do not conflict with it. It is more permissive than Goodin's account, but it certainly does not give equal recognition to the obligations arising from both general and special duties, and it is not clear that general duties are always in this kind of priority relationship with duties to people with whom we are in special relationships, as we will suggest in the section "Challenges for Reconciliation, or Challenges for Rooted Cosmopolitanism" below.

Another Constraining Strategy: Finding Room for Particularism/Patriotism, Constrained by "Deontic" Duties

A third strategy deployed by cosmopolitans entails acknowledging the value of special relationships from the outset. This view does not simply acknowledge the value of relationships to a flourishing human life but also attaches inherent value to these relationships. For these cosmopolitans, the need for human relationships is a basic human need, just like food, shelter, and protection from violence; in other words, human relationships do not occupy a subordinate role in the hierarchy of needs. As a result, a commitment to moral egalitarianism entails a commitment to special relationships. This strategy shares with the first constraining strategy (according to which, as above, cosmopolitanism limits the scope of special relationships) the notion that the extent to which these relationships may be prioritized is constrained by a commitment to egalitarianism; that is, we find a commitment to special relationships from within cosmopolitanism, just as we find the limits that must be placed on these relationships from within cosmopolitanism. Arash Abizadeh and Pablo Gilabert (2008, 357) write: "If the value of relationships is constitutive of, and so conditional on, the value of human well-being, then from a moral point of view the justification of relationships such as friendship must also be compatible with respect for the well-being of each human being, and not just those party to the relationship." A consequence of this view is that, as cosmopolitans, we are committed to doing what we can do in order to protect *everyone's* capacity to access valuable human relationships.

Abizadeh and Gilabert argue that it is a mistake to assert a "genuine tension"[9] between the cosmopolitan commitment to equal moral worth and the duties that are said to derive from special relationships.[10] Rather, a commitment to equal moral worth, however defined, necessarily requires recognizing the valuable contribution made by relationships to an individual's well-being.[11] Special relationships are therefore just one among the many "basic goods" that are essential to a flourishing human life (Abizadeh and Gilabert 2008, 354). To the extent that a tension can be said to exist, it is between the general and special duties to which an individual is committed; any flourishing life is defined by both of these sets of duties. The basic strategy here is to find room, within a sophisticated cosmopolitanism, for special ties and the duties to which they give rise, and thereby address the concern that a cosmopolitanism that fails to recognize these ties will be implausible and will, additionally, fail to track the moral complexity of our lives. While we are sympathetic to this "room-finding" account, and think that it is right to acknowledge the central role of both general and special duties in a flourishing life, the precise version that Abizadeh and Gilabert articulate is, we believe, somewhat problematic.

The central problem with their view is that they ultimately say that special duties are duty creating only when they are valuable, that *special duties have force only when they are constrained by general duties* (Abizadeh and Gilabert 2008, 365). As with Tan's account (2004), conflicts are to be resolved in favour of general duties. Without elaborating a full critique of this account, suffice it to say here that it is not at all clear that general duties override special duties when they conflict; as Samuel Scheffler has observed, it seems, in fact, that our general duties are frequently in tension with duties that arise from the value of certain kinds of relationships, in ways that cannot be resolved by simply asserting an automatic priority for general duties, which is how Abizadeh and Gilabert proceed.[12] Instead of describing special duties as having moral value if they derive from valuable relationships (as a result discounting, as we also would do, the duties that may appear to arise from objectionable relationships), Abizadeh and Gilabert describe an associative duty as a moral duty only if it is *constrained* by deontic values. They write (2008, 358): "One must have *moral* reason to value the relationship. And one has moral reason to value a relationship only if it does not violate certain moral constraints." The value of the relationship does not derive simply from its being valuable considered independently; its value depends additionally, and for Abizadeh and Gilabert more importantly, on its consistency with a set of (unspecified) deontic constraints. As a result, special duties are moral if and only if they meet a set of "deontic constraints"; thus, for them as for Tan, general duties always have priority over special duties.

Moreover, beyond the observation that they are more demanding than duties of non-harm, what exactly these deontic constraints consist of remains unspecified – in part, they have no choice but to leave these unspecified, since they fail to outline the precise content of the egalitarianism to which they are committed. They write: "Special responsibilities cannot arise from relationships that involve undermining or neglecting *others'* fair access to the basic goods that are constitutive of *their* well-being" (Abizadeh and Gilabert 2008, 358). In this account, special duties are necessarily subject to deontic constraints, and Abizadeh and Gilabert are thus endorsing what we have described elsewhere as a Blanket Priority Thesis (BPT) (Lenard and Moore 2009, 403). According to the BPT, duties that derive from a commitment to equal moral worth, which Abizadeh and Gilabert (2008) term "general duties" or "deontic duties," have blanket priority over the duties that derive from special relationships. We have thus moved far from their starting point, which suggested an equal consideration of special and general duties, since both derive from a commitment to equal moral worth, to the view that general duties are to be prioritized over special duties when conflict emerges. Abizadeh and Gilabert may have recognized the value of special relationships, and the duties to which they give rise, but the value they are accorded is subject to constraints in such a way that their *independent value* is not recognized. In the end, they have "erased" the supposed tension between special duties and general duties by arguing for the necessary priority of general duties.

To see the problem here, suppose we imagine that my daughter is gifted and that, to realize her talents and abilities and enable her to flourish, she must be provided with an expensive enrichment education. Suppose we also think that our general duties to others are fairly rigorous, that is, that they include not only negative duties of non-harm but also demanding positive duties, such as ensuring equal access to society's basic goods, including education, health care, and so on. If this is the case, it may well be that my limited resources are such that I cannot discharge both sets of duties: I cannot meet my positive duties while providing my daughter with the kind of education that would allow her to flourish. In this case, there *is* a conflict between the duties I owe to my daughter and my general duties to ensure that others have "fair access to the basic goods that are constitutive of *their* well-being" (Abizadeh and Gilabert 2008, 358). If it is at least plausible that there is a dilemma here – that is, that the latter does not automatically constrain the former – then it is also not clear that in this case general duties (to all) should be prioritized over special duties (to a daughter). It is not enough to state a Blanket Priority Thesis, since it fails to capture, and resolve, the most complex dilemmas that inevitably arise over the course of one's life.

The difference between our position and that of Abizadeh and Gilabert is subtle, but it will be significant in guiding us in our attempts to resolve tensions between special and general duties in the right way. We agree with them that our special duties must be grounded in relationships of value, but it does not follow from this that to have moral value, they must be *constrained by* general duties. The question of the proper relationship between special duties and general duties is of course a deeply contested one, but it cannot be resolved by describing the priority of general duties over special duties as a conceptual truth. It is simply not clear that *all* special duties – to family or friends and even to co-nationals – must be constrained by any and *all* general duties, even if they must be grounded in moral value. Nevertheless, their general insight – that an adequate cosmopolitanism is one that must find room for special relationships and attachments and the obligations to which these relationships give rise – is one that we accept and is at the core of the general idea of the rooted cosmopolitanism that we describe next.

Challenges for Reconciliation, or Challenges for Rooted Cosmopolitanism

Thus far we have tried to articulate what is probably an intuitively obvious position, that cosmopolitanism and special duties are not in fact antithetical but are deeply connected; that any plausible theory must articulate both the importance of our connections to others and our fundamental moral equality; and that the most interesting questions surround precisely how to strike a balance between the two. We have also suggested that both cosmopolitans and non-cosmopolitans have actually been moving toward this middle position – toward acknowledging that everyone has equal moral worth *and* that relationships and commitments are very important to us and often give meaning to our lives, and therefore that a flourishing life is composed of both general duties (to everyone) as well as special duties (some of which arise from our relationships).

In this section, we will suggest that reconciling the duties that derive from special relationships, such as those we have to co-nationals, with those that derive from the demands of global justice will face some particularly thorny issues, one of these being the fact that people are strongly attached to particular *places*. We use this particular issue in part to highlight the point above, not to claim that it is in some way unique. Consider the proposal that the profits from the oil presently being extracted in the Niger Delta be redistributed to Africa's poor, rather than (as it presently is) serving to enrich the Nigerian elite. The proposal is an attempt to address the serious problems of poverty and deprivation faced by many of Africa's poorest citizens. This proposal – which reflects a commitment to equal moral worth, and the general duties to which this commitment gives rise – comes into unfortunate conflict with the claims made by the vulnerable indigenous communities living in the Niger Delta region. These claims – to self-government and to the control of resources that this self-government would entail – are based in part on their history and attachment and relationship to each other and to place, and to their culture, all of which will be threatened (further) by this proposal.[13] This sort of case can be viewed as a conflict between general duties and particular duties, that is, between commitments arising from our equal moral worth, and the consequent legitimate claims of redistributive justice on the part of poor Africans that stem from this commitment, and the particular attachments and history and way of life of the indigenous people, who also make a claim (of justice) to that land under which oil has been discovered.

In many ways, the luck-egalitarian cosmopolitan literature response to this kind of debate does not guide us well. Territorial rights (rights over land) are often discussed as if they are an affront to justice and to the general duties that a commitment to justice demands, at least in the sense that the earth is obviously differentially endowed. This differential distribution of resources seems like an arbitrary advantage conferred on some people (who happen to live on rich and fertile land) compared with others who live in landlocked deserts. For example, in developing luck-egalitarian cosmopolitan arguments, many theorists refer to the arbitrary distribution of natural resources among countries. Charles Beitz argues that the distribution of natural resources among countries is analogous to, but even more powerful than, arguments premised on the arbitrary distribution of talents among people. He writes that "the fact that someone happens to be located advantageously with respect to natural resources does not provide a reason why he or she should be entitled to exclude others from the benefits that might be derived from them" (Beitz 1999, 138). The parties to the international original position, from which principles of international justice are derived, would think that the resources (or the benefits derived from them) "should be subject to a resource redistribution principle" (Beitz 1999, 138) and would therefore argue, on luck-egalitarian grounds, for redistribution of (benefits) to natural resources. A similar argument is made by Thomas Pogge, who treats unequal access and control over natural resources as a straightforward unfairness. One of the arguments for his proposed global resource dividend is predicated on the idea that citizens of many different countries all over the world should benefit from the resources in a particular country. Indeed, Pogge (2008, 439) writes: "This payment they [the resource rich] must make [the global resource dividend] is called a dividend because it is based on the idea that the global poor own an inalienable stake in all limited natural resources." He also writes that it should be conceived of as compensation: "The better-off enjoy significant advantages in the use of a single, natural resource base from whose benefits the worse-off are largely, and without compensation, excluded" (443). Here it seems that the better-off and worse-off are conceived of as the global well-off and the global poor. For this argument to work, we must assume that the world's poor have some basic (pre-institutional) entitlement to the world's natural resources, which dovetails with the luck-egalitarian intuition that people are entitled to the products of their choices, but not of their natural endowments.

However, this way of characterizing the debate – where land is viewed simply as resources, which can be converted into unequal wealth – recognizes only the general duties at stake. So, although the view is consistent with the luck-egalitarian cosmopolitan literature, it does not acknowledge the legitimate stake that indigenous or national minorities also have in their land. The claim of people (indigenous people, national minorities) to be collectively self-determining is not simply a claim to control the collective aspects of their existence and to extract resources from the geographical domain that they occupy, but it is a claim to be self-determining *over particular pieces of land,* and this claim will necessarily entail the privileging of insiders' needs in some cases. The groups in question are typically settled on particular pieces of land, are attached to them, and seek jurisdictional control over that particular geographical space. The fact that people care about particular bits of land, and believe themselves to be engaged in a project that demands recognition of at least some special duties to insiders, makes the reconciliation of the demands of global justice – to treat everyone across the globe fairly – with particularist aims and attachments, commitments and relationships, challenging, if not impossible. It is not sufficient simply to dispense equal amounts of goods: it matters, fundamentally, for many people *where* they are self-governing and over which pieces of land, and different lands will almost inevitably contain different kinds and quantities of resources. Moreover, some cultures – such as the Amazonian Indians or the Bedouins or the indigenous communities of the Niger Delta – seek to preserve their particular culture and way of life, and part of this may involve refraining from developing the resources that happen to be located on their land, for to do so would undermine the way of life they seek to preserve. It is hard to see how the contours of cosmopolitan justice can address this issue in the abstract.

Let us conclude this discussion by way of two fairly cryptic thoughts. First, it is unsatisfactory for cosmopolitan justice theorists to assume that all such links to territory, and the special duties to which these links give rise, can be ignored or assumed away as stemming from unfairness or ignorance. This would make cosmopolitan theory unsatisfactorily utopian, in the worst sense, in being a theory for people not as they are but as the theorist would prefer them to be. Second, recognition of this attachment that some groups and cultures have for particular pieces of land, and the relationship of that land to meaningful collective self-determination, means that some groups will seek to *prevent* their resources from being developed. This is clearly in tension with the very pressing claims of the global poor to access the resources they need in order to address their severe deprivation.[14] It is not clear, at least in a general way, which duties should be prioritized. Much depends on the importance of the land to the people who are making a special claim to it, and how this is balanced against the importance of the resources to the global poor. But it is not obvious that there is an easy and general (rather than contextually nuanced) answer to this kind of dilemma. We think this takes us into the realm of political and moral judgment, rather than to an easy priority thesis of the kind the cosmopolitans we have considered appear to advocate.

Conclusion

In this chapter, we have been interested in the relationship between cosmopolitan justice and particularist relationships and attachments, particularly the attachment of people to particular political communities. We have argued that the initial cosmopolitan interpretation of nationalism as fundamentally antithetical to cosmopolitanism was fundamentally wrong, and we expressed sympathy for the more sophisticated attempts of cosmopolitan justice theories to incorporate people's relationships and attachments into a fuller account of cosmopolitan theory. We considered three attempts to reconcile general and special duties, and argued that the instrumental strategy and Tan's constraining strategy are problematic, and that the "room-finding" strategy described by Abizadeh and Gilabert – who argued, correctly, that we have both general duties to others and special duties that arise from particular relationships and attachments, and that give meaning to our lives – is more promising. It is not clear, however (because not substantively developed), how exactly Abizadeh and Gilabert intend to pursue this reconciliation, and the language of "deontic" duties constraining special duties suggests a Blanket Priority Thesis, which is very similar to Tan's constraining strategy and is therefore similarly problematic.

We have also suggested, but did not argue fully for, the position that it may not be possible to develop a clear reconciliation of general and special duties in the abstract rather than on a case-by-case basis. We tried to illustrate this by examining the attachments that people may have for land, and the ways in which luck-egalitarian global justice theory views land compared with the way in which indigenous or national groups view land. We argued that a general reconciliation may not be possible but that it might be possible to develop some principles for thinking the cases through, and then to examine them on a case-by-case basis.

Notes

1   In fact, there is an increasingly prominent fourth strategy, which aims to ground justice in associations and then argues that the global economic order constitutes just such an association. While not technically a reconciliation strategy, since it views global duties as special or associative duties, it tends to ignore how these duties relate to the duties that arise in non-global, more particularist associations. For one example of such an attempt, see Moellendorf 2009. We evaluate this strategy in general in Lenard and Moore (2011).

2   First, there is no doubt that both the original nineteenth-century nationalists and their contemporary counterparts share a vision of global (albeit non-cosmopolitan) justice that includes a number of universalist ideals. The original

nationalists, such as Mazzini, argued that protection of the cultural life of the community was compatible with a number of universalist values, and the structure of this argument, and the limits that the foundational appeal sets on the argument, suggests that it is compatible with a weak cosmopolitan claim that all people are, at a fundamental level, of equal moral worth. Indeed, for both nineteenth-century nationalists such as Mazzini and contemporary liberal nationalists, the claim is not that *my* language and *my* culture are superior to others and therefore entitled to be embraced by the political order. The claim is a much more generalizable one: that my language, culture, and identity are important to me, just as yours are important to you. The idea was one of the (basic) equality of all nations. Indeed, Mazzini was explicit that the "brotherhood of man" was the basis for the "brotherhood of Italians." In his view, "the question of *nationalities*, rightly understood, is the Alliance of the Peoples." The imperative of Italian nationalism, then, was situated within a broader conception of global justice in which different national identities were given due recognition. This was the fundamental idea behind the League of Nations, and subsequently underlay the composition of the United Nations General Assembly (by contrast, the Security Council, with its five permanent members, reflects historical and contemporary power dynamics). This was a morally progressive idea in practice, because it helped to challenge the hegemony of existing powers. It is a generalizable principle in the sense that it assumes that all people are similarly situated in important, group-based relationships.

3 Philosophical non-cosmopolitans such as David Miller and John Rawls accept the idea that all persons have basic rights. The acceptance into their theories of an idea of human rights is at its core the acceptance of moral cosmopolitanism, because human rights are ascribed to all human beings simply in virtue of their humanity, or personhood. They are individualistic and inclusive; in other words, they embody the fundamental norm of moral cosmopolitanism, which recognizes individuals as fundamental units of moral concern. In some ways, this just reveals that the definition of moral cosmopolitanism trumpeted by its defenders (Charles Beitz and Thomas Pogge, for example) is so inclusive as to fail to leave anyone outside its ambit. There is some disagreement on how to arrive at a philosophically coherent list of human rights. Although the idea is enshrined in documents such as the Universal Declaration of Human Rights (and subsequent conventions), which were in large part a reaction to the atrocities of the Holocaust, they include many different kinds of rights, some of which seem very fundamental (right not to be tortured) whereas others seem like an aspirational good (the right to just and favourable conditions of work and to protection against unemployment). See *Universal Declaration of Human Rights*, GA Res. 217(III), UNGAOR, UN Doc. A/810 (1948); *International Covenant on Civil and Political Rights*, New York, 16 December 1966, 999 U.N.T.S. 171 (entered into force 23 March 1976); *International Covenant on Economic, Social and Cultural Rights*, New York, 16 December 1966, 993 U.N.T.S. 3 (entered into force 3 January 1976); and *Convention on the Prevention and Punishment of the Crime of Genocide*, Paris, 9 December 1948, 78 U.N.T.S. 277 (entered into force 12 January 1951). When we refer to "rights," we are referring to a claim that takes the following form: A has a right when A has an interest sufficiently important to warrant holding others to be under some duties to respect it. Duties are not therefore mere correlates of rights; rights ground duties

(Raz 1986, 166ff.). See also the very useful account set out by Ivison (2010, 239-55).

4   It is a striking feature of the global justice literature that almost everyone, cosmo-politans and non-cosmopolitans alike, endorse some form of a non-exploitation principle, which implies a fundamental commitment to transactional justice, and a commitment to human rights. It is not entirely clear what the concept of "exploitation" refers to: while many people believe that there is something like exploitation, and that it is wrong, it is difficult to identify an independent account of what counts as exploitation (unless one is a Marxist, in which case exploitation necessarily occurs at the hands of the owners of the means of production). Most people use "exploitation" as a kind of emotive word for an agreement or interaction that is profoundly unfair. It is not an independent concept because, in its central uses, it is derived from an account of fairness – fairness both in the sense of a conception of fair starting points and an account of fair processes. If an agreement between X and Y is unfair – that is, it is an agreement made from an unfair or unequal initial position and through a process that also is unfair – then we can clearly identify the violation of a duty of justice (i.e., a duty not to exploit others). When both the starting point and the process are unfair, we might say that the agreement was uncoerced but exploitative. In this context, the term "exploitative" means something like "severely unfair." Such varied theorists as Pogge (2008, 206) and Miller (2007, 266-67) appeal to some kind of non-exploitation principle. Interestingly, Miller is sensitive to the difficulties of calling the unfair process and unfair terms "exploitation." For an account of "exploitation" that distinguishes exploitation from mere unfairness (through the concept of "rights"), see Wellman 2005.

5   This is clear in Miller's endorsement of the non-exploitation principle. If exploitation does mean something like profoundly unfair, then, although there are some problems in identifying its precise contours, the concept of unfairness that is at the heart of the prohibition on exploitation contains within it the (cosmopolitan) idea that all persons are fundamental units of moral concern. It contains within it a fundamentally individualist and universalist conception of fairness by which to consider the justice of our transactions or agreements. And if liberal nationalists and statists both agree with the non-exploitation principle, then they too share this fundamentally cosmopolitan principle. Liberal nationalists, like Miller, in upholding the non-exploitation principle as a principle of transactional justice, are not violating cosmopolitan principles but are relying on them as a central principle of justice. They are arguing that people and nations, or one's own political community, ought not to act purely in the national interest without regard for the interests of others: rather, one's agreements and activities have to be constrained by the non-exploitation principle, which, as we have suggested, is fundamentally a principle of fairness.

6   This point is made by Tan (2004, 178).

7   This is not true of contractual duties, which are also "special" duties, and which can be explained in terms of the exercise of our autonomy. See Scheffler 2003.

8   Here, Tan is responding to Miller's claim that self-determination implies responsibility and that this is in tension with an egalitarian global redistribution of wealth and resources. Miller's words (1995, 108) are: "To respect the self-determination of other nations also involves treating them as responsible for

decisions they may make about resource use, economic growth, environmental protection and so forth, which should give us pause when advocating a more egalitarian global redistribution of wealth and resources."

9   Scheffler (2003) does the same in his influential account of associative duties.

10 This argument has been subjected to a more in-depth critique in Lenard and Moore 2009.

11 Although we do not discuss this ambiguity here, it should be clear that each of these articulations of what is entailed by a commitment to equal moral worth will give rise to quite distinct requirements. As we argue in our Reply to Abizadeh and Gilabert, we suggest that this ambiguity about the content of the equality to which they are committed makes it difficult to understand what they mean by "deontic duties" later in their essay (Lenard and Moore 2009).

12 It is clear in Scheffler's work (2003), too. He accepts, as Abizadeh and Gilabert acknowledge, that "the mere existence of a relationship that one values non-instrumentally is not sufficient to ground special responsibilities: one must also *have reason* to value the relationship, or, to put it differently, the relationship must in fact be non-instrumentally valuable" (Abizadeh and Gilabert 2008, 356).

13 Of course, the destruction of these communities is already well under way, as the Nigerian government forcefully evicts citizens living on land under which oil can easily be extracted.

14 This is referred to by Kolers (2009) as a "stream of benefits" theory, and he presents good arguments for why this is necessary.

References

Abizadeh, Arash, and Pablo Gilabert. 2008. "Is There a Genuine Tension between Cosmopolitan Egalitarianism and Special Responsibilities?" *Philosophical Studies* 138 (3): 349-65.

Arneson, Richard. 2008. "Rawls, Responsibility and Distributive Justice." In *Justice, Political Liberalism, and Utilitarianisms: Themes from Harsanyi*, ed. by Maurice Salles and John A. Weymark. Cambridge: Cambridge University Press.

Beitz, Charles. 1999. *Political Theory and International Relations*, rev. ed. Princeton, NJ: Princeton University Press.

Brock, Gillian. 2009. *Global Justice: A Cosmopolitan Account.* Oxford: Oxford University Press.

Goodin, Robert. 1988. "What Is So Special about Our Fellow Countrymen?" *Ethics* 98 (4): 663-86.

Ivison, Duncan. 2010. "Human Rights." In *Ethics and World Politics,* ed. by Duncan Bell, 239-55. Oxford: Oxford University Press.

Kolers, Avery. 2009. *Land, Conflict, and Justice: A Political Theory of Territory.* Cambridge: Cambridge University Press.

Kymlicka, Will. 1996. *Multicultural Citizenship: A Liberal Theory of Minority Rights.* Oxford: Oxford University Press.

Lazar, Seth. 2009. "Responsibility, Risk, and Killing in Self-Defense." *Ethics* 119 (4): 699-728.

Lenard, Patti Tamara, and Margaret Moore. 2009. "Ineliminable Tension: A Reply to Abizadeh and Gilabert's 'Is There a Genuine Tension between Cosmopolitan Egalitarianism and Special Responsibilities.'" *Philosophical Studies* 146 (3): 399-405.

–. 2011. "Cosmopolitanism and Making Room (or Not) for Special Duties." *Monist* 94 (4): 615-27.

Mazzini, Guiseppe. "Europe: Its Condition and Prospects." In *Essays: Selected from the Writings, Literary, Political and Religious of Joseph Mazzini,* ed. by William Clark, 266. London: Walter Scott, 1880.

Miller, David. 1995. *On Nationality.* Oxford: Oxford University Press.

–. 2007. *National Responsibility and Global Justice.* Oxford: Oxford University Press.

–. 2009. "Social Justice versus Global Justice." In *Social Justice in a Global Age,* ed. by Olaf Gramme and Patrick Diammond, 23-37. Cambridge: Polity Press.

Moellendorf, Darrel. 2009. *Global Inequality Matters.* Basingstoke, UK: Palgrave Macmillan.

Nagel, Thomas. 2005. "The Problem of Global Justice." *Philosophy and Public Affairs* 33 (2): 114-47.

Pogge, Thomas. 1989. *Realizing Rawls.* Ithaca, NY: Cornell University Press.

–. 2008. "Eradicating Systemic Poverty: Brief for a Global Resource Dividend." In *The Global Justice Reader,* ed. by Thom Brooks, 439-52. Oxford: Blackwell.

Rawls, John. 1971. *A Theory of Justice.* Cambridge, MA: Harvard University Press.

Raz, Joseph. 1986. *The Morality of Freedom.* Oxford: Clarendon.

Raz, Joseph, and Avishai Margalit. 1990. "National Self-Determination." *Journal of Philosophy* 87 (9): 439-62.

Scheffler, Samuel. 2003. *Boundaries and Allegiances: Problems of Justice and Responsibility in Liberal Thought.* Oxford: Oxford University Press.

Tamir, Yael. 1993. *Liberal Nationalism.* Princeton, NJ: Princeton University Press.

Tan, Kok-Chor. 2004. *Justice without Borders: Cosmopolitanism, Nationalism, and Patriotism.* Cambridge: Cambridge University Press.

Wellman, Christopher H. 2005. *A Theory of Secession: The Case for Political Self-Determination.* Cambridge: Cambridge University Press.

4

Universality and Particularity in the National Question in Quebec

Joseph-Yvon Thériault

One's native country forms the necessary initiation into the universal country.

– Jules Michelet

Quebec: Rooted or Unrooted?

Viewed from a distance, Quebec and its French Canadian past appear to be the prototype of an anti-cosmopolitan identity. Francis Fukuyama (2007) recently said of Quebec that it was the political and theoretical source in Western democracy of an identity politicization that rendered the civic nature of liberal democracy problematic. In an earlier text, he even made of Quebec the ultimate test of the "end of history" hypothesis. Quebec, he said, an old liberal democracy – the British type of parliamentary institution had existed there since 1791 – located a few hundred kilometres from the most dynamic centre of capitalism in the past two centuries (New York) could well, by asserting its political independence, overturn the hypothesis wherein liberal democratic societies would prefer the comfort of global governance, which heralds the end of history, at the risk of a politics based on a "thymos" (Fukuyama 1992).

Although the 1995 referendum on Quebec independence almost replied in the negative to the "end of history" test – 49.6 percent of the electorate voted in favour of proposed sovereignty – almost reversing Fukuyama's thesis, most observers close to Quebec's political reality would contest that assertion of an anti-cosmopolitan Quebec. Rather, they would agree with the opposite statement made by, among others, Will Kymlicka (1998a), according to which Quebec today, the one arising from the Quiet Revolution of the 1960s, largely adheres to a civic and liberal conception of its identity. This would thus make Quebec's political identity an eloquent example of a cosmopolitan pluralism or rooted cosmopolitanism – that is, a society that adheres to the moderns' values of universalism while accommodating a cultural diversity within.

Kymlicka cites Quebec, like Scotland, or even Catalonia, as examples of national minorities – nations that are not nation-states and that, while claiming their identity from the standpoint of a cultural nationalism, still maintain that they are a political space for a civic integration of plurality. The interpretation could even be broadened to a larger group of other nations that have a state – nation-states – which, while including their nationalism in a societal culture, nevertheless follow a policy that recognizes diversity. I do not feel I am betraying Kymlicka's analysis by stating that the American style of integration model, the one to which Fukuyama refers, or even the one described by David Hollinger (1995) in *Postethnic America* and that makes of the United States of America a microcosm of universal cosmopolitanism – if it does not prove to be entirely false for the United States (as we will see afterward), the latter being somewhat exceptional – is widely unsuitable for describing the historical experience of most of the world's other societies (see Kymlicka 1998b). Liberal democracies can combine the principles of universalism, individualism, and freedom into specific forms of cultural integration representing one or more societal cultures. This is why liberal nationalism can usually be defined as a rooted cosmopolitanism.

These arguments fail to sway Hollinger, who, particularly in reference to Quebec, responds to Kymlicka with two counter-arguments. The first is that the effect of such a position is "to relax the tension between the tribe and the claims of the human, and to carve out a political space in which the tribe simply rules" (Hollinger 2002, 233). The tribal temptation would not be foreign to Quebec, where Hollinger tells of the refusal to name a bridge in honour of an Italian immigrant in order to preserve the name of two French families. Here is an example, he points out, of a "crude ethnic chauvinism" to which any insertion of a cultural or societal dimension into liberal nationalism would likely lead. The attentive observer of the Quebec scene will easily dismiss this as an example of a news item that is completely unrepresentative of Quebec's policy of managing pluralism.[1]

The other refutation Hollinger offers to contest the rooted cosmopolitanism of Quebec liberal nationalism appears to be more serious. The argument here is reversed. It no longer involves finding in Quebec nationalism an ethnic chauvinism specific to every particularizing nationalist reference, but seeing in it the affirmation of a banal form of civic nationalism fully compatible with universal cosmopolitanism.

What I find remarkable about this account is its implication that Quebec is potentially a civic nation virtually identical to the United States of America, except that the official language is French instead of English. What, other than linguistic particularism, makes Quebec by Kymlicka's description here any more a national minority in Canada than New Jersey or Colorado is a national minority in the United States of America? (Hollinger 2002, 234)

I will focus especially on this latter issue here. If, to open itself up to cosmopolitanism, every nationalism must rid itself of a substantial conception of the nation in favour of a purely civic conception, it makes impossible, on a national scale, the very existence of a rooted cosmopolitanism or, as Hollinger prefers to call it, cosmopolitan pluralism. Since the civic nation recognizes only universal values, any particularist conception of identity is then removed from politics and returned to an ethnic, or even tribal, dimension. Thus Hollinger's double conclusion: either Quebec establishes itself as a civic nation, in which case it has no more legitimate claim to political recognition than New Jersey or Colorado, or it plunges into a "crude ethnic chauvinism," as the story of the bridge-naming episode recalls. In either case, rooted cosmopolitanism is an impossibility, as in any liberal democracy.

More nuanced in his words, Jürgen Habermas (1995, 107-48) was nevertheless not far from making such a proposal when, in response to Charles Taylor's argument according to which Quebec's desire for political recognition, though based on a hypergood, is compatible with the ideas of liberal democracy, he replied: yes, but under those conditions a sovereign Quebec will still have to submit those conceptions of the good to the court of the universal. In other words, every liberal democracy must give priority to a form of civic nationalism, "constitutional patriotism," over every substantive, cultural, or societal nationalism. Such an obligation would in the end only slightly differentiate the state that Quebec nationalists covet from other liberal democracies.

Paradoxically, Fukuyama's affirmations, Hollinger's conclusions, and, by extension, Habermas's predictions do not fall very far from the most influential currents prevalent among Quebec intellectuals in the past few years. Indeed, most Quebec intellectuals and political leaders who support sovereignty now reject the idea that the sovereigntist project is based on ethnic nationalism, or even on any particular societal culture. This position has been evident since the defeat of the first referendum on Quebec sovereignty (1980) and especially exacerbated following the second one (1995), where, on the evening of the defeat, the leader of the sovereigntist camp, Jacques Parizeau, Quebec's premier at the time, blamed the defeat on "money and the ethnic vote." The very next day, he was forced to resign, and the sovereignty sphere of influence attempted then to shift the nationalist discourse to one that would be seen as more in step with the prevalent hegemonic discourse about the basic civic nature of what links people together in the modern world. From then on, it insisted on the essentially civic culture of the new Quebec nationalism, its zero-ethnicity character, its total submission to universal values, its promotion of an internal pluralism, and its adherence to the values of "interculturalism" – the term preferred over "multiculturalism" to express the recognition of the cultural contribution made by immigrants.[2] In short, the idea of a Quebec oddly resembling post-ethnic American cosmopolitanism, as described by Hollinger – which, from an identity perspective, would effectively distinguish it little from New Jersey – became the template by which Quebec nationalist intellectuals read their situation.

An eloquent example of this can be found in the popularity of the idea of Americanity in 1980s Quebec.[3] This term, little used in the Anglo-American world,[4] means, for Quebec intellectuals, a belonging to America, not adhesion to the American societal culture (Americanization). It is something deeper, upstream of societal culture, a kind of essence that American societies would have because of their status as New World societies, societies arising from recent immigration, societies without long memories, based, consequently, on the imaginary of a radical newness. By thus dissociating the US societal culture, that born of the United States' specific historical experience, from the culture arising from membership in America as the experience of newness, one arrived at the description of Americanity – a culture that Quebecers and Americans would share. Americanity then designated a reality where every societal culture would disappear to make way for the networked society, the autopoesis of systems, the cold world of machines, identity as a simple individualized "bricolage."

Through such a conception of Americanity, Quebec and the United States would represent a kind of unrooted cosmopolitanism. These "new" societies would never have been, strictly speaking, national realities, at least not like the nation as a place of fixing identity boundaries, as those would have been established in the Old World. Although, for thinkers of Americanity, the nation as a place of fixing identity was the case in traditional Quebec, that of French Canada before the 1960s, it was in the form of an elite discourse with a false awareness of its true essence.

Aside from that exception, the historical period of the French Canadian nationalist, which was fleeting and regrettable according to the thinkers of Americanity, Quebec and the United States, since their foundation, during the very process of building a people through migration and the frontier experience, drafted the open, postnational, universalist, cosmopolitan nature of their societies. Recognizable here is the thesis of the American exceptionalism of Manifest Destiny, according to which, from its earliest beginnings, America would either support a project of universal emancipation or, as Hartd and Negri (2000) more recently think, proclaim a form of globalized, postnational governance – the Empire.[5] Through Americanity, Quebec's dream would participate in such an exceptionalism; it too would proclaim an unrooted cosmopolitan pluralism.

Less radical, but involved nevertheless in the same effort to define Quebec nationalism in opposition to a particular societal culture, is the recent report from the Consultation Commission on Accommodation Practices Related to Cultural Differences (Bouchard and Taylor 2008). The two eminent intellectuals who co-chaired the commission, the philosopher Charles Taylor and the historian Gérard Bouchard, one being globally recognized for his philosophic defence of multiculturalism,[6] the other for his rewriting of Quebec's historical path through the prism of Americanity,[7] were mandated to hold public consultations and advise the government of Quebec about the direction of policies governing plurality. The report sees the Quebec identity as a form of secular insecurity due mainly to the minority situation of the francophone group in North America. It encourages Québécois of French Canadian background to abandon such insecurity so they can see Quebec as a society open to plurality.

For the commissioners, such openness to plurality does not mean the abandonment of common values. When it comes to defining them, however, they are limited to the abstract values of a procedural liberalism: "democracy," which includes the values of gender equality; a "religious neutrality" of the state open to publicly recognizing the practice of multiple religions, which the report calls open secularism; and a "common language," which is French in this case.[8]

Once again, except for French and not English being the common language of citizenship, nothing here would refute Hollinger's argument, according to which a Quebec thus conceived would have no more characteristics and legitimate claim to political recognition than New Jersey or Colorado. Quebec under this definition does not have the features of a "pluralism cosmopolitanism" or a rooted cosmopolitanism. Indeed, if Quebec's nationalist affirmation is based only on the universalist ideals of liberal democracy, its "nationalism" is ultimately an unrooted cosmopolitanism, which Hollinger calls "universalism-cosmopolitanism." In fact, for Hollinger, rooted cosmopolitanism could not exist; only the civic nation – a microcosm of universal cosmopolitanism on a national scale – can contain the sectarian excesses produced by the pathos of the tribes involved in any social reality.

The Nation: A Rooted Cosmopolitanism

I believe this paradox to be false. The tension between "the claims of the tribe" and the "claims of the human," which is nothing less than the tension specific to the modern political world, is not resolved by the permanent victory of one of its poles, in Hollinger's case the "claims of the human." Indeed, even if politically modernity decrees that henceforth the human will take precedence over the tribe, this affirmation could never have been at the centre of the effective history of any modern society. This non-realization is not due to, as liberal progressive thought generally affirms, a kind of immaturity or unfinished project of modernity, a project that universal cosmopolitanism would finally realize (Habermas 1997, 38-55). It is due to the way that we have conceived and practised politics and democracy since the Enlightenment. The unfinished project of modernity is, so to speak, included in the very idea of modern democracy.

To back this thesis, I will use a socio-historical type of argument – democracy as process – rather than a philosophic one – democracy as a moral universal project. This brief recap of the effective history of modern democracies will better explain how rooted cosmopolitanism can be considered a response to the unfinished nature of political modernity and how it is in the nation that such a process can best be observed. Based on these considerations, I will then return to the presence of such a process in the history of Quebec (French Canadian) nationalism.

It is fair to say that the modern political project, the one born of the European Enlightenment, was clearly marked by the desire to base politics on the authority of universal moral norms. That is why Kant (1795), already taking stock of the Enlightenment, was able to make the universal cosmopolitan state the only perspective of political emancipation. Such a proposition has a very broad political scope; it now makes legitimate political authority depend not on the transcendence of gods, not on the tradition of ancestors, not on social relationships of power, but on a purely abstract principle: a reason of which all humans are said to be capable of making public use. As Claude Lefort stated, since power thus uprooted is located in an "empty place," it will be the source of endless dispute, of a penalty of decreed illegitimacy for all groups or opinions claiming a legitimacy to hold power. Thus can be described the origin of modern democracy. In its primary version, it effectively disrupts all "tribal affiliations" as the sources of political legitimacy; it could not construct them as an ultimate place of sovereignty (Lefort 1986, 1998).

But this is only half the effective history of modern democracies. Democratic reality quickly challenged the absolute postulate of the sovereignty of reason. Men and women who were supposedly depositories of such reason turned out to be more complex than the philosophers of modern reason had assumed. They had to navigate through social relationships – of class, sex, and so on – religious feelings, feelings of ethnic, national, and other affiliations, and all kinds of ideologies, which sociology was to confirm in the early nineteenth century. A little later, Sigmund Freud would teach that those citizens, new depositories, as beings of reason, of modern sovereignty, actually carried a subconscious that was largely inaccessible to reason and yet explained part of human action. In fact, what sociology, like psychoanalysis, taught us was that what was excluded from the abstract thought of the Enlightenment, declared irrelevant for guiding humanity, had largely survived it. And, that it did not involve remnants, traditions as yet unexhausted, but actually a kind of permanence related to the anthropological – cultural – nature of political man, who could not be reduced to a being of reason (Gauchet 1999, 162-207).

These are the cultural dimensions, in the broad sense, that include the relationships of power, the identities, and the affects that survive the declaration of the abstract man of the Enlightenment, that will form the other half of democracy. Even more, these substantial dimensions of togetherness are as if revived, stimulated by the very effect of the declaration that power is now found in an empty place. Every individual, faction, group, and class can, in a world where power is said to belong to nobody and thus can be owned by everybody, legitimately claim to be an equal stakeholder in such ownership. Democratic reason will in the end prove to be a source of endless dispute because of the plurality of the subjects populating the political space, all claiming to be stakeholders of the empty place of power.

The nation must be included in this historical dynamic of modern democracy, which, by legitimizing power in the abstract human, stimulates the awakening of a concrete humanity. The nation is absent from the theorizing of the thinkers of the modern social contract. The merging of citizens into a particular *demos* is, among the latter, purely contingent, related to the functional nature of old monarchic boundaries that were essentially non-democratic. The political horizon of liberal democracy is the humanity and the cosmopolitanism of the moderns. From a civilizational, even cosmopolitical, perspective, democracy is reduced to the moral universalism of human rights and the procedural-technocratic management of humanity. The realization of these principles does not necessitate the division of humanity into nations. The other, non-political dimensions of modern civilization, the marketplace and science, are also foreign elements on all national fronts (Gauchet 2004). This is how modern civilization has come to have this totally original characteristic of the history of humanity – that is, being based on asocial, literally inhuman principles, inhuman because they are not cultural. Other known civilizations, the Christian world, the Muslim civilization, and Hinduism, for example, were based on the representation of a concrete cultural humanity. The civilizational horizon and cultural dimension of humanity coincided in the latter, with the consequence that the deployment of humanity (civilization) and identity (culture) were joined.

Modernity severs this link between civilization and culture (Gauchet 2004).[9] By seeking the culture of the civilizational place, the modern world is preventing humanity from being a place of meaning, which is literally impossible given, as I pointed out, the cultural dimension of human nature. This impossibility of cosmopolitanism did not escape Kant, who, seeing that nature had bestowed on men different languages and religions, concluded that the Universal Republic would have to be limited to being a federation of republics.

Politically speaking, democracy is what opens this gap between civilization and culture. It is also through democracy that the gap thus created will be closed again. Indeed, although modern democracy is based on the abstract human – power as an empty place – it is in the name of power to the people, as opposed to power to fractions, that such a regime establishes itself. And the reference to the people is still somewhat concrete, included in a context, referring to a substantive We – *We the People*. The unexpected creation of the nation, here in the sense of a reality not conceived of by the thinkers of modern democracy, plays a key role in this process that rearticulates what political modernity disarticulates – the abstract human and the concrete people. This introduction of the concrete human into democracy took place in the early nineteenth century, along with the consolidation of the democratic era. In effect, though the nation was absent from the theorizing of Enlightenment thinkers, though it was also absent from the first democratic revolutions, particularly the American Revolution and the French Revolution, it would be affirmed everywhere in the early nineteenth century, to the extent that it became possible to say, afterwards, that although not all nations were democratic, all modern democracies were national (Manent 2001, 85-99).

The nation thus gave modern democracy the cultural weight it was missing. But let there be no mistake. It was not the return of the tribe in a democratic world that had been seeking it. The nation was everywhere, in the liberal democracy, an intermediary between the particular and the universal, between the shuttered, closed world of family, clan, tribe, village, and such affiliations and the unrooted world, abstract subject of modern civilization. Consequently, contrary to the rigidity of traditional affiliations, the nation sought to be a historical agent, a vehicle of modern civilization: all nations affirmed that they had singularly conducted the modern civilizational project, that they were agents of progress (Gauchet 2004). If this is obvious in the first national narratives of dominant democracies (Michelet in France, Bancroft in the United States), it is also true, as will be seen, for a small nation without a state such as French Canada. The nation will be defined everywhere as a place that is large enough and far enough away from tribal affiliations to accommodate within itself a diversity particular to modern societies but sufficiently historical to be the political community that is the vector of modern civilization and sufficiently aware of itself to transform the sharing of a common law into citizen solidarity. In short, the nation is established in history as a project of rooted cosmopolitanism or, in other words, unfinished modernity.

Of course, this framework deserves to be historicized. The nations of the nineteenth century defined this cultural substrate in a kind of historical essence of peoples. At the least, it was the task of nascent history to try to confirm the continuity of the national spirit in an ancient past. Contemporary nationalism insists, however, on the constructed nature of the national bond, thus on a more fluid national fact that is more open to diversity. But whether the origin of the nation is sought in an essence of peoples or in the social relationships inherent in the contemporary world, the nation is established everywhere as the vehicle that gives meaning to the progress of modern society. This is why, moreover, although the ties between nation and liberal democracies were largely unthought in modern political history, today's questioning of the nation, especially by unrooted cosmopolitanism, leads to a questioning of the political community likely to give meaning to civilizational progress in a postnational world (Kymlicka and Straehle 1999, 65-88).

If the preceding analysis is fair, from the perspective of the effective history of democracy, a civic nationalism – a kind of microcosm at the scale of a people of a universal republic or an unrooted cosmopolitanism – never existed. Hollinger is wrong to see the United States as the incarnation of such a reality. He greatly minimizes the historical experience and cultural requirements – above all the language – shaping the American national identity. His blindness is partly excusable. The American national imaginary, as was pointed out above, is exceptional because of the fact that the American nation, more than any other, merged into a civilization. It claims to alone represent civilization, progress, and democracy. Such a claim was plausible because of the diverse origins of the American population, the country's continental nature, and the status of dominant power quickly acquired by America. It is nevertheless an ideology, in the sense of a false awareness of reality: like other modern nations, the United States is a cultural version of modern civilization, not civilizational universality.

Such a claim of alone personifying the universal is not permitted for most nations. Because of the non-hegemonic nature of their presence in the world, such a claim is not really credible. They cannot claim their national narrative in the name of the universal. Having to satisfy the integration requirements of modern societies without being able to rely on such a claim to represent the universal, they had to eradicate from history a rich past, sometimes at the cost of a certain amount of historical truth. This is even truer of what would be called small nations, such as Quebec. In other words, although the great powers – colonial, France, England; imperial Russia; and now the United States – can mask the cultural dressing they operated on modern civilization, these small cultures have had to emphasize it. By thus making visible – too visible – such a cultural dressing, the small nations have opened themselves up to the accusation of turning their backs on the universal. Consequently, they must continually respond to the demand made of them by the great powers to justify how this surplus of history they are exhibiting is not tribal.[10]

Return to Quebec

I will now return to the question of Quebec. Here Hollinger will be proved right: it is not by affirming its civic character that Quebec nationalism confirms its rooted cosmopolitanism, where it acts by imitating large societies that alone can claim to embody the universal in them-selves. By the same token, it makes illegitimate any reference to culture to establish its claim of political autonomy. Paradoxically, recalling the old French Canadian nationalist, the one before the Quebec nationalism that arose from the Quiet Revolution of the 1960s, will better explain how Quebec nationalism participates in a rooted cosmopolitanism. Aside from an actual claim to civic nationalism, such rooted cosmopolitanism remains present in today's Quebec nationalism.

The origin of French Canadian nationalism is typical of the paradox, described above, between nation and democracy. Its formulation in the early nineteenth century is tied directly to the erection of institutions of modern democracy. In 1791, London granted Lower Canada a Legis-lative Assembly, the first institution of a representative democracy within Quebec's existing boundaries, the first political affirmation of the exist-ence of a people in that territory. Very early on, however, a question arose concerning the definition of the people to whom this right to legislate had been granted. Were the "Canadien" people thus what was called the old French people who made up the vast majority of the population of the territory? Were the people the English colonists, a minority but who claimed to represent the future, both demographically and politically, on this territory? As Lord Durham stated when asked by London in 1838 to formulate recommendations for putting an end to the troubles that had afflicted the colony in 1837 and 1838: "I expected to find a contest between a government and a people: I found two na-tions warring in the bosom of a single state" (Lampton 1912, 16). Two peoples, in other words, who claimed that their difference should be seen as a depository – a vehicle – of the institutions of modern democracy.

In this dispute, Durham sided with the "English" people, who, he felt, were more capable of handling the institutions of liberalism and better represented the cultural future of the continent, a future that was decid-edly English. He said that the "French Canadian" people were a people without a history, that is, a people poorly suited to the enjoyment of modern freedoms because of the old, obsolete character of its culture inherited from France before the time of the Revolution. This explains why he forced the union of Lower and Upper Canada and proposed that the English government wait for the minorization of French Canadians, through assimilation and immigration, before granting the new colony a government that was fully responsible before the people's parliament.

The French Canadian nationalism that then took shape and lasted until the 1960s was both a resigned acceptance of the Durham Report

(Lampton 1912) and a refutation of it; a resigned acceptance that put off, for more than a century, any real separatist political claim. That represented, to use Fernand Dumont's expression, a withdrawal to "the reserve," where, to compensate for the impossible political institution-alization, the focus was placed on its historical cultural boundaries, particularly those of its French and Catholic heritage.[11]

For all that, such a withdrawal does not imply that the group became ethnicized. French Canadians have never represented themselves as immigrants on American soil. It is "French Canadian society" that has inherited the French and Catholic culture, not the individual as such whose identity is "Canadien." The representation of their identity is not the result of immigration; it is national. Guillaume Lévesque (1848, 292), on returning from exile following his sentencing for having taken part in the Rebellion of 1837-38, already expressed this distinction between the "country" – a nation, *la patrie* – to be defended and the identity we now refer to as "ethnic": "In all cases, native country *[patrie]* for us is not what *home* is for our English compatriots, and try as we might to bring with us our family and establish ourselves in a foreign country, we will never find our native country *[patrie]*, while their home can fol-low them anywhere because that word does not seem to include the country."

Lévesque here is typical of the French Canadian elites, who presented the historical path of the group very differently from that of the legions of immigrants settling in Anglo-Saxon America in the nineteenth cen-tury. The latter immediately agreed to get involved in the civilizational Anglo-American world, to be ethnicized in the American melting pot, while they – the French Canadians – represented themselves as a separ-ate nation that claimed to be, like the Anglo-American civilization, a vehicle of modern progress. Following in the footsteps of American Manifest Destiny, French Canadians were said to be bearers of a provi-dential mission on American soil, and their national project would be defined as a civilizational project.[12] This was their way of refuting Lord Durham's argument that they were a people "without a history," that is, a group incapable, like modern nations, of bringing about civiliza-tional progress.

Many examples can be given of such a rooted cosmopolitanism found in a national narrative, which, because of its distance from politics, was often considered the prototype of the ethnic nation or even of an ethnic group. I will simply present two of them still extant in contemporary nationalism to recall how this old national reference was "modern" in the sense of seeing the nation as being a cultural vehicle of universal civilization.

The first is that of François Xavier Garneau, who wrote the first major history of Canada (French Canada), the first volume of which was published in 1845. It has often been said of Garneau that his goal was to respond explicitly to Durham's argument stating that French Canadians have no history. He responds to it, in the literal sense, by writing their history, but also, in a more theoretical sense, by affirming that such a history shaped the French Canadian group into a national community, that is, into an agent of modern history. Compared with, he says, "the Germans, the Dutch, the Swedes [who] are established by groups in the United States, and who imperceptibly melted into the greater mass with no resistance, without even a word to reveal their existence in the world" (Garneau 1845, 25; author's translation), French groups sought to defend their nationality. Drawing on modern historiography, in the style of people like Vico and Michelet, "who see the nation as the source and the goal of all power," Garneau (1845, 13) thus seeks to show that the history of French Canada is only an application of a broader principle, that of modern progress being realized by and through the nation. That is the real goal of his historical quest – not to confirm the past but to show that such a past was a vehicle of progress. The historical experience he describes thus is really that of a rooted cosmopolitanism before the term existed.

Yet another, perhaps more surprising, instance of such a rooted cosmopolitanism can be found in Henri Bourassa's famous reply to the words of Monsignor Bourne, the Archbishop of Westminster, in Notre Dame Cathedral in Montreal in 1910 (see Lacombe 2002). Surprising because the reply, which was to quickly be considered a kind of political manifesto of French Canada, originally had a basically religious goal, which attempted to confirm the closing of French Canadian nationalism, not its opening up to history.

A man of politics, Henri Bourassa was the leading proponent of the idea of Canada as a political pact between two cultural nations – the English Canadian and the French Canadian. To Monsignor Bourne's words stating that North American Catholicism, if it was to expand, had to leave its French localism and take on the dominant language of the American continent (English), Bourassa replied that history did not work that way. To spread, universal Catholicism had to fit into an earthly "moral order." History had ensured that the vehicle of Catholicism in North America was French Canadian society. That was the source of its spread to the rest of America. Dismantling that vehicle by proposing the Anglicization of the Catholic Church, was, for Bourassa, to hinder the spread of universal Catholicism, to put an end to its expansion. What this argument teaches is that even from a religious viewpoint, what set French Canada apart as a nation was not its localism but actually the fact that such a localism was the historical vehicle of a universal culture.

The substantial contents of historical French Canadian nationalism that we have just seen appear to be a far cry from what we now consider acceptable as the core of a societal culture. Not open enough, too close to an essentialist vision of culture, too reliant on a religion. It would also be too closed in on itself, too *tricoté serré*, too tight-knit, to use a Quebec expression that defines the old French Canadian identity. Not open enough to either a global humanism or the presence within itself of diversity that will make it a kind of microcosm, on a national scale, of the universal. In other words, the rooted cosmopolitanism of the French Canadian nation, like nationalism in general, was clearly able to represent itself as a vehicle of modern progress, but might it not be at the cost of a certain identity closure that would make it more "rooted" than "cosmopolitan"? These kinds of statements would also be true for most Québécois, even among today's proponents of a cultural nationalism, who effectively redefined, after the 1960s, in a more historical, more secularized manner, the values now at issue in such a societal culture.

That is partially true. It is fair to say that every nationalism exhibits a form of national egoism, a closure, that, when exacerbated, results in closing itself off to the other, whether the external or internal stranger. The history of nationalism has given us proof of this; the possibility of its degenerating into a confrontational closure is very real. Moreover, the negative dimension associated with nationalism since the Second World War is largely the result of such drifts, much as the emphasis on exchanges, migrations, and international communications today lends little credibility to a national narrative too tied to a descent community.

But this is not the natural gradient of the effective history of the modern nation; it is one of its risk lines, one of the possible ways it could drift, along with abandonment in a universalism without subjectivity. Those who wanted to close the nation off to the idea of universal humanity (Nazism) or, on the contrary, to make it the only place of the universal realization of humanity (Communism) had to quit democracy, and, by the same path, the modern idea of the nation. They had to quit it because the nation is primarily a modern construction, the main strength of which is to connect cosmopolitan values to a societal culture. It is through the presence of such a connection that we associated French Canada with a rooted cosmopolitanism, without denying, however, that along this continuum it was closer to particularism than to the universal.

It is through such a process, through the work of the paradox of modern democracy, that the national experience is indissociable from the democratic experience. The plurality of nations falls under the heading of a universal civilization. A nation without a project of openness cannot be a rooted cosmopolitanism because it will not then be built around the impossible incompletion – the unfinished nature of modernity – of a permanent link between the universal and the particular. Although such may have been the danger of nationalisms in the nineteenth century – the closure to openness – it does not appear to be the problem of either Quebec or contemporary nations. Their possible departure from rooted cosmopolitanism is more likely today through their dilution in universalism than their substantialization in a societal culture.

Furthermore, the substance of the modern nation does not reflect core values that a national narrative could simply list. This was no truer in the nineteenth century than it is today. The values of modern nations are the values of modernity. The societal culture reflects rather a tradition, a national conversation, fraught with both battle and consensus, where modern ideals and values have found a way. Although tradition feeds on and manufactures identity, it is not an identity but a historical group of institutions – from school, through a situated public space, to Parliament – that formed a human plurality into a political community, so the narrative of that voyage forms the narrative of a rooted cosmopolitanism. And there is the impasse of today's Quebec nationalism, as I stated at the outset; both its detractors and its proponents are vainly seeking the values that would particularize it, when they should be seeking the political community – the historical institutions – that conveys them.

Conclusion

The goal of this discussion of French Canada's case was not to confirm a substantial aspect of the common culture as a kind of permanent trait of what would have to be called national. On the contrary, I wanted to show how national culture is only a kind of mediation between the contextualized, constantly changing nature of human culture and the moderns' ideal of a universal standard of justice. It is as a vehicle of universal progress that French Canada has represented itself as a nation.

This process of mediation is a characteristic of the effective history of democracy, a kind of rooted cosmopolitanism. Today's Quebec, like most liberal democracies, is defining itself less and less as a singular way of realizing the universal by insisting on the civic dimension of its identity. To remain there, however, to reiterate just the values of civic nationalism, means that nationalism becomes merely a universal cosmopolitanism. It becomes rooted cosmopolitanism when it is defined less by its values than by the vehicle – the political community – that conveys those values in a national tradition.

Seeking to put an end to this mediation by resolutely choosing the human over the substantive dimension of humanity – the "tribe," in Hollinger's words – would be to break with what has been at the centre of democracy as process for two centuries. Democracy would thus lose the collective subjects – the vehicles – by which it would realize itself.

I do not want to make Quebec a sort of anti-test of the end of history. Its inability to assume a rooted cosmopolitanism, in the trail of what was the national intention of French Canada, is not in itself a major issue for contemporary democracy. In such a case, Quebec as a particular vehicle for realizing universal democracy would be removed for the benefit of democratic societies – Canadian or American. But we can see Quebec as a generic case for the cosmopolitanization of democracy. The Quebec question, then, is the same as the question asked of universal cosmopolitanism by rooted cosmopolitanism: Who are the people to whom democracy must give power: concrete or abstract?

Notes

1 Hollinger refers here to "On the Ethnic Battlefield, the French Retake a Bridge," *New York Times,* 23 February 2004, A4. This event does not seem to have had any public resonance in Quebec, where, however, linguistic issues are widely discussed.

2 For an overview of such recent civic definitions of Quebec's political culture, see Bariteau 1998; Bouchard 2000; Maclure 1998.

3 For a more detailed description of the meaning of Americanity in Quebec's recent intellectual history, see Thériault 2005.

4 One of the rare references in Anglo-American literature is that of Quijano and Wallerstein (1992). Americanity as the "deification and reification of newness" is here associated with the idea that America would have introduced the idea of a world perpetually announcing the World-system.

5 For further reading on American exceptionalism, see Lipset 1997.

6 Taylor 1995.

7 Bouchard 2000.

8 For a more in-depth analysis of the commission's issues concerning this question, see Thériault 2010.

9 For a socio-historical analysis of how this distinction began in modernity, especially in Germany, see Elias 1982.
10 For a longer discussion on this issue, see Finkielkraut 1999; and Boucher and Thériault 2005.
11 Dumont 1993. This text is still the best introduction to the history of Quebec (French Canadian) nationalism in the nineteenth century.
12 In 1953, the great French Canadian national historian, Lionel Groulx, inaugurated a Chair of "French-Canadian Civilization" at Université de Montréal.

References

Bariteau, Claude. 1998. *Québec 18 septembre 2001*. Montréal: Québec Amérique.
Bouchard, Gérard. 2000. *Genèse des nations et cultures du Nouveau monde*. Montréal: Boréal.
Bouchard, Gérard, and Charles Taylor. 2008. *Building the Future: A Time for Reconciliation*. Report to the Consultation Commission on Accommodation Practices Related to Cultural Differences. Quebec: Government of Quebec.
Boucher, J., and J.Y. Thériault, dir. 2005. *Petites sociétés et minorités nationales, enjeux et perspectives comparées*. Québec: PUQ.
Dumont, Fernand. 1993. *Genèse de la société québécoise*. Montréal: Boréal.
Elias, Nobert. 1982. *The Civilizing Process. Vol. 2: State Formation and Civilization*. Oxford: Blackwell.
Finkielkraut, Alain. 1999. *L'ingratitude. Conversations sur notre temps*. Montréal: Québec Amérique.
Fukuyama, Francis. 1992. "Comments." *Journal of Democracy* 3 (4): 23-28.
–. 2007. "Identity and Migration." *Prospect*, issue 131 (25 February).
Garneau, François Xavier. 1845. *Discours préliminaire. Histoire du Canada. Depuis sa découverte jusqu'à nos jours*. Québec: N. Aubin.
Gauchet, Marcel. 1999. *The Disenchantment of the World: A Political History of Religion*. Trans. by Oscar Burge. Princeton, NJ: Princeton University Press.
–. 2004. "Le problème européen." *Le Débat*, no. 129 (March/April): 50-67.
Habermas, Jürgen. 1995. "Struggles for Recognition in the Democratic Constitutional State." In *Multiculturalism and the Politics of Recognition*, ed. by Charles Taylor, 107-48. Princeton, NJ: Princeton University Press.
–. 1997. "Modernity an Unfinished Project." In *Habermas and the Unfinished Project of Modernity*, ed. by Seyla Benhabib and Maurizio Passerin d'Entrèves, 38-55. Cambridge, MA: MIT Press.
Hardt, Michael, and Antonio Negri. 2000. *Empire*. Cambridge, MA: Harvard University Press.
Hollinger, David A. 1995. *Postethnic America: Beyond Multiculturalism*. New York: Basic Books.
–. 2002. "Not Universalist, Not Pluralist: The New Cosmopolitans Find Their Own Way." In *Conceiving Cosmopolitanism, Theory, Context, and Practice*, ed. by Steven Vertovec and Robin Cohen, 227-39. New York: Oxford University Press.
Kant, Immanuel. 1972 (1795). *Perpetual Peace: A Philosophical Essay*. New York: Garland Publishing.
–. 1984 (1784). *Idea for a Universal History from a Cosmopolitan Point of View*. Indianapolis, IN: Bobbs-Merrill Company, 1963.

Kymlicka, Will. 1998a. *Finding Our Way: Rethinking Ethnocultural Relations in Canada.* Toronto: Oxford University Press.

–. 1998b. "American Multiculturalism in the International Arena." *Dissent* (Fall): 73-79.

Kymlicka, Will, and Christine Straehle. 1999. "Cosmopolitanism, Nation-States, and Minority Nationalism: A Critical Review of Recent Literature." *European Journal of Philosophy* 7 (1): 65-88.

Lacombe, Sylvie. 2002. *La rencontre de deux mondes.* Québec: PUL.

Lampton, John George, Earl of Durham. 1912. *Report on the Affairs of British North America.* Oxford: Clarendon Press.

Lefort, Claude. 1986. *The Political Forms of Modern Society: Bureaucracy, Democracy, Totalitarianism.* Cambridge, MA: MIT Press.

–. 1998. *Democracy and Political Theory.* Cambridge, MA: MIT Press.

Lévesque, Guillaume. 1848. "De l'influence du sol et du climat sur le caractère, les établissements et les destinées des Canadiens. Institut canadien de Montréal [1848]." Reprinted in James Huston, ed., *Le répertoire national,* vol. 4, Éditeur J.M. Valois, 1893.

Lipset, Seymour Martin. 1997. *American Exceptionalism: A Double-Edged Sword.* New York: W.W. Norton.

Maclure, Jocelyn. 1998. *Récits identitaires. Le Québec à l'épreuve du pluralism.* Montréal: Québec Amérique.

Manent, Pierre. 2001. *La nation et le travail de la démocratie.* Paris: Fayard.

Quijano, Anibal, and Immanuel Wallerstein. 1992. "Americanity as a Concept, or the Americas in the Modern World-System." *International Social Science Journal* 44 (4): 549-57.

Taylor, Charles. 1995. *Multiculturalism and the Politics of Recognition.* Princeton, NJ: Princeton University Press.

Thériault, Joseph-Yvon. 2005. *Critique de l'américanité. Mémoire et démocratie au Québec.* Montréal: Québec Amérique.

–. 2010. "Entre républicanisme et communautarisme: La Commission Bouchard Taylor, une synthèse ratée." In *Penser la diversité au Québec,* ed. by B. Gagnon, 143-55. Montréal: Québec Amérique.

5
Rooted Cosmopolitanism: Unpacking the Arguments
Daniel Weinstock

Taken at a very high level of abstraction, rooted cosmopolitanism is an appealing notion. It appears to possess the virtue of moderation. Cosmopolitanism *sans phrase* seems an austere and overly demanding moral stance to some, disconnected as it would appear to be from the ties of kith and kin. But too much rootedness suggests an equally unattractive insularity and a lack of moral concern for those with whom one does not share "thick" ties, such as those of family, religion, or nation. Put them together and presumably you get the best of both worlds, a cosmopolitanism tempered by an acknowledgment of one's situatedness, a moral particularism capable of acknowledging broader allegiances.

Before concluding that we should all therefore become rooted cosmopolitans, we should beware that our attraction to the notion does not trade on its abstraction and lack of specificity when expressed in such general terms. For when we examine the matter more closely, it turns out that both terms in the phrase have been given a plurality of meanings, both in common parlance and in the philosophical literature.

There are, to begin with, a great many senses associated with the term "cosmopolitanism." In recent years, it has been taken to denote an abstract expression of the equal moral value of all human agents, and it has also been seen as implying specific duties flowing from that equal moral value. Moreover, it has been defined as involving the affirmation of an agent's allegiance to humanity as a whole over and above the allegiance that she might feel to this or that community (Nussbaum 1996). Some theorists have viewed cosmopolitanism as, at least in part, a doctrine about cultural identity (Appiah 2005, 2006; Waldron 1992, 2000). And it has been interpreted as a political rather than a strictly moral doctrine, one that claims that we either already do, or at any rate that we ought to, view the world as a whole as constituting a single polity subject to common norms of justice (Beitz 1979; Pogge 2002). Each of these families of views about cosmopolitanism possesses internal distinctions and nuances, and, of course, they have complex relationships with one another. For example, need one identify with humanity as a whole in order to accept that one has obligations toward all members of humanity? Is moral cosmopolitanism a prerequisite for political cosmopolitanism?

The semantic indeterminacy of the term is increased by the multiple meanings that have in the philosophical literature attached to the notion of "rootedness." At least four senses have been given to the notion that our cosmopolitanism should be qualified or moderated by a consideration for the fact that we are "rooted" (whether or not those who have advanced the notion use the term "rooted"). For some, the notion is an epistemic one. We are, according to this view, limited in our ability to realize the cosmopolitan duties we might have by what we know, and perhaps even more strongly by what we can know. For others, the primary sense to be given to the term is motivational: we must define cosmopolitanism, or at least the scope of our cosmopolitan duties and obligations, in a way that makes it compatible with the constraints posed by human moral motivation. A third sense of rootedness is moral. According to this view, our cosmopolitanism must coexist in some complex relationship with duties and obligations that flow from some particularly important forms of "thick" human relationships. Finally, rootedness has been taken to denote the fact that at least certain kinds of obligation – most notably those to do with justice – flow from aspects of our political institutions. Inasmuch as political institutions do not bind all of humanity together, but only define subsets of humanity, it would follow that we must qualify our cosmopolitanism by due appreciation of the bounds of justice.

The multiplicity of senses potentially attaching to the notion of rooted cosmopolitanism, given the various meanings that can be ascribed to its constituent concepts, means that the evaluation of the notion is a much more arduous task than may at first blush have appeared. For the purposes of this chapter, I will therefore adopt the following simplifying assumption. I will adopt a well-known definition of cosmopolitanism that has been introduced by Thomas Pogge (2002). According to this definition, *all* human agents have *equal* moral worth, and *only* human agents have moral worth. Furthermore, that all human agents possess human status implies that they have this status for *everyone*. In Pogge's view, that is, the affirmation of equal moral worth is not just an abstract axiological claim. Rather, it has implications for each and every one of us.

This last claim might seem controversial to some. But note that as stated, the claim is not that all are owed equal treatment but rather, more modestly, that they are owed equal consideration (cf. R. Miller 1998). Thus, Pogge's definition of cosmopolitanism merely requires that differential treatment be justifiable in a way that is compatible with the equal moral status of all agents. At most, it establishes a *prima facie* claim for equal treatment, but one that can be defeated by other considerations – epistemic, motivational, political, moral – provided these considerations do not contradict the core cosmopolitan belief in the equal moral worth of all human agents.

So my strategy in this chapter will be to keep the meaning of cosmopolitanism (artificially) fixed on the definition given to it by Pogge. I will then run through the various senses of the concept of rootedness that can be inferred from the recent literature in order to make clearer the meanings of rooted cosmopolitanism that emerge from these different senses, and the philosophical problems that they give rise to.

Epistemic Rootedness

To begin with, rootedness can denote an epistemic condition. To be rooted epistemically may mean at least two things. First, it can mean that, given our epistemic position, there are limits on what we can know, in the sense that there are limits on the amount of information that we can come to acquire. Second, it can mean that rooted as we are in a certain set of concepts through which we apprehend the world, there are limits on the degree to which we can understand phenomena that require a conceptual vocabulary quite different from ours to render intelligible. To be rooted in the first sense implies that there are limits on the information we can acquire, or on the amount of information we can reasonably be *expected* to acquire. To be rooted in the second sense means that there are limits on how we process the information that we acquire.

Epistemically rooted cosmopolitanism involves a full acknowledgment of the moral force of cosmopolitanism claims. The limits that it imposes on cosmopolitan duties are not born of countervailing moral considerations but rather of epistemic feasibility constraints. According to the first construal of epistemic rootedness, we are, as finite knowers, limited in the information we can acquire, and some of our informational deficits impact on our ability to live up to what our cosmopolitan obligations would be in epistemically ideal circumstances. If we accept that "ought implies can," it follows that we must forgo some of our cosmopolitan obligations and gear our moral action toward duties with respect to which we are in an epistemically better position. To put it concretely, we should perhaps respond in the first instance to the ethical claims made on us by those nearest to us, not because these moral claims are weightier but because we dispose of the information (about their needs, about the resources that we might need to bring to bear in order to respond to their needs, about the institutional mechanisms that we can avail ourselves of in order to deliver those resources effectively, and so on) that we need to respond to their needs.

Although he does not build his case for it entirely on epistemic grounds, Robert Goodin's model of "assigned responsibility" provides us with possible grounds for justifying some form of national partiality that are at least partly epistemic in nature. Starting from a cosmopolitan position, we can see that everyone does better if they are provided with a set of institutions that have primary responsibility for the satisfaction of their legitimate claims, rather than having everyone viewing themselves as equally responsible for everyone else (Goodin 1988). Goodin's argument is far from being a defence of the status quo. He is not claiming that the way in which responsibility is currently being distributed between the nation-states of the world assigns responsibility in a manner that is compatible with the equal moral status of all. But he does claim that, partly for epistemic reasons, there might be *some* way of organizing humanity into smaller units of concern that would.

Even as thoroughgoing a cosmopolitan as Andrew Kuper has, in the context of a critique of Peter Singer's views (1972) – according to which we act well toward the world's poorest people simply by engaging in massive resource transfers toward them – emphasized the degree to which living up to cosmopolitan responsibilities involves the mobilization of dizzying amounts of sociological, political, and economic information so as to ensure that well-intentioned action reliably activates the causal levers most likely to conduce to good consequences actually resulting from these actions (Kuper 2002).

Now Kuper does not draw from the informational deficits that we may very well suffer from the conclusion that we ought to turn our backs in any way on our cosmopolitan obligations. But he does claim that these obligations are best pursued by indirect, institutionally mediated means, which do not require that we forgo self-interest but perhaps rather that we pursue it in different ways (for example, by consuming goods in a way that will stimulate the economy of poor countries rather than by forgoing consumption for the sake of charity). Kuper's argument dovetails with Goodin's in that, as opposed to Singer, who believes that our cosmopolitan responsibilities are best realized when we accept direct responsibility for individuals in dire need, he also believes that taking epistemic limitations into account will moderate the degree to which we ought to act directly for the good of persons situated at a great distance.

According to the second construal, it might be the case that the cultural difference that separates us from the distant others toward whom cosmopolitanism inclines us is such that we simply lack the conceptual apparatus required to fully comprehend their needs. Our characterization of the cosmopolitan duties that we may have toward them is inextricably tied to our conceptual scheme. Given this conceptual rift, attempts at fulfilling obligations risk being culturally insensitive at best, counterproductive at worst. Epistemically rooted cosmopolitanism construed in this second way moderates our cosmopolitan duties by claiming that we do better by focusing on the needs of those with whom we share a "thick" conceptual vocabulary.

David Miller has in recent writing developed a view such as this. Though he does not deny that we have moral obligations toward distant others, he claims that there is a particular kind of obligation – an obligation of *justice* – that makes sense only among people who share a common normative vocabulary. In Miller's view (2005), justice has to do with goods that are not necessarily understood or valued the same way across cultures, and justice cannot gain an epistemic foothold unless there is at least prior broad agreement on the nature and importance of the goods that institutions of distributive justice allocate.[1]

Even more cosmopolitan-minded philosophers, such as Amartya Sen (2009), have been impressed by the challenges of meeting cosmopolitan obligations in a world marked by conceptual and normative pluralism. While arguing that the capabilities approach is an appropriate metric by which to assess states of justice and injustice, he is loath to fill in the details of how this abstract notion should be specified in diverse cultural contexts, preferring to allow democratic processes internal to specific societies to provide detail.

Should we be epistemically rooted cosmopolitans in either (or both) of the foregoing senses? Let me begin with the second sense of epistemically rooted cosmopolitanism, which claims that there are reasons to do with the concepts through which claims and arguments of justice are necessarily assessed to limit the purview of considerations of justice to those with which we share a conceptual repertoire.

A first observation about epistemic rootedness in this sense is that it overstates the degree to which the citizens of modern, pluralistic nation-states are actually united in their way of conceptualizing and evaluating the goods that principles and institutions of justice aspire to allocate fairly. First, the street-level multiculturalism of many modern societies makes it the case that much of the conceptual plurality that Miller sees at the international level is at least to a significant degree echoed domestically. Think of the different value ascribed by different immigrant groups to a good such as education – these different evaluations most likely point back to evaluations that were prevalent in their countries of origin, and that, at least for a couple of generations, are transported to their new homes.

Second, modern societies are not only culturally but also morally pluralistic. A healthy civil society will be one in which a great many political opinions will be voiced, political opinions that often embody very different ways of conceptualizing different goods relevant to justice. "Left-wing" and "right-wing" opinion parts, among other things, on the question of what the goods are that should be distributed by market mechanisms. Basic political divisions that are present in all even moderately free polities would thus seem to belie the assertion that national spheres encompass consensuses on the terms under which political and economic justice are transacted.

Thus, if conceptual division is not an obstacle to the setting up of tolerably well functioning institutions at the level of modern nation-states that encompass highly pluralistic mass societies, there is no reason to think that it should be an obstacle to transnational justice.

The first sense of epistemic rootedness that I surveyed suggests that there are limits on what we can know that should give us pause before we translate abstract moral cosmopolitanism (which neither sense of epistemic rootedness denies) into a theory of obligation that negates ties of kith and kin and considerations of self-interest on cosmopolitan grounds.

Assessing the plausibility of this position requires that we dig deeper conceptually and distinguish three ways in which the idea that there are limits on what we know can affect the duties that we have. The first way in which we can be said to be limited in what we know is purely factual. In this interpretation, most people that cosmopolitan conceptions of obligation would target as givers simply do not know enough about the needs of their putative beneficiaries to carry out their responsibilities adequately.

If this is the sense in which we are epistemically rooted, it can clearly be remedied to a significant degree, most notably through educational institutions. Education in most advanced industrialized societies has been thought of since the nineteenth century as *national* education, that is, as education designed to foster a sense of national identity. If cosmopolitans are correct, perhaps we should now refocus education so as to provide citizens of affluent nations with more knowledge about other societies, particularly about societies whose members have the greatest needs. It is thus not surprising that cosmopolitan educational reform is the principal practical implication drawn by Martha Nussbaum (1996, 1997) from her ethical cosmopolitanism.

A second sense that can be given to this kind of epistemic rootedness would claim that there are more hard-wired limits on what we can know about the plight of distant others and about the resources and institutional mechanisms through which aid might be delivered to them. In this view, because we are finite knowers, it would be a mistake to assume in conceiving of the nature and extent of our moral obligations that we can know enough to live up to our moral responsibilities effectively.

While plausible on its face, this statement of our epistemic limitations ignores the fact that in the transnational context our moral actions are always institutionally mediated. The disagreement between Singer and Kuper does not have to do with the question of whether individuals can, unaided, act in such a way as to effectively aid distant others in need. Singer believes that the resource transfers that the rich engage in should be done through institutions such as Oxfam, which have developed the epistemic competence as institutions that isolated individuals cannot be expected to have. In matters that have to do with the carrying out of our cosmopolitan obligations, as in a great many other matters, we must guide our actions by epistemically trusting others who we have good reason to believe possess the required expertise.[2] The epistemic division of labour and the mediation of institutions make it the case that our epistemic potential is greater than we might think it is when we focus on the situation of the individual knower.

This is not to say that institutions are foolproof in quarrying information relevant to the carrying out by the citizens of rich countries of their cosmopolitan obligations. They face a raft of obstacles, ranging from internal organizational issues to difficulties in predicting how aid programs will (or will not) translate into improvement of the situation of the global worst-off once local institutions are brought into the picture (Wenar 2005). In principle, however, these obstacles are not insuperable. One of the principal objectives that interdisciplinary research in international ethics ought to be pursuing has to do with the design of aid institutions, with a view to overcoming the kinds of obstacles that have been known to plague even the most effective of them.

Motivational Rootedness

The second sense of rootedness mooted above has to do with our motivations. In this view, there are psychological limits to the degree to which we can be expected to realize cosmopolitan obligations. Our psychological makeup inclines us to be sensitive to the needs of specific others with whom we are engaged in certain kinds of relationships. Since living up to our obligations requires that we be motivated to do so, it follows that our cosmopolitan obligations must be moderated so as not to demand more of us than we are, as human agents with a certain psychological set of dispositions, capable of giving.

The motivational rootedness under discussion here should not be confused with rational egoism. The view is not that we are never, absent non-moral motives, motivated to act morally. Rather, it is that our *moral* motivation inclines us to certain categories of agents and not others, or, at the very least, that we feel a greater degree of motivation to respond to the moral needs of some. So motivationally rooted cosmopolitanism, as we might call it, does not require that cosmopolitan obligations somehow be shown to dovetail with non-moral motivation. Rather, it requires that obligations that we might have toward the distant needy not be perceived as crowding out the obligations to which we are motivationally more responsive. In Samuel Scheffler's words (2001, 83), "if the idea of global justice is to make headway among the affluent, the widespread resistance to that idea cannot be dismissed as just a manifestation of simple self-interest."

Defenders of the motivationally rooted cosmopolitan position divide along at least two dimensions. First, some theorists view human moral motivation as malleable, while others take it to be fixed, at least to a significant degree. Second, some philosophers believe that our motivations, and more broadly our emotional responses to others, are not just brute facts but rather evidence in favour of the moral distinctions toward which they point. That is, if I feel more motivated to respond to the needs of my children than I do to those of other children, or if the plight of my countrymen moves me to a greater degree than does that of people from other lands, it is because I have good reason to ascribe greater importance to these relationships. In this view, our emotional responses are an epistemic key, or at any rate as good an epistemic key as we can hope to get, to access moral truth (D. Miller 1993). Predictably, theorists are more likely to see our motivational makeup as fixed if they see it as reflecting some underlying set of moral reasons than if they see it as simply a brute fact with merely psychological significance.

Rooted cosmopolitans who believe (1) that agents must be motivated in order to fulfill their moral duties; (2) that agents are not presently motivated to fulfill cosmopolitan obligations; (3) that our motivations are malleable; and (4) that our motivations do not point back to some underlying moral truths or sets of reasons to which people have reason to give their allegiance – such rooted cosmopolitans are likely to believe that the moral force of cosmopolitanism is undiminished by its necessary (given 1) rootedness in human moral motivation, and that the main philosophical task facing the rooted cosmopolitan is not to rethink cosmopolitanism in the light of its rootedness but rather (given 3) to reshape human moral motivation so as to make us more amenable to our cosmopolitan obligations. A number of proposals have been made in this connection. Martha Nussbaum (1997, 50-83) has famously argued that we must rethink liberal education so as to cultivate an identification and allegiance toward humanity as a whole. Andrew Dobson (2006) has argued that cosmopolitan obligations should, in order to fill the "motivational deficit," be seen not so much as a matter of living up to moral obligations to distant others with whom we are not otherwise implicated, but rather as involving the rectification of harms in the creation of which we are causally involved.

Another route has consisted in denying (1). There is after all a risk of overemphasizing the degree to which human agents respond to unalloyed moral motives in living up to the obligations they have toward people with whom they are involved in "special relationships." After all, we rely on coercion to get people to pay the taxes that are needed in order to set up the welfare institutions through which we purportedly manifest our solidarity toward our fellow nationals (Weinstock 1999). Even the supposed "naturalness" of parental duties are subtly and sometimes not so subtly undergirded by incentives and sanctions, both formal and informal. There is therefore no reason not to avail ourselves of the fairly reliable mechanisms of human self-interest in order to anchor cosmopolitan obligation in human motivation. One way in which this might be done is to emphasize the degree to which many goods most sought after by citizens of affluent nations – security, environmental sustainability, health – are in fact "globally public," in that they cannot be had by members of rich nations unless the world's poor possess them as well (Kaul et al. 1999; Weinstock 2009).

Theorists who deny either (3) or (4) will hold that cosmopolitanism must be redefined so as to accommodate truths about human moral motivation. Those who deny (4) will argue that the locution "rooted cosmopolitanism" denotes the fact that we are subject to the pull of distinct irreducible sources of moral obligation. In the section "Political Rootedness," I will discuss the various ways in which it has been suggested that this pluralism should be managed. As for those who deny (3) and affirm (4), the need to moderate cosmopolitan claims will be motivated purely by prudential considerations. For example, Peter Singer has argued that if it turned out that the requirement that affluent individuals give money to the poor up to the point where any further bequest would make them less well-off than those that they are benefiting were to turn people off charitable giving altogether, then we should adjust the level at which we expect people to give to the highest point compatible with their not losing the motivation to give (Singer 1972).

But if the manner in which human moral motivation is viewed as a factual contingency rather than as imbued with independent moral value, theorists who view moral motivation as imposing a factual rather than a moral constraint on the strength and scope of cosmopolitan obligations should also be willing to countenance the use of state institutions in order to motivate people to act on behalf of the global public good, just as they have in the past been used to motivate action on behalf of the national common good. Lea Ypi (2008, 66-67) has recently argued for this form of "state cosmopolitanism," holding that the stable fulfillment of cosmopolitan obligations depends on their being able to rely on the coercive institutions of the state, and on the state's public education system's inculcation of cosmopolitan values among citizens so as to allow even those who may at the outset have been recalcitrant "progressively [to] learn to live with them because they reflect the transformation of collective institutions that members consider valuable."

Political Rootedness

The third sense of rootedness, and thus of rooted cosmopolitanism, that I would like to examine is what I refer to as political rootedness. By this I mean a cluster of positions that incorporate the following two claims: (1) There are certain kinds of obligations (call them "political obligations") that human agents have toward one another by virtue of features of the political institutions that they share, that they do not have toward people who stand outside these institutions; and (2) these obligations appropriately limit (or trump) the claim of obligations not born of such political institutions. Rooted cosmopolitanism thus refers to one of three possible positions:

1 *Exclusive politically rooted cosmopolitanism.* According to this view, the political institutions of the nation-state possess features that are not possessed by the institutional (or non-institutional) contexts that bind people together across state boundaries, and therefore political obligations rooted in nation-state institutions are weightier than obligations born of these other contexts.
2 *Inclusive politically rooted cosmopolitanism.* This is the view that whatever features of the nation-state context warrant the obligations claimed for fellow nationals by exclusive politically rooted cosmopolitanism are also possessed by the transnational institutional framework, and that whatever political obligations characterize the relationships among fellow citizens within a nation-state should also obtain transnationally.
3 *Aspirational politically rooted cosmopolitanism.* This view affirms that people bound together in certain kinds of institutional frameworks are morally bound to one another by virtue of features of those institutional frameworks in ways that do not obtain outside of them. What institutions there are, however, should not be viewed as a brute fact, but should instead be answerable to moral considerations. Thus, according to this view, we have the responsibility to bring about the institutions that ought to be.

The debate between exclusive and inclusive politically rooted cosmopolitans has gone through a number of epicycles over the years. It began with the claim made by Rawlsians such as Charles Beitz (1979) and Thomas Pogge (1992) to the effect that if the presence of a "basic structure" in the Rawlsian sense calls for the establishment and enforcement of standards of justice to regulate the interactions of individuals living within that structure, then such standards should apply transnationally because there is today a global basic structure, which might not function exactly as a national basic structure does, but which is just as thoroughgoing and pervasive in its impact as the institutions of the nation-state.

Some defenders of the view that there are aspects of nation-state institutions that make talk of certain kinds of obligations – most notably obligations of distributive justice – apposite that are not pertinent to the transnational sphere have attempted to show that theorists like Beitz and Pogge had misunderstood the aspects of the basic structure by virtue of which political obligations obtain (Heath 2005).

Many theorists have adopted the tack that consists in a continuing attempt to identify further aspects of the nation-state's institutions by virtue of which they generate special obligations among compatriots that do not obtain among agents who do not live under common political institutions. Thus, Michael Blake (2001) has argued that it is the legitimacy of state coercion that requires that people who are potentially subject to that coercion be treated as equals; Thomas Nagel (2005) has held that it is the fact that the state involuntarily subjects us to norms, the legitimacy of which depends on our being able to question arbitrary inequalities, that are instantiated under them; Andrea Sangiovanni (2007, 20) has maintained that requirements of equality among compatriots stem from the fact that their participation in shared institutions "provide[s] us with the basic conditions and guarantees necessary to develop and act on a plan of life, but not to noncitizens who do not"; and Richard Vernon (2010) has suggested that it is by virtue of the risks that we visit on each other through the setting up of state institutions that we must treat fellow citizens as equals in ways that do not apply to non-citizens.

It would be laborious to run through each one of these arguments in turn to assess whether they succeed on their own terms. What I want to suggest is that these terms are too simplistically drawn if they hope to be able to defeat the inclusive and the aspirational politically rooted cosmopolitan arguments.

In essence, each one of the arguments canvassed above has roughly the same form. The argumentative burden is taken by their authors to involve: (1) the identification of some aspect of nation-state institutions that is not possessed by the transnational setting; and (2) the demonstration that this aspect of national institution requires the application of standards of justice according to which all who fall under the institutions are to be treated as equals.

Let us accept for the sake of argument that these various exclusivist arguments succeed in passing the argumentative hurdles laid out in (1) and (2). Do (1) and (2) succeed in defeating the inclusive and aspirational politically rooted cosmopolitans?

In my view, they do not. In order to do so, at least two further claims would have to be established, beginning with the following: (3) The transnational sphere is not characterized by any *other* features that generate obligations of distributive justice.

In other words, defenders of exclusive politically rooted cosmopolitanism need to show that the features of nation-state institutions that generate the requirement of equality are not just sufficient but also necessary conditions of egalitarianism.

Let us assume for the sake of argument that that requirement of the argument against the inclusivist can be made good. Let us assume, in other words, that the exclusivist has been able to show that there is no feature of the institutions, practices, and rules that currently govern the global sphere that warrant egalitarian treatment. He would, in order to successfully defend his position, also have to establish: (4) What states and institutions there are not answerable to normative considerations.

This is far from being an obvious claim (cf. Tan 2004). Kant famously argued that when people interact with one another in such a way as to affect each other's basic interests, they have a right to bring each other under lawful relations. That is, in order to prevent their interactions from ultimately being grounded in brute force, and thus ruled according to the law of the strongest, people have to provide themselves with laws and institutions through which they recognize each other as autonomous moral equals (Kant 1998; Ripstein 2009). In order to refute this argument, the defender of the exclusivist position would have to show either that interactions among the world's peoples are not sufficient for the claim to be made that they have a pervasive impact on people's well-being, or that it is not the case that force and the rule of the strongest are the operative principles in relations among peoples where common laws and institutions are absent.

Neither of these claims seems particularly plausible on its face. Now Kant famously did not argue for a world state. His argument called for common laws and institutions, something that in his view could be achieved through a confederation of republican states. Most cosmopolitans have followed him in holding that it is a failure of institutional imagination to suppose that the need for institutions through which to regulate transnational relations is tantamount to the need for a nation-state-like state. So perhaps the defender of exclusive politically rooted cosmopolitanism can argue that the institutions that are required in order to bring "lawfulness" (in the Kantian sense) to transnational relations do not possess features by virtue of which the people who live under them ought to be treated as equals, as equality is construed by theories of social justice. This seems a difficult line to tread. Indeed, what is the requirement that human relations previously governed by force come to be governed by shared institutions subject to the at least hypothetical consent of those involved in the relationship if not a demand for justice?

Moral Rootedness

A final sense of rootedness that has been prominent in the philosophical literature will, in the context of this chapter, be termed "moral." By moral rootedness I mean the idea that certain kinds of relationships are by their very nature characterized by special obligations. The idea, expressed with the greatest philosophical precision in recent years by Samuel Scheffler, is that there are certain kinds of relationships that we find ourselves in (rather than relationships that we have chosen) that we have reason to value, and that, independent of any explicit undertaking on our part within them, involve special obligations. Part of what it means to be engaged in a relationship such as this is that it involves special obligations (Scheffler 2001). These relationships presumably include (among others) ties of family, of religion, of nationhood, and perhaps more generally of tradition (Scheffler 2010).

Of the forms of rooted cosmopolitanism explored thus far, morally rooted cosmopolitanism is the only one that views rootedness as placing a full-bloodedly normative consideration in opposition to cosmopolitanism. The reasons to moderate cosmopolitan demands in light of the requirements of rootedness were, in a sense, morally contingent. That is, none of the forms of rooted cosmopolitanism considers that, were we able to overcome whatever obstacles stand in the way of a full affirmation of cosmopolitan duty, we ought to refrain from doing so. The morally rooted cosmopolitan does not believe that we ought to set aside the moral demands of rootedness.

Morally rooted cosmopolitans can part company on at least three issues. First, though it is criterial for the family of positions that the special obligations we have by virtue of our relationships are not ones that we take on through some contractual or quasi-contractual act of the will, some morally rooted cosmopolitans deny, while others affirm, that the relationships that human agents value, and that they take as giving rise to special obligations, are self-validating. That is, some theorists may accept that the class of obligation exists, but deny that human agents are infallible in determining what the relationships are that generate them. They may be impressed by the historical record, which would seem to include instances of relationships – based, for example, on race – that were formerly taken to generate special obligations but that are viewed as valueless today.

Second, "special obligation" theorists who believe that human agents can be mistaken as to the kinds of relationships that they see as giving rise to special obligations will obviously differ as to the relationships that actually do generate special obligations. They all agree, for example, that ties of family are a paradigmatic example, but will tend to disagree as to the other kinds of relationships that are in relevant respects sufficiently "like" the family so as to legitimate the perception that agents might have that they involve special obligations.

The status of national belonging is interestingly ambiguous in this connection. While the nation has in the course of history been represented as linking its members together in a manner at least similar to that in which a family binds kin together, it is, at least in its modern incarnation, an abstraction when compared with the face-to-face relations that people entertain with family members, neighbours, and the like (Appiah 2006). One can well imagine a special obligation theorist defending the moral claims born of the kind of proximity and immediacy that characterizes family against the claims made on behalf of the nation, in much the same way that nationalist theorists today defend national partiality against the "abstract," *gesellschaftliche* claims of the cosmopolitan.

Third, morally rooted cosmopolitans will differ in the manner in which considerations of rootedness moderate cosmopolitan moral demands. A moderate version of the position would have it that the demands of rootedness and those of equal cosmopolitan regard coexist, and that there is no a priori way in which to adjudicate their conflicting claims. This is Samuel Scheffler's view (2001, 64): "[T]he problem is that both associative duties and the values that generate opposition to them exert genuine authority within our moral thought, so that what might otherwise be a mere clash of philosophical positions is instead a deep conflict within contemporary moral life." A stronger conception of the rootedness in rooted cosmopolitanism would have it that special obligations trump the obligations that stem from our bare humanity.

In current debates about the limits of cosmopolitanism, national partiality has emerged as the most morally significant form of rootedness. National belonging is seen by some theorists as valuable not only by virtue of the functions of the nation-state that fellow citizens are both responsible for and subjected to, but just by virtue of the kind of relationship that shared nationality represents. In this view, we owe things to fellow nationals that we do not owe to members of humanity at large, just by virtue of the kind of relationship that shared nationality amounts to (D. Miller 2005).

Morally rooted cosmopolitan theorists who ascribe this level of importance to the associative duties born of shared nationality must respond to the following challenges. First, they must (against the particularist who views associative duties as stemming from relationships much closer to home) give an account of what it is about shared nationality that legitimates the associative duties that people assume it gives rise to. The response that some such theorists might be tempted to give – to wit, that people's perceptions of what the associative duty-generating relationships that they have reason to value are – places them in an awkward position, given the historical record that, as was suggested above, contains instances of relationships having been valued and having been seen as giving rise to duties that are today seen as morally egregious.[3]

Second, to the extent that they are liberals, they must explain why the central liberal normative commitment, to the effect that "the right is prior to the good," fails to obtain at the global level. Some morally rooted cosmopolitans have claimed that one has a prerogative to pursue the goods that give shape to one's life even if this is to the detriment of the needs of distant others, or to expend what might otherwise be seen as disproportionate resources on the interests of one's children (R. Miller 2010). The claim first articulated in these precise terms by Rawls that the right is prior to the good does not deny that one can devote greater resources to the pursuit of one's own good or that of one's children than to the pursuit of the good of strangers within one's own polity. It merely claims that considerations of justice appropriately constrain what that good is. The bounds of the good are defined by one's fair share of resources, rather than the other way around.

A liberal view such as this does not deny that there are associative duties. Reverting to the third distinction among types of morally rooted cosmopolitanisms that one can identify, it merely claims that such duties must coexist with claims of justice rather than trumping them.

The question that the morally rooted cosmopolitan who ascribes great moral importance to claims of national partiality must answer is why this priority is reversed once one transcends the bounds of the nation-state; that is, why it is that the obligations that we have toward distant others are defined as what is left over once one has indulged the relationship-relative prerogatives one takes oneself to have. *Prima facie,* the liberal nationalist preserves coherence by adopting a moderate rather than a strong position on the limits that prerogatives of national partiality impose on cosmopolitan demands.

In sum, to the extent that we are *nationally* morally rooted cosmopolitans, it would seem that the most philosophically plausible variant of the position is one that does not see claims born of national belonging as self-validating, and that views the relationship between claims of national partiality and equal concern for distant others as being one in which the latter conditions the former, rather than the former trumping the latter.

Notes

1 It should be noted that Miller develops a great many other arguments elsewhere in his critique of cosmopolitanism.
2 On the necessary role of trust in epistemic contexts, see Coady 1992. For a bracing account of reasons for epistemic distrust in the context of humanitarian aid agencies, see Wenar 2005.
3 For a good examination of arguments in favour of seeing patriotism as an associative duty, see Moore 2009.

References

Appiah, Kwame Anthony. 2005. *The Ethics of Identity.* Princeton, NJ: Princeton University Press.
–. 2006. *Cosmopolitanism: Ethics in a World of Strangers.* New York: W.W. Norton.
Beitz, Charles. 1979. *Political Theory and International Relations.* Princeton, NJ: Princeton University Press.
Blake, Michael. 2001. "Distributive Justice, State Coercion, and Autonomy." *Philosophy and Public Affairs* 30: 257-96.
Coady, C.A.J. 1992. *Testimony: A Philosophical Study.* Oxford: Oxford University Press.
Dobson, Andrew. 2006. "Thick Cosmopolitanism." *Political Studies* 54 (1): 165-84.
Goodin, Robert E. 1988. "What's So Special about Our Fellow Countrymen?" *Ethics* 98 (4): 663-86.
Heath, Joseph. 2005. "Rawls on Global Distributive Justice: A Defence." In *Global Justice, Global Institutions,* ed. by Daniel Weinstock, 193-226. Calgary: University of Calgary Press.
Kant, Immanuel. 1998 (1797). *Metaphysics of Morals,* ed. by Mary Gregor. Cambridge: Cambridge University Press.
Kaul, Inge, Isabelle Grunberg, and Marc Stern, eds. 1999. *Global Public Goods: International Cooperation in the 21st Century.* Oxford: Oxford University Press.
Kuper, Andrew. 2002. "More than Charity: Cosmopolitan Alternatives to the 'Singer Solution.'" *Ethics and International Affairs* 16 (1): 107-28.
Miller, David. 1993. "In Defense of Nationality." *Journal of Applied Philosophy* 10 (1): 3-16.
–. 2005. "Against Global Egalitarianism." *Journal of Ethics* 9 (1): 55-79.
Miller, Richard W. 1998. "Cosmopolitanism Respect and Patriotic Concern." *Philosophy and Public Affairs* 27: 202-24.
–. 2010. *Globalizing Justice: The Ethics of Poverty and Power.* Oxford: Oxford University Press.
Moore, Margaret. 2009. "Is Patriotism an Associative Duty?" *Journal of Ethics* 13 (4): 383-99.

Nagel, Thomas. 2005. "The Problem of Global Justice." *Philosophy and Public Affairs* 33: 113-47.

Nussbaum, Martha. 1996. "Patriotism and Cosmopolitanism." In *For Love of Country? Debating the Limits of Patriotism*, ed. by Joshua Cohen. Boston: Beacon Press.

–. 1997. *Cultivating Humanity: A Classical Defense of Reform in Liberal Education.* Cambridge, MA: Harvard University Press.

Pogge, Thomas. 1992. *Realizing Rawls.* Ithaca, NY: Cornell University Press.

–. 2002. *World Poverty and Human Rights.* Cambridge: Polity Press.

Ripstein, Arthur. 2009. *Force and Freedom: Kant's Legal and Political Philosophy.* Cambridge, MA: Harvard University Press.

Sangiovanni, Andrea. 2007. "Global Justice, Reciprocity, and the State." *Philosophy and Public Affairs* 35 (1): 3-39.

Scheffler, Samuel. 2001. *Boundaries and Allegiances: Problems of Justice and Responsibility in Liberal Thought.* Oxford: Oxford University Press.

–. 2010. "The Normativity of Tradition." In *Equality and Tradition: Questions of Value in Moral and Political Theory.* Oxford: Oxford University Press.

Sen, Amartya. 2009. *The Idea of Justice.* Cambridge, MA: Harvard University Press.

Singer, Peter. 1972. "Famine, Affluence and Morality." *Philosophy and Public Affairs* 1: 229-43.

Tan, Kok-Chor. 2004. *Justice without Borders: Cosmopolitanism, Nationalism and Patriotism.* Cambridge: Cambridge University Press.

Vernon, Richard. 2010. *Cosmopolitan Regard: Political Membership and Global Justice.* Cambridge: Cambridge University Press.

Waldron, Jeremy. 1992. "Minority Cultures and the Cosmopolitan Alternative." *University of Michigan Law Review* 25: 751-92.

–. 2000. "What Is Cosmopolitan?" *Journal of Political Philosophy* 8 (2): 227-43.

Weinstock, Daniel. 1999. "National Partiality: Confronting the Intuitions." *The Monist* 82 (3): 516-41.

–. 2009. "Motivating the Global Demos." *Metaphilosophy* 40 (1): 92-108.

Wenar, Leif. 2005. "The Basic Structure as Object: Institutions and Humanitarian Concern." In *Global Justice, Global Institutions*, ed. by Daniel Weinstock, 253-78. Calgary: University of Calgary Press.

Ypi, Lea. 2008. "Statist Cosmopolitanism." *Journal of Political Philosophy* 16 (1): 48-71.

6

We Are All Compatriots

Charles Blattberg

One does not have to be a cosmopolitan to see that there is something seriously wrong with a world in which, whenever the slightest conflict arises between the needs of the local and those of the global, the former almost always prevail. To cite what should be a well-known example: even though it would take a shift of only 1 percent of global income from the First World to the Third in order to eliminate extreme poverty altogether, the shift does not take place (Pogge 2008, 223, 257, 264). This, surely, is a blatant injustice. For we are, after all, talking about *1 percent* – a figure that represents a minuscule difference to the lives of people in the First World but is a matter of life and death for millions in the Third.

Why, then, is such an appalling reality allowed to stand? Without necessarily discounting the many by now standard answers to this question – including ignorance, selfishness, insensitivity, futility, and complacency – I want to offer one of my own. It is an answer, moreover, that has something of an ironic tragedy about it for it aims to place the blame squarely on cosmopolitans and their allies, particularly on the abstract or rootless ways in which they tend to assert their positions. All of which is to say that if I were a cosmopolitan, I would be a rooted cosmopolitan. And yet this also means that in order to be a good rooted cosmopolitan, I would be a patriot. Let me explain.

Patriotism, as I conceive of it, is distinct from nationalism in that it is a political philosophy rather than political ideology. Only nationalism, then, should be placed on par, not to mention often in competition, with all of the other political ideologies – including cosmopolitanism, of course, but also liberalism, conservatism, socialism, feminism, green ideology, and so on. What makes ideologies different from philosophies is that the latter are, or should be, concerned chiefly with the kinds of

dialogue that people ought to engage in when responding to their conflicts, whereas the former aim to provide direction regarding the kinds
of things that we should be saying *within* those dialogues. What makes
patriotic political philosophy unique, moreover, is that it favours that
form of dialogue known as conversation, and this means that it can be
said to try to get us to respond to a conflict without ever having to invoke
an ideology. Those who converse aim to reconcile, rather than merely
accommodate, their differences, to develop, rather than compromise,
their values, and if there is to be a hope of doing this they will need to
listen to *each other* instead of to a preconceived doctrine such as an
ideology. They listen, moreover, not out of respect for some universal
principle such as that each person has equal moral worth but because
they hope to learn something about how they might better fulfill their
own values. That said, conversations tend to break down, which is why
patriots recognize that it will often become necessary to negotiate instead,
to weigh the values against each other, and this can mean turning to
ideologies for guidance about how to do so since they tell us how values
should be ranked. Crudely put, liberalism favours the liberty of the individual, socialism equality, conservatism controlled change, and so on.
Thus, although patriots can come to endorse any of these ideologies,
they will do so only once it has been determined that, in the case of a
given conflict, conversation is no longer viable – if it ever was (Blattberg
2009, ch. 1).

I call this approach patriotic because, despite being decidedly modern,
it has roots in that ancient, classical republican conception of politics
according to which a patriot is someone who aims to fulfill the common
good that he shares with his fellow citizens. Modern patriots accept that
women can do this at least as well as men, but we are also more aware
than our forebears were of how diverse a political community can be,
and so of why it must be legitimate – and not merely a sign of corrup-
tion – for parties to negotiate whenever conversation is deemed impossible. There no longer being any hope of reconciliation, it is surely right
to try to arrive at a balanced accommodation, to accept that the values
in conflict have taken on a zero-sum or adversarial, as distinct from
merely oppositional, relationship (Blattberg 2009, ch. 12) and so that
it will be necessary to perform a sort of "damage control" on the common good.

Now those, patriotic or otherwise, who turn in such cases to cosmopolitanism surely do so because they hope to give more weight to global
values over local ones. Alas for the cosmopolitan, we live in a world in
which most people adhere to precisely the opposite priority, for most

tend to care more about the persons or things that are closer to them (Hume 2007, 207, 309-10). This does not always have to be so – I grew up in a province, Ontario, whose citizens long prided themselves on identifying with Canada first – but it is certainly the norm. Perhaps this explains why cosmopolitans have tended to adopt rootless versions of their ideology, since if the domination of local circles of concern is to be overcome, many believe, those circles must be transcended and so ethics needs to be placed on an abstract footing.

It is precisely here, however, that we have reason to speak of an ironic tragedy, because when cosmopolitans favour abstraction, they end up doing two self-defeating things: first, they virtually guarantee that any conflict between the global and the local will take an adversarial form, thus ruling out reconciliation; second, they "disempower" the values, especially their own, by sapping their ability to motivate people to uphold them. And the effect of the latter, given the conflict's adversarial nature, is to ensure that the global values will almost invariably lose out when weighed against the local.

Hence that 1 percent.

The Problem with Abstraction

There is another way, however, one based on what we might call a "global patriotism." But before giving an account of it, I need to say something about the very idea of abstraction as well as about how it both undermines conversation and disempowers values. To abstract, as I understand it, is to consider something apart, to separate it in that sense from something else, and there are basically two ways in which this can be done with regard to our values: we can either separate them out from each other or separate them from ourselves (and doing the former, it is worth adding, automatically means doing the latter). Normally, values exist for us in a more or less integrated state, as parts of a whole, which is how they are expressed when we are engaged in everyday practices. This is also when they are at their most powerful, their most motivating, since they can draw support from a variety of considerations and so are the stronger for it. "To realise the relative validity of one's convictions," Isaiah Berlin (1969, 172), quoting Joseph Schumpeter, once wrote, "and yet stand for them unflinchingly is what distinguishes a civilised man from a barbarian." What I am suggesting goes further: it is precisely when we assume the relativity of our convictions, and so see them as embedded within the contexts of our practical lives, that we are most able to stand for them unflinchingly. For "the practical," as we might call it, is the domain where we are "plugged into" our values, allowing them to serve as the "sources of our selves," as Charles Taylor (1989) would put it.

When we abstract, however, we take either our values or ourselves out of the practical and put them into what we might call "the aesthetic." This happens to the values when we separate them out, since it leads us to take a disengaged stance toward them and that "pushes" them out of the practical. Many think, however, that doing so amounts to treating them in a naturalistic, as distinct from aesthetic, way instead, since this is the very same disengagement that natural scientists take toward their objects of study. And it is true that, ever since at least Galileo, scientists have focused on the context-free properties of things by employing a resolutive-compositive method: a phenomenon is atomized, separated out into its component parts, and these are then logically compounded in order to provide the sought-for explanation (Wallace 1984, 118-26). Unlike things in nature, however, values cannot fully exist outside of a context. To chop them up by, say, defining each with a set of necessary and sufficient conditions only renders them ersatz since it removes all that is "authentic" about them, using this term in the sense of Walter Benjamin (1968, 221) to refer to the qualities that something accrues because of its history.

When we abstract by separating ourselves from our values, which is what comes from taking on a special kind of disinterested attitude, then the effect is to move *us* toward the aesthetic, because that is the direction we go whenever we forgo our practical interpretations of the world and do one of at least three things instead: savour, imagine, or play. By savour I refer to the act of taking pleasure in a thing's beauty, in how it appears to our senses not as relevant to our practical values but, as Kant (1987, especially section 39) described, for its own sake. When we imagine, by contrast, we use the capacity that Vico (1968) called *fantasia* in order, say, to make or grasp metaphors or "to put ourselves in another's shoes," as the saying goes (Cohen 2008). Metaphors are figures of speech that suggest a similarity with things whose literal denotations can direct our attention sometimes very far away from our own practical contexts, as can looking at the world from someone else's perspective – especially, of course, when that someone is a fictional character or even an animal (Horowitz 2009). Finally, when we play, or at least play games, we conform to sets of rigid and systematic rules that, because they must also be followed for their own sake instead of for the game's ability to serve practical ends, establish domains that stand apart from our practical lives (Huizinga 1950, especially 8-10; Riezler 1941).

Now many cosmopolitans can be said to prefer the "separating out" kind of abstracting, since many favour the language of human rights, and what are rights if not atomized representations of our values, items that tend to be placed on unranked schedules or lists (Blattberg 2009, 45)? This, as I said, has the effect of separating us from the values as well, and if there are cosmopolitans who do that because they favour savouring, then it is probably because they share with Elaine Scarry (1999) the belief that the experience of the beautiful can evoke a sense of ethical fairness. More, however, are surely attracted to the imagination instead, since they agree with all those for whom its ability to bring empathy and compassion makes it "the great instrument of *moral* good," as Shelley (1977, 488) famously put it. Think of the many who invoke the ethic of the Golden Rule, which is present in virtually all of the world's major religions; or the Scottish Enlightenment's moral sentimentalist tradition (Krause 2008; Slote 2009); or that of American pragmatism (Fesmire 2003; Rorty 1993); or, finally, stories whose metaphors are said to be able to get us to think and act differently.[1] Because, as the writer Cynthia Ozick (1989, 283) once put it regarding the latter: "Through metaphorical concentration, doctors can imagine what it is to be their patients. Those who have no pain can imagine those who suffer. Those at the centre can imagine what it is to be outside. The strong can imagine the weak."

Others, however, turn instead to play, this being the favoured approach of most political theorists today. To them, justice requires that we conform to the systematic rules of a theory of justice, and such rules are comparable to those of a game, one that we are all expected to play fairly. Of course, doing so may also require the imagination, whether to follow the construction of the theory or simply to accept all of the hypotheticals necessary for adopting it.[2] Thus does John Rawls, for example, call on us to use our imagination at least twenty-three times in his *A Theory of Justice* (1971). But then, once we have agreed to his theory as the best way of affirming justice "for its own sake" (Rawls 1971, 9; 1996, 50, 54, 92, 148-49), the game may begin: "In much the same way that players have the shared end to execute a good and fair play of the game, so the members of a well-ordered society have the common aim of cooperating together to realize their own and another's nature in ways allowed by the principles of justice" (Rawls 1971, 527; 1996, 204).

As I have suggested, however, all of these various forms of abstraction undermine conversation, which is our best hope for justice. They do so because in order to converse we need to remain fully connected to our context, as only in this way can we express how the conflict impacts on our practical concerns as well as listen intently to what our interlocutors in that context have to say. When we separate out the values involved and conceive of them as independently distinct things, however, we are led to view their conflict as the product of a "clash" or "collision," and this is a fundamentally adversarial event. Faced with it, the best we can do is to balance the values against each other, that is, to struggle to reach an accommodation, to negotiate rather than to converse. Instead of listening with an open mind in the hopes of developing a shared understanding, we find ourselves putting pressure on each other to make concessions and to compromise, our aim, as Rousseau would put it, being to persuade rather than to convince.

There are at least two basic reasons for this, one pragmatic and the other conceptual. When we conceive of our opponents as adversaries, as threatening to do harm to our values, then we will simply feel too defensive, too insecure, to listen to them with an open mind. This is the pragmatic reason. And when the values in a conflict are seen as separate instead of as parts of a whole, then there is no reason to think that we and our opponents share any part of that whole, and so a common good. But it is none other than the common good that must be the topic of a conversation, since to converse is to assume that the values in conflict are "within" it, indeed, that it is a whole that, at least to some degree, is present in every part. Only in this way can it make sense to try to develop interpretations of the values that show them to be present within each other, thus further integrating rather than compromising them. Only if we can transform the whole so as to smooth out or harmonize its regions of tension – this being how we must conceive of the conflicting values (and not, again, as if they were separate things clashing or colliding) – can there be a hope of genuinely reconciling the conflict, of arriving at interpretations that everyone will perceive as being more true to the values than when the conflict began. This, then, is the conceptual reason why separating values out precludes conversation.[3]

Needless to say, conversation as so understood is an extremely difficult, not to mention fragile, affair. That is why the other form of abstracting, whereby we separate ourselves from the values by taking on a disinterested attitude, will also virtually guarantee its failure. Savouring a context's beauty (if there is any) will do this since it interferes with our ability to concentrate on the meanings of the values conflicting within it, and this is exactly what we must do if there is to be a hope of transforming them through reinterpretation. Imagining ourselves in another's shoes has the same effect, for it is *our* values, *our* identities, that need to be transformed if there is to be reconciliation. Finally, treating a conflict as if it were part of a game not only brings with it its own adversarial, because competitive, spirit but also requires us to respect a rigid system of rules, and that cannot help but impose limits on any reconciling transformations. This does not concern those such as Rawls (1996, 157) since they believe that, at least when it comes to the fundamental issues that are the purview of a society's basic structure, the "work of reconciliation" has already been completed by the theorist. But that is a mistake, and it is one which makes conversation not only superfluous but also impossible. In sum, then, while the move to the aesthetic can certainly entertain, it will not necessarily edify since it draws our attention away from ourselves and the common good, distracting us from the concentration necessary for conversing about it (Benjamin 1968, 239; Postman 1985).

Abstraction, I have claimed, not only undermines conversation but also disempowers our values. One way that it has this "unplugging" effect is well known, for it has become commonplace that the use of technical language, with its precise, independently distinct terms, encourages a sense of anonymity, of disconnection from self, and this makes it easier for people to behave in ways that they normally would not.[4] Think of military jargon: "collateral damage" for the deaths of civilians, "incontinent ordnances" for wayward bombs, "traumatic amputation" for the blowing off of arms and legs. Soldiers employ this terminology because they know that it makes it easier for them to do what they are ordered to do.[5] Or, to take a less dramatic example, consider the recent discovery by behavioural economists that the use of technical terms (e.g., "derivatives") by stock market traders has the effect of distancing them from the everyday, practical reality of their clients' money, and this makes it easier for them to steal it (Ariely 2008; Mazar et al. 2008, 633-44).

That rights talk can similarly disempower is suggested by the fact that in Canada today, although our Charter of Rights and Freedoms (1982) contains no positive, economic rights, and although we are a signatory to the UN Universal Declaration of Human Rights (1948), which does, our government redistributes over ten times more wealth to the Canadian poor than it does to far worse off, indeed severely impoverished, foreigners (Blattberg 2009, ch. 3). So while Canadians recognize that people the world over have a right not to live in poverty, it seems we are far more willing to have our non-rights-based policies take precedence.

Perhaps this is why, even though rights talk has achieved a near-paramount status in world politics today, many have begun to remark on a seemingly paradoxical phenomenon, namely, that the more states ratify human rights treaties, the more they seem to violate human rights (Hafner-Burton and Tsutsui 2005, 2007; Powell and Staton 2009). This is no paradox, however, if we recognize that rights talk's abstract, because atomic, nature interferes with our practical ethical motivations. It is because human rights advocates miss this that they fail to see the contradiction in speaking of "great progress in our moral norms and conduct" on the one hand and "a rather catastrophic moral situation on the ground" on the other (Pogge 2008, 3). Talk of human rights, cosmopolitans should thus accept, does not strengthen our global obligations – it does the opposite.

The same result comes from trying to affirm those obligations by abstracting ourselves out of the practical. While I do not have the space here to go into much detail about how the various forms of the disinterested attitude can have this effect, I do want to say something about each of them. To begin with beauty, Scarry's basic claim (1999, 95) is that our experience of it can lend support to a theory of distributive justice very much like that of Rawls. But this seems extremely hard to credit, and not only because beautiful art was often used to great effect by dictators in the twentieth century.[6] For Virginia Postrel (2003) seems to me to be on to something when she suggests that today we are more concerned about beauty than ever. Yet it is far from certain that we can say the same about justice.

As for imaginative ethics, its chief weakness is simple: seeing may not lead to feeling, which is to say that empathy may not produce compassion. Citing research on psychopaths showing that they are quite capable of the former without, of course, having much if any sense of the latter, Bruce Maxwell (2008, 151) has even written of what he calls "the fallacy of the Golden Rule." Now while this may just be symptomatic of their illness, it is nevertheless important to recognize that there exists a significant distinction here, one that should lead us to question the assumption that empathy and compassion are necessarily linked.[7]

And even if they are, this compassion is a notoriously fickle thing. Notice the stipulation at the end of novelist Maggie Gee's statement (2009) that "ideally, fiction can make both its creators and its readers kinder – at least for the duration of the book." Gee continues:

> I add that proviso because of course the fictional world is not the real one. We are freed in this infinitely yielding imaginary space from all

the frustrations and annoyances of every day, the intransigence of real life human beings acting as free and unpredictable agents, the demands they make on us, the way they bring out the worst in us and make all our attempts at empathy no more than partial successes.

But surely any viable ethics must be capable of maintaining its power in face of "the frustrations and annoyances of every day." My claim is that it can do so only if it remains directly connected to the practical. So whereas ostensibly rooted cosmopolitans such as Kwame Anthony Appiah (2005, 242) tell us that "nothing could be more powerful than the human imagination," I would suggest that, on the contrary, almost every (practical) thing is.[8] And what else should we expect, given that the aesthetic is a domain of numerous classic tropes and archetypes that, like anything, become boring with repetition?[9] Just think of our tendency to become numb to Holocaust imagery if we have seen too much of it. Formulas for imaginative empathy such as the Golden Rule, then, can never support anything more than a "second-best" form of justice. The Talmud makes this point in a particularly striking way:

> On another occasion it happened that a certain heathen came before Shammai and said to him, "Make me a proselyte, on condition that you teach me the whole Torah while I stand on one foot." Thereupon he repulsed him with the builder's cubit which was in his hand. When he went before Hillel, [the latter] said to him, "What is hateful to you, do not do to your neighbour: that is the whole Torah, while the rest is the commentary thereof; go and learn it." (Epstein 1961, 31a)

Hillel's laconic response suggests that he knows that the Golden Rule is, at best, a simulacrum of justice; better to "go and learn it" instead.

I would say the same of theories of justice, which are also formulas of a sort. And indeed it appears that most citizens are already aware of this since few are willing to accept theory as a means of guiding political practice (Miller 1999). Perhaps this is because they sense that making a game of politics fails to take it, and so our commitment to justice, seriously enough (Blattberg 2010).

The Patriotic Alternative
The first goal of patriotism, as we have seen, is reconciliation, which is why the first thing that a patriot will do when faced with a conflict between the global and the local is refuse any and all abstractions in favour of conversation. Because the patriot knows that only conversation can

make a win-win situation – one that gives every value its full due – possible. Instead of the zero-sum balancing of negotiation, then, patriots strive to integrate values by virtue of a transformation-through-reinterpretation of the common good.

Once again, however, we need to be aware that there is anything but a guarantee here. And when the conversation breaks down, the patriot will indeed turn to negotiation and so to balancing the values against each other. But at least this negotiation will take place on a wholly contextual, rather than abstract, plane, meaning that all of the values involved will be more or less empowered. Yet doesn't this mean that the local values will continue to win out over the global? Not necessarily. For the global will, for the first time, remain properly connected to a genuine community, a historical common good shared by persons with unique identities, rather than to abstractions such as rights-bearing human beings or individuals with whom we have come to empathize thanks to the mercurial spotlight of a sensationalist media.[10] All of which is to say that the global community will no longer be undermined by attempts to transcend – as opposed to expand – our practical circles of concern.

So no longer will there be any reason to heed those, such as Rajan Menon (2009, 235-37, 244), for whom the global community must be able to "empathize with" people in need as well as to prevent violations of its "core principles" by asserting the "primacy of universal obligations" – to Menon, unsurprisingly, it is because the global community has not been able to do these things that it should be seen as no more than "virtual" and the claim otherwise as but "an instance of the wish fathering the thought." But this is the wrong wish, because instead of principles and other abstractions[11] what that community needs is to be referred to in ways that help us conceive of it as a concrete, practical entity, as something that is a part of who we are.

Stories, both fictional and non-fictional, can help us to do this, but not if we focus on their metaphors; rather, we need to interpret them in ways that relate them to our practical lives. And it is not as though we should do this only with stories that focus directly on issues of worldwide relevance, such as genocide, the environment, or the recent economic crisis. For as the novelist Graham Swift has pointed out, references to the local can also have a very wide reach:

> If we are all, at least in our minds, travellers, if to write or to read a book is to go on a mental journey, then it is also true that books themselves travel. One proof of this is that books get translated, something which could hardly happen if the experience being purveyed could not be

recognized and felt to be true in more than one place. Writers are always trying to touch, to grasp the universal. And the way not to do this, it seems to me, is to write the avowedly universal, global, cosmopolitan book – the sort of book that ought to be written in Esperanto. The key to the universal is always the local, if only because it's a universal truth that all experience is and must be local, all experience is placed. If I read a book set in China or Peru, or indeed Nice, a great many local references may pass me by, but that doesn't matter, it even helps, because through them I nonetheless sense the true, the genuinely local texture of life as it's really lived. (Swift 2009, 310-11)

And as we might interpret Leonard Cohen on this quality, the key is for a reference to be specific and contextual rather than general and abstract:

That's advice that a lot of good writers have given me and the world. You don't really want to say "the tree," you want to say "the sycamore" ... We seem to be able to relate to detail. We seem to have an appetite for it. It seems that your days are made of details, and if you can get the sense of another person's day of details, your own day of details is summoned in your mind in some way rather than just a general line like "the days went by." It's better to say "watching Captain Kangaroo." Not "watching TV." Sitting in my room "with that hopeless little screen." Not just TV, but the hopeless, little screen. I think those are the details that delight us. They delight us because we can share a life then. It's our sense of insignificance and isolation that produces a great deal of suffering. (Zollo 1997, 340)

Notice how Cohen associates this delight with sharing, with relating what one is hearing or reading to one's everyday, practical concerns, not with imaginatively leaping out of that everyday and into someone else's. The fundamental goal, as Swift (2009, 309) has put it, is to be "led back in the end, with something more than we started with, to ourselves."

What both Swift and Cohen are saying, then, is that the proper way to benefit from such stories – at least when our goal is edification and not merely entertainment – is to approach them hermeneutically rather than aesthetically, critically rather than empathically, for only this allows them to contribute to the development of a durable, rather than fickle, form of caring. Such caring is what accompanies the sharing of a good in common with others, which can, after all, be the basis of a kind of friendship – and friendship is, of course, a thoroughly practical, as distinct from natural or aesthetic, thing. It is friends, moreover, or at least good ones, who always try to respond to their conflicts with conversation. That is why whenever conversations take place between the citizens of the same state, we may identify the civic or political community expressed by that state, by its laws and institutions, with the common good that they share. And it is why when those conversations reach across borders we have reason to speak of a global common good, hence of a global patriotism.

Of course, unlike friendships between two people, when it comes to politics one does not have to actually *like* the person or persons one is conversing with, only to recognize that there are good reasons for caring about them. What is required, we might say, is sympathy (rather than empathy). And this is something that, once again, comes from engaging a hermeneutical form of practical reason, one that, it is worth mentioning, shares a great deal with Aristotle's notion of practical wisdom *(phronēsis)*.[12] For while Aristotle does give *phantasia* an important role within *phronēsis*,[13] he means something very different by the term than does Vico. This becomes clear when we appreciate that Aristotelian *phantasia* is a selective, discriminatory capacity rather than one that we might associate with fantasy; as Martha Nussbaum (1990, 77) has described, "its job is more to focus on reality than to create unreality."[14] And it is only by doing this well that we can bring about the *dispositions* that are appropriate to given contexts, hence that form of caring that I am calling sympathy.

Thus, by shunning abstractions rooted cosmopolitans can make way for the empowerment of their values and so, for perhaps the very first time, give them comparable weight with local ones when balancing them against each other becomes unavoidable. What is required is certainly not more abstract principles such as the newly minted "responsibility to protect,"[15] since we need ways of affirming the global as a genuine community. These could include replacing the relatively recent and abstract notion of "crimes against humanity" with one that refers to a form of "treason against the world" instead, since this would be a far more powerful way of proscribing widespread or systematic violations of what we might call "the minimal global ethic" (Blattberg 2009, ch. 10). Or we could have the United Nations issue everyone a passport in order to encourage those holding it alongside, say, a Canadian one to weigh the obligations that each represents more equitably when they turn out to be irreconcilable. For if we Canadians can care for over thirty million of our compatriots, then surely this is a number without limit, which is to say that it must be possible to feel an attachment to billions and not only millions.

An Illustration: Refugees

It would be wrong to say very much more about how patriots would deal with such issues here, in the "abstract," since whether a dialogue takes the form of conversation or negotiation, it will always require an actual context, not to mention real interlocutors, if it is to be genuine. It is not for the armchair political philosopher, however committed to practical contexts, to dictate a potential dialogue's terms, nor to say very much about the conclusions that might be reached. Still, in order to further illustrate my approach, I want to conclude with a look at what has become a major area of tension between the global and the local – namely, refugees. My argument, in essence, is that the dominance of abstractions, particularly human rights, has encouraged states to let in fewer refugees than they should. I begin by describing Michael Walzer's account of the politics of immigration admissions, since his is generally taken to reflect the conventional or orthodox view. I then show how that view is biased against refugees and how human rights talk is largely responsible for such bias. The other abstract alternatives do not fare much better, however, since the support they are able to provide refugees remains weak at best.

Walzer (1983, 52) has summed-up his position as follows: "The members of a political community have a collective right to shape the resident population – a right subject always to the double control that I have described: the meaning of membership to the current members and the principle of mutual aid." Walzer is sometimes misinterpreted as asserting that, except in the case of those who can demonstrate some kind of special political affinity to the state they are trying to enter, refugees have no moral claim whatsoever on that state and so must rely on its charity or some other such supererogatory virtue (Singer and Singer 1988, 121). As we can see from the quotation above, however, he distinguishes between the question of *who* is to decide immigration policy, a power he awards to each sovereign state, and *what* is the basis on which that decision should be made. It is with regard to the latter that he recommends the twofold criteria of a citizenry's self-interpretation, and so of the kinds of people that it believes should be eligible for membership, on the one hand and the duty to come to the aid of those in need, on the other. Yet note that Walzer (1983, 51) conceives of the latter as something that "can only modify and not transform" the former. Evidently, he wants to give priority to the local community over mutual aid, although this is not to be an overriding priority since it is something he is willing to compromise.

The two, then, are to be negotiated, balanced against each other. And that is precisely what tends to happen in practice today, even when we are dealing with only those refugees who have managed to reach a state's borders in order to claim asylum. One might think that this contravenes international law since, as Article 14 of the UN Universal Declaration of Human Rights states, "everyone has the right to seek and to enjoy in other countries asylum from persecution," and as Article 31 of the UN Convention Relating to the Status of Refugees (1951) implies, all such people must be given a fair hearing to determine whether they are genuine refugees and be allowed to stay if they are. Every signatory state, however, is permitted, indeed expected, to interpret the definition of who is a refugee in its own way, and it goes without saying that the narrower the interpretation, the fewer refugees will be let in. Thus, given the large number of asylum claims, this can only mean that large numbers of genuine refugees are, *de facto* if not *de jure,* being turned away. Walzer is consequently right to recognize that their needs are being compromised to a degree, for they are being balanced against the political community's understanding of its own needs and membership. Whether he is right to approve of this is another story.

For that balance is, again, unduly weighted against the refugees. One of the reasons for this is that the mutual aid side of the equation tends to be articulated in the language of rights and, as we have seen, rights talk has a counterproductive, because divisive and disempowering, effect. It has such an effect in this case in particular because it emphasizes the refugee's separation from the community, as Walzer (1983, 32-33) also does when he describes mutual aid as an "*external* principle for the distribution of membership" (emphasis added), one relevant to "strangers," individuals with whom one does not "share a common life." So this is why, when it comes to a country's weighing of the rights of refugee claimants against what it perceives to be its own needs, we cannot expect there to be much of a contest.

Of course, many are dissatisfied with the status quo, hence with approaches like Walzer's that essentially endorse it, but they tend to make the mistake of advocating equally abstract alternatives. Think of all those who call on us to accept their theories of justice. When it comes to the matter of immigration admissions, playing according to a given theory's rules is often said to result in the surmounting of the conflict between mutual aid and the political community's sense of itself.[16] This is because the latter, at least when it comes to democratic states, ends up being interpreted in terms of principles that are fully compatible with mutual aid. Kant (1983, 118), for example, does precisely this when he asserts a conception of cosmopolitan right according to which no one trying to get into a country may be turned away should it lead to his or her "destruction." Or we might cite Joseph Carens's survey (1995) of the theories of Rawls, Robert Nozick, and utilitarians, which concludes with the claim that, properly understood, all support the case for open borders.

Both Kant's and Carens's approaches are abstract, however, since they are not driven by actual cases of conflict and so are not grounded in any particular context. And that, it seems to me, is precisely why so few people are willing to go along with them. Faced with this, theorists understandably become frustrated and sometimes even turn to *ad hominem* arguments. Here, for example, are Peter and Renata Singer (1988, 128): "We regard the *status quo* as the outcome of a system of national selfishness and political expediency, not as the result of a considered attempt to work out the moral obligations of the developed nations in a world with ten million refugees." But all this only leaves the values underlying mutual aid with very little support – no more, that is, than may come from following Rawls's suggestion (1971, 339) that we "imagine what a society would be like if it were publicly known that this duty was rejected" – which is to say, little support indeed.

At least, however, it would be more than could be provided by a refugee policy that was driven by something like Scarry's conception of justice as beauty. I would say the same of all those approaches that encourage us to use our imaginations in order to empathize with refugees' suffering, for they would leave the basic, zero-sum structure of the conflict between an external principle of mutual aid and an internal sense of communal self-government intact, since their goal is to do no more than add weight to the former by getting us to experience it in a different way. Thus do the Singers (1988, 111-13, 128), for example, open their article on the ethics of refugee policy by asking us to imagine what we would do if we had a say over whether to let desperate people into a luxury shelter following a nuclear war (three proposals are presented – admit 10,000 outsiders, 500, or none – and we are confronted with the question of how many tennis courts we would be willing to give up in order to provide them with a radiation-free place to sleep). But any change in perspective or feelings that may result can, as I suggested above, never be other than fickle, which is precisely why this approach will ultimately fail to bring about the justice required.

Instead of invoking abstractions, then, the patriot will try to reinterpret mutual aid in a way that allows it to be understood as something *internal* to the political community's sense of itself. This means beginning with the actual refugee-driven conflicts faced by the community and asking how they might be reconciled through conversation. When successful, we would be able to say that the community's conception of its common good, and so its 'members' concrete, particularistic circles of concern, will have been expanded instead of traded off against some universal principle.

If I think of how this might be done by the two political communities to which I, in addition to the global, feel a particular sense of attachment – Canada, of course, but also Israel – then I would suggest the following. Beginning with the latter, I believe that a real difference could be made if Israelis, both Jewish and Arab, were encouraged to think about refugee claims while keeping in mind not, say, the obligations that stem from some doctrine of universal human rights but the histories of both the many Jewish refugees who fled from Arab lands, or from the Nazis during the Second World War, and the many Palestinians who either fled from or abandoned their homes during modern Israel's founding (Morris 2004; Proudfoot 1956; Shulewitz 2000). The result, I believe, would be a far more open refugee policy than is the case today (even if it would be one understandably shaped by Jewish concerns about the demographic balance between the country's two national communities; Blattberg 2009, ch. 6). And such a policy would not have to represent a compromise of the country's sense of itself in favour of some external principle; on the contrary, nothing would be more internal, more authentically true, to its ideals.

I would say the same of a Canada that opened its doors to more refugees. We Canadians already welcome more immigrants per capita than perhaps any other country, but by choosing more of them from among the world's refugees we would better acknowledge our citizenry's membership in the global community of persons. It is often said that the identity of a community is partly constituted by what it is not, by the contrast between "us" and "them." That this is all too easy to do between local communities is clear. But what of the global community? If it includes all of the others, then from what can it be distinguished? Here it seems to me worthwhile to turn to some of the ideas present within Canadian Aboriginal traditions, particularly those grounded in animistic cosmologies, for they suggest a way of relating man to the other animal species, and indeed to all other parts of nature, that allows us to conceive of their similarities and differences along the lines of those that exist between communities (Bringhurst 1999; Robinson 1992).

To the degree that this can help us to conceive of the global community as not only distinct from and but also a part of Canada, then we Canadians will surely want to let more refugees into the country. Not, again, because we see them as bearing certain rights, nor because it would be something beautiful or imaginative or playful to do. No, we would do so because it would be a way of being more true to ourselves, to who we really are. And even if this were not the case, it would still mean conceiving of mutual aid as part of a shared common good, hence empowering it far more than it has ever been before. How much more? That depends, of course, but we can be sure of one thing: it will be at least 1 percent.

Notes

1 For example, Singer (2009) opens his book's first chapter by asking us what we would do if we saw a small child drowning in a pond but wading in and pulling him out would ruin our new pair of shoes and make us late for work. He then draws an analogy with the nearly 10 million children under five who die each year from poverty-related causes. Singer's regard for the ethical role of stories is also evident in the book he edited with Renata Singer (2005). Lodge (2002) can be said to sum up this approach when he quotes Ian McEwan on the terrorist attacks of 11 September 2001: "If the hijackers had been able to imagine themselves into the thoughts and feelings of the passengers, they would have been unable to proceed ... Imagining what it is like to be someone other than yourself is at the core of our humanity. It is the essence of compassion and the beginning of morality."

2 This accounts, it seems to me, for Habermas's recommendation (1990) that we adopt a "hypothetical attitude." To Habermas (1982, 253), the work of developmental psychologist Laurence Kohlberg supports the idea that, at its highest stages, moral consciousness requires us to be willing and able to "consider moral questions from the hypothetical and disinterested perspective."

3 For more on this transformative conception of practical reason, see Blattberg 2000, especially ch. 3.

4 I consider this an example of what psychologists call a "situationist" phenomenon, wherein aspects of our circumstances or environment influence our behaviour. See, for example, Milgram 1974 and Zimbardo 2007.

5 According to the psychologist Fromm (1973, 23): "There is good clinical evidence for the assumption that destructive aggression occurs, at least to a large degree, in conjunction with a momentary or chronic emotional withdrawal." Other forms of emotional distancing are discussed by Grossman (1996, 156-70).

6 This is one of the reasons Dutton (2000, 259) gives for rejecting Scarry's claims.

7 For as Isenberg (1973, 163) has put it, in aesthetics "sameness of vision" may or may not be followed by a "community of feeling."

8 Appiah (2006, 85) also makes the mistake of claiming that "conversations across boundaries of identity – whether national, religious, or something else – begin with the sort of imaginative engagement you get when you read a novel or watch a movie or attend to a work of art that speaks from some place other than your own." As I shall explain below, to assume that conversation begins with imagination is to miss its hermeneutical, and so practical rather than aesthetic, basis. For practical dialogues must take place between interlocutors, "between" being one way of translating the ancient Greek *dia-*, whereas imagining, as we have already noted, is "disinterested," from the Latin *dis-* ("not"), *inter-* ("between"), and *esse* ("to be").

9 On the tropes and archetypes, see Frye 1957. On how the boredom of repetition is the bane of the aesthetic life, see Kierkegaard 1987.

10 On the problems with the former, see Blattberg (2009, ch. 3) as well as the original critiques of rights as abstractions advanced by Bentham, Burke, and Marx (reproduced in Waldron 1987). As for the problems with the latter, see Boltanski 1999 (chs. 9-10) and Moeller 1999.

11 On why principles are ineffective (or worse) for ethics, see Blattberg 2009 (ch. 8) and Dancy 2004.

12 See Gadamer 1989 (220-22, 312), although Gadamer would, of course, reject my Kantian claim that the aesthetic constitutes a distinct domain; hence his blurring of Aristotle and Vico.

13 See Aristotle (1941, 427a61-429a9, 431b2-19). According to Noel (1999), *phantasia*'s role in *phronēsis* is twofold: first, that of laying out an ideal as an end goal, and, second, that of comparing options in order to arrive at the best judgment.

14 Note, however, that both Nussbaum and Noel appear not to distinguish enough between this non-aesthetic *phantasia* and what today we call imagination.

15 See International Commission on Intervention and State Sovereignty 2001, and Evans 2008.

16 For the surmounting of conflict is precisely what a theory of justice is supposed to provide: "If we are to succeed in finding a basis of public agreement, we must find a new way of organizing familiar ideas and principles into a conception of political justice so that the claims in conflict, as previously understood, are seen in another light" (Rawls 1999, 393).

References
Appiah, Kwame Anthony. 2005. *The Ethics of Identity.* Princeton, NJ: Princeton University Press.

–. 2006. *Cosmopolitanism: Ethics in a World of Strangers.* New York: W.W. Norton.

Ariely, Dan. 2008. "How Honest People Cheat." *Harvard Business Review* Blog Network, 29 January. http://blogs.harvardbusiness.org/cs/2008/01/how_honest_people_cheat.html.

Aristotle. 1941. *De Anima,* trans. by J.A. Smith. In *The Basic Works of Aristotle,* ed. by Richard McKeon, 535-603. New York: Random House.

Benjamin, Walter. 1968. "The Work of Art in the Age of Mechanical Reproduction." In *Illuminations: Essays and Reflections,* ed. by Hannah Arendt, trans. by Harry Zohn. New York: Schocken Books.

Berlin, Isaiah. 1969. "Two Concepts of Liberty." In *Four Essays on Liberty,* 118-72. Oxford: Oxford University Press.

Blattberg, Charles. 2000. *From Pluralist to Patriotic Politics: Putting Practice First.* Oxford and New York: Oxford University Press.

–. 2009. *Patriotic Elaborations: Essays in Practical Philosophy.* Montreal and Kingston: McGill-Queen's University Press.

–. 2010. "Taking Politics Seriously – but Not Too Seriously." Social Science Research Network, http://papers.ssrn.com/sol3/papers.cfm?abstract_id=1723387.

Boltanski, Luc. 1999. *Distant Suffering: Morality, Media and Politics,* trans. by Graham D. Burchell. Cambridge: Cambridge University Press.

Bringhurst, Robert. 1999. *A Story as Sharp as a Knife: The Classical Haida Mythtellers and Their World.* Vancouver: Douglas and McIntyre.

Carens, Joseph H. 1995. "Aliens and Citizens: The Case for Open Borders." In *Theorizing Citizenship,* ed. by Ronald Beiner, 229-53. Albany, NY: SUNY Press.

Cohen, Ted. 2008. *Thinking of Others: On the Talent for Metaphor.* Princeton, NJ: Princeton University Press.

Dancy, Jonathan. 2004. *Ethics without Principles.* Oxford: Oxford University Press.

Dutton, Denis. 2000. "Mad about Flowers: Elaine Scarry on Beauty." *Philosophy and Literature* 24 (1): 249-60.

Epstein, Isidore, ed. 1961. *The Babylonian Talmud: Tractate Shabbath,* trans. by H. Freedman. London: Soncino Press.

Evans, Gareth. 2008. *The Responsibility to Protect: Ending Mass Atrocity Crimes Once and for All.* Washington, DC: Brookings Institution Press.

Fesmire, Steven. 2003. *John Dewey and Moral Imagination: Pragmatism in Ethics.* Bloomington, IN: Indiana University Press.

Fromm, Erich. 1973. *The Anatomy of Human Destructiveness.* New York: Holt, Rinehart and Winston.

Frye, Northop. 1957. *Anatomy of Criticism: Four Essays.* Princeton, NJ: Princeton University Press.

Gadamer, Hans-Georg. 1989. *Truth and Method,* 2nd ed. rev., trans. by Joel Weinsheimer and Donald G. Marshall. New York: Crossroad.

Gee, Maggie. 2009. "Britain's Got Talons." *Prospect Magazine,* June. http://www.prospectmagazine.co.uk/2009/06/britainsgottalons/.

Grossman, Dave. 1996. *On Killing: The Psychological Cost of Learning to Kill in War and Society.* Boston: Little, Brown.

Habermas, Jürgen. 1982. "A Reply to My Critics." In *Habermas: Critical Debates,* ed. by John B. Thompson and David Held, 219-83. Cambridge, MA: MIT Press.

–. 1990. *Moral Consciousness and Communicative Action,* trans. by Christian Lenhardt and Shierry Weber Nicholsen. Cambridge, MA: MIT Press.

Hafner-Burton, Emilie M., and Kiyoteru Tsutsui. 2005. "Human Rights in a Globalizing World: The Paradox of Empty Promises." *American Journal of Sociology* 110 (5): 1373-1411.

–. 2007. "Justice Lost! The Failure of International Human Rights Law to Matter Where Needed Most." *Journal of Peace Research* 44 (4): 407-25.

Horowitz, Alexandra. 2009. *Inside of a Dog: What Dogs See, Smell, and Know.* New York: Scribner.

Huizinga, Johan. 1950. *Homo Ludens: A Study of the Play Element in Culture.* Boston: Beacon Press.

Hume, David. 2007. *A Treatise of Human Nature,* vol. 1, ed. by David Faye Norton and Mary J. Norton [2007, 1739-40]. Oxford: Oxford University Press.

International Commission on Intervention and State Sovereignty. 2001. *The Responsibility to Protect.* Ottawa: International Development Research Centre.

Isenberg, Arnold. 1973. "Critical Communication." In *Aesthetics and the Theory of Criticism,* 156-71. Chicago: University of Chicago Press.

Kant, Immanuel. 1983. "To Perpetual Peace: A Philosophical Sketch." In *Perpetual Peace and Other Essays,* trans. by Ted Humphrey, [1983, 1784], 107-43. Indianapolis, IN: Hackett.

–. 1987. *Critique of Judgment,* trans. by Werner S. Pluhar, [1987, 1790]. Indianapolis, IN: Hackett.

Kierkegaard, Søren. 1987. "The Seducer's Diary." In *Either/Or: Part I,* trans. by Howard V. Hong and Edna H. Hong, 301-445. Princeton, NJ: Princeton University Press.

Krause, Sharon R. 2008. *Civil Passions: Moral Sentiment and Democratic Deliberation.* Princeton, NJ: Princeton University Press.

Lodge, David. 2002. "Consciousness and the Novel." In *Consciousness and the Novel: Connected Essays,* 1-91. Cambridge, MA: Harvard University Press.

Menon, Rajan. 2009. "Pious Words, Puny Deeds: The 'International Community' and Mass Atrocities." *Ethics and International Affairs* 23 (3): 235-45.

Maxwell, Bruce. 2008. *Professional Ethics Education: Studies in Compassionate Empathy.* Dordrecht, Netherlands: Springer.

Mazar, Nina, On Amir, and Dan Ariely. 2008. "The Dishonesty of Honest People: A Theory of Self-Concept Maintenance." *Journal of Marketing Research* 45 (6): 633-44.

Milgram, Stanley. 1974. *Obedience to Authority: An Experimental View.* New York: Harper and Row.

Miller, David. 1999. "Distributive Justice: What the People Think." In *Principles of Social Justice,* 61-92. Cambridge, MA: Harvard University Press.

Moeller, Susan D. 1999. *Compassion Fatigue: How the Media Sell Disease, Famine, War, and Death.* New York: Routledge.

Morris, Benny. 2004. *The Birth of the Palestinian Refugee Problem Revisited.* Cambridge: Cambridge University Press.

Noel, Jana. 1999. "*Phronesis* and *Phantasia:* Teaching with Wisdom and Imagination." *Journal of Philosophy of Education* 33 (2): 277-86.

Nussbaum, Martha. 1990. "The Discernment of Perception: An Aristotelian Conception of Private and Public Rationality." In *Love's Knowledge: Essays on Philosophy and Literature,* 54-105. Oxford: Oxford University Press.

Ozick, Cynthia. 1989. "Metaphor and Memory." In *Metaphor and Memory: Essays,* 265-83. New York: Knopf.

Pogge, Thomas W. 2008. *World Poverty and Human Rights: Cosmopolitan Responsibilities and Reforms,* 2nd ed. Cambridge: Polity Press.

Postman, Neil. 1985. *Amusing Ourselves to Death: Public Discourse in the Age of Show Business.* New York: Penguin.

Postrel, Virginia. 2003. *The Substance of Style: How the Rise of Aesthetic Value Is Remaking Commerce, Culture, and Consciousness.* New York: HarperCollins.

Powell, Emilia Justyna J., and Jeffrey K. Staton. 2009. "Domestic Judicial Institutions and Human Rights Treaty Violation." *International Studies Quarterly* 53 (1): 149-74.

Proudfoot, Malcolm Jarvis. 1956. *European Refugees 1939-52: A Study in Forced Population Movement.* Evanston, IL: Northwestern University Press.

Rawls, John. 1971. *A Theory of Justice.* Cambridge, MA: Harvard University Press.

–. 1996. *Political Liberalism,* 388-414. New York: Columbia University Press.

–. 1999. "Justice as Fairness: Political not Metaphysical." In *Collected Papers,* ed. by Samuel Freeman. Cambridge, MA: Harvard University Press.

Riezler, Kurt. 1941. "Play and Seriousness." *Journal of Philosophy* 38 (19): 505-17.

Robinson, Harry. 1992. *Nature Power: In the Spirit of an Okanagan Storyteller,* ed. by Wendy Wickwire. Vancouver: Douglas and McIntyre.

Rorty, Richard. 1993. "Human Rights, Rationality, and Sentimentality." In *On Human Rights: The Oxford Amnesty Lectures,* ed. by Stephen Shute and Susan Hurley, 111-34. New York: Basic Books.

Scarry, Elaine. 1999. *On Beauty and Being Just.* Princeton, NJ: Princeton University Press.

Shelley, Percy Bysshe. 1977. "A Defence of Poetry." In *Shelley's Poetry and Prose,* ed. by Donald H. Reiman and Sharon B. Powers, 478-508. New York: W.W. Norton.

Shulewitz, Malka Hillel, ed. 2000. *The Forgotten Millions: The Modern Jewish Exodus from Arab Lands.* London: Continuum.

Singer, Peter. 2009. *The Life You Can Save: Acting Now to End World Poverty,* 111-30. New York: Random House.

Singer, Peter, and Renata Singer. 1988. "The Ethics of Refugee Policy." In *Open Borders? Closed Societies? The Ethical and Political Issues,* ed. by Mark Gibney. New York: Greenwood Press.

–, eds. 2005. *The Moral of the Story: An Anthology of Ethics through Literature.* Oxford: Blackwell.

Slote, Michael. 2009. *Moral Sentimentalism.* Oxford: Oxford University Press.

Swift, Graham. 2009. "I Do Like to Be Beside the Seaside." In *Making an Elephant: Writing from Within,* 291-312. New York: Knopf.

Taylor, Charles. 1989. *Sources of the Self: The Making of the Modern Identity.* Cambridge, MA: Harvard University Press.

Vico, Giambattista. 1968. *The New Science of Giambattista Vico,* trans. by Thomas Goddard Bergin and Max Harold Fisch. Ithaca, NY: Cornell University Press.

Waldron, Jeremy, ed. 1987. *Nonsense upon Stilts: Bentham, Burke and Marx on the Rights of Man.* London and New York: Methuen.

Wallace, William A. 1984. *Galileo and His Sources: The Heritage of the Collegio Romano in Galileo's Science.* Princeton, NJ: Princeton University Press.

Walzer, Michael. 1983. *Spheres of Justice: A Defense of Pluralism and Equality.* New York: Basic Books.

Zimbardo, Philip G. 2007. *The Lucifer Effect: Understanding How Good People Turn Evil.* New York: Random House.

Zollo, Paul. 1997. "Leonard Cohen: Los Angeles, 1992." In *Songwriters on Songwriting,* 329-50. Cambridge, MA: Da Capo Press.

Part 2
The Practice of Rooted Cosmopolitanism

7

Cosmopolitanizing Cosmopolitanism? Cosmopolitan Claims Making, Interculturalism, and the Bouchard-Taylor Report

Scott Schaffer

Recent trends in Anglo-North American social theorizing have shown that one of the primary concerns for theorists is the normatively oriented exploration of how we relate to others in the world. Whether theorists choose to emphasize cosmopolitanism's political aspects regarding the organization of states and human rights in the world or its ethical aspects relating to how those of us in the global North orient toward others, whether in our midst or across the globe, it is clear that how we live with or near others, and how we treat them, has returned to the fore of social theorizing. Yet, save for a small number of scholars who have examined the ways in which cosmopolitan strictures inform lived social practices (Portes 2000; Skrbis and Woodward 2007), there have been relatively few case study-based analyses or theoretical discussions about the ways in which cosmopolitanism operates on the ground. Although I do not necessarily subscribe to the view that social theory should be subjected to the scientific method, I believe that for those theorists working to develop such a normative and prescriptive theoretical perspective, it is important to explore how it is that cosmopolitanism is and has been lived, in order to better refine the extent to which we can say or suggest that people should live cosmopolitan lives.

Such an opportunity is afforded us thanks to the recent examination of immigration, social integration, and societal accommodations afforded to immigrants in the province of Quebec. The Consultation Commission on Accommodation Practices Related to Cultural Differences (la Commission de consultation sur les pratiques d'accommodement reliées aux différences culturelles, or CCPARDC), headed by the philosopher Charles Taylor and the Québécois sociologist Gérard Bouchard (2008, 33), was commissioned by the government of Quebec to explore "accommodation practices related to cultural differences, [and] analyse the attendant issues bearing in mind the experience of other societies." However, rather than simply examining the data regarding the extent to which new immigrants to Quebec had requested some form of accommodation of their particular customs or beliefs by institutional or professional practices, as was their initial mandate, Bouchard and Taylor went much further in their consultations and their report, expanding their inquiry into the study of the cultural, economic, and social conditions within which immigration to Quebec, the integration of newcomers into the life of the province, and the reaction of Quebecers to new immigrants took place. The resulting report, *Building the Future: A Time for Reconciliation* (referred to hereafter as the Bouchard-Taylor Report), not only represents the result of wide-ranging consultations with the Quebec public and the contributions of scholars to the commission's work but is also a case study within which we can explore the ways in which cosmopolitan policies and cosmopolitan practices are frequently detached from one another.

One of the logics of cosmopolitan thinking has to do with the ways in which local, national, and global identities and interactions with others at each of these levels of analysis begin to take on an isomorphic quality. The way we conceptualize ourselves and interact with others in our multiethnic city, as citizens of a country that interacts with other nations on the planet, and how we orient to those suffering halfway around the world, all begin to take on a similar morphology. Appadurai's development of the concept of the ethnoscape (1992, 192-93; 1996), the "landscape of persons who make up the shifting world in which we live: tourists, immigrants, refugees, exiles, guest workers, and other moving groups and persons," reflects the deterritorialization not only of money and commodities but also of people (Hannerz 1992); distinguishing between cosmopolitans who travel the world consuming cultures and transnationals, those who relocate themselves in a diasporic manner and face economic and social hardships in doing so, still manages to identify a common characteristic of each group, namely, the cultural hybridity developed as a response to their particular situation (Werbner 1997, 11-12). And Robbins (1998, 2-3) argues that since we are not connected solely to one place but "to all sorts of places, causally if not always consciously, including many that we have never travelled to," cosmopolitanisms should be seen as plural, "both European and non-European ... weak and underdeveloped as well as strong and privileged." In these formulations and others lies one commonality – the realization that, whether at home or abroad, a first-class traveller on a transoceanic flight or a transnational guest worker, we exist in a world that presses on us frequent contact with others from elsewhere in that world. In short, we could say that, both at home and elsewhere in the world, we exist in a state of *la mixité*, a concept that carries more with it than a mere descriptive state of "diversity" and captures the experience of the mixing *(la brassage)* of peoples having to grapple with one another's existence (Genestier 2010, 21-23).

As well, we have to recognize that cosmopolitanism itself carries little value unless we come to understand it not simply as a theoretical discourse or set of normative prescriptions but also as grounded in and, we hope, guiding a variety of lived experiences of the world (Malcomson 1998; Skrbis and Woodward 2007). The very notion of rooted cosmopolitanism that undergirds this book embodies this; the notion that we are simultaneously rooted, acting within and embodied in a particular location and context while maintaining moral and ethical commitments to others with whom we will never have contact, all the while ensuring a continuity of our ethical action, suggests that this isomorphism of lived experiences of the social world is at the heart of new conceptions of cosmopolitanism. As a duty of openness to the Other, cosmopolitanism as an ethical program arises in both domestic and foreign contexts, and is engaged whether the Other appears on the cosmopolitan's home turf due to migration or the cosmopolitan appears on the Other's home turf. I begin this work with the premise that even though the Bouchard-Taylor Report never once mentions cosmopolitanism (in either the English or French versions), its authors' efforts to articulate the principles of interculturalism on Quebec's home turf embody a cosmopolitan ethos.

To my mind, the importance of the Bouchard-Taylor Report lies precisely in the tacit exploration of the detachment of cosmopolitan policy and practice in the province of Quebec, and highlights one of the crucial issues that lurks in the shadows of cosmopolitan social thought – namely, the question of *how to get people to act in a cosmopolitan manner.* The problem, as I intend to show here, is that, to date, cosmopolitanism as an ethic and as policy has not yet fully had a mechanism for claims making; that is, theorists have not yet conceptualized how it is that people might make claims against those who purport to have a cosmopolitan ethics or politics. The Bouchard-Taylor Report's examination of the provincial policy of interculturalism, accommodation practices in the public and private sectors of Quebec, and the insecurities of Quebecers regarding the purported agenda of newcomers to the province give us the basis for thinking through the problem of cosmopolitan claims making, and thereby give us a crucial additive to this body of normative theory. To put it another way, what is needed, and what the Bouchard-Taylor Report gives us, is a way of cosmopolitanizing cosmopolitanism.

In order to paint a picture of this process, I will first detail what I mean by cosmopolitanism, focusing primarily on its ethical aspects and highlighting the issues that can appear when it becomes official state policy. Then I will develop my notion of cosmopolitan claims making, a process in which self-proclaimed cosmopolitans can be called on by the others to whom they are attempting to relate to adhere more firmly to their stated ethical principles. Turning then to the case of accommodation practices in Quebec, I show the ways in which the practices and processes detailed at length in the Bouchard-Taylor Report represent a cosmopolitan claims-making process. Finally, I will highlight the ways in which the issues raised in the Bouchard-Taylor Report speak to the possibilities of normative cosmopolitanism, showing how it is that the detachment of cosmopolitan policy and lived practice presents issues that can be addressed only by recalling the phenomenology of any form of ethics – that it requires a degree of responsibility and accountability, one that, while contained in the official policy of interculturalism, has not yet become a part of how we conceptualize cosmopolitanism.

It should be noted, though, that this examination represents only half of the study needed regarding issues of accommodation in Quebec and cosmopolitan thought as a whole. To be sure, the ethical element of cosmopolitanism addresses one crucial social justice element of our time – namely, what Nancy Fraser (1997) and Axel Honneth (2007), among others, have termed the issue of recognition. The other component of the problem of social justice in our time, one that Fraser and Honneth both recognize as intimately bound up with the problem of recognition, is the problem of redistribution (Fraser 1997; Fraser and Honneth 2003; Honneth 2007). Both scholars, the most insightful on the problem of the relation between recognition and redistribution in our time, make the claim that any substantive critique of society must attend to, as Honneth puts it, "the socio-structural causes responsible for a distortion of the social framework of recognition" (Honneth 2007, 74). Space limitations here prevent me from following through on this exploration; however, as the Bouchard-Taylor Report specifically, though in a limited manner, deals with the issue of inequality (particularly through "labour market integration" [Bouchard and Taylor 2008, 259]), it is clear that the inclinations of scholars such as Fraser and Honneth about the link between recognition and redistribution are correct, and further study is needed on this matter.[1]

Cosmopolitanism: Ethics, Orientation, Accountability

The essential premise behind the establishment of a commission of inquiry is the failure of some type of policy or societal process and the need to rectify that failure. From the Krever Commission on the failings of the blood system, to the Somalia Commission of Inquiry that dealt with the actions of members of the Canadian Airborne Regiment during peacekeeping operations in that country, to the Arar Commission on the actions of the Canadian government with regard to the treatment of Maher Arar by the United States, the Canadian government, as well as provincial authorities, have relied on impartial investigations of commissions of inquiry to address structural- or individual-level failures in the operation of social institutions.

The intent was no different in the case of the Bouchard-Taylor Commission. The commission's mandate specified that the core goal of the commission of inquiry was ultimately to "formulate recommendations to the government to ensure that accommodation practices conform to Québec's values as a pluralistic, democratic, egalitarian society" (Bouchard and Taylor 2008, 17); as Bouchard and Taylor interpreted their mandate, this meant an examination of the interculturalism model of social and cultural integration. Given their experience as theorists of political and social justice and expertise on modes of dealing with difference, this led them to extend this mandate in three directions. First, it led them to develop principles for improving the integration of newcomers to Canada into Québécois society; second, they examined the creation of practical guidelines for dealing with the accommodation of cultural practices different from those of the host society; and finally, they provided a deeper understanding of the structural and intergroup issues that were undermining the successful integration of newcomers, including the anxiety Quebecers feel as a "majority minority," or as a group that is both the majority within Quebec and a national minority within Canada (Bouchard and Taylor 2008, 35, 41-42, 187; Kymlicka 2000, 189). In many ways, the question I see at the heart of the Bouchard-Taylor Commission's inquiry was this: *To what extent is a model of sociocultural integration that demands an openness to newcomers and strangers operating in a just manner, and how can the findings of this commission contribute to the amelioration of the issues that stand in the way of this openness?* Effectively, this question is the question posed by theorists of what I would call *ethical* or *normative* cosmopolitanism.

To my mind, the ethical/normative project of cosmopolitanism prioritizes a fundamental question, one that undergirds and makes possible the cultural and political projects discussed in the introduction to this book, namely: *How do we foster an idea and a practicable map of the good life that embodies the values represented by cosmopolitan thought?* Even before figuring out how we can foster the intellectual and cultural capacities for engaging with human differences that might make possible the creation of inclusive modes of governance, theorists need to identify ways in which to highlight a cosmopolitan orientation to the world as an ethical good in its own right.[2] As the most recent incarnations of cosmopolitan thought develop as a response to the late twentieth-century processes of globalization, it would make sense that two of the fundamental premises of a normative cosmopolitanism would be that we take the world, to borrow Appiah's term (2005, 217), as a "shared hometown," and that that world is one characterized by a plethora of human differences in beliefs, values, and practices embodying those values. Rather than following the global village trope, in which cultural and intellectual differences appear to be flattened out through the processes of globalization, normative cosmopolitans working in this new tradition focus on the welter of human differences, the recognition of a variety of modernities, and what Lemert (2004, 54) calls "plural oughts," a situation in which the diversity of extant situations and the Others living in those situations demand a grappling with the ethical obligations that each of those "oughts" requires. Taken together, these two premises demand by all accounts a new way of conceptualizing ethical relations and ethical reasoning.

As discussed elsewhere in this book, normative cosmopolitanisms developed thus far can be seen to have focused on four key elements: (1) the issue of space, particularly regarding the orientation of cosmopolitans to those in the space around them; (2) the fostering of a hermeneutics of the Other, wherein the cosmopolitan orients to those in the social space on their own political, cultural, and ethical terms; (3) the fostering of autonomy and conversation predicated on impartialist reasoning, detaching the moment of cosmopolitan engagement from any particular mode of thought; and (4) the preservation or creation of dignity, mutual recognition, and trust as the core concerns of the cosmopolitan moment.[3] Taken together, this would seem to demand that ethical cosmopolitans, when moving through the globe or thinking of how they want Others in the world treated, would make every effort to engage Others on their own terms when in their social space, with attention being paid to the socio-historical conditions that pertain to and structure the cosmopolitan/local relationship, and calls on the cosmopolitan to recognize the autonomy of Others and the dignity of their lives and social practices, all with the goal of collectively developing new, more just ways of living with one another in the world that preserve, rather than eliminate, human differences.

Depending on the particular space within which the encounter occurs, one of these individuals is expected to make a greater effort to engage the other and to understand the other's positions and practices. If the cosmopolitan appears on the Other's home turf, then it is the cosmopolitan who has a duty toward openness to the Other; it is the duty of the cosmopolitan to be cosmopolitan, to make the effort to engage the Other on his or her own terms, yet the Other has no concomitant duty specified. If the Other appears on the cosmopolitan's home turf, as in the case of migration, the cosmopolitan still has a duty toward openness to the Other; in this case, however, the openness is limited by the "home field advantage" of the cosmopolitans, who in being hospitable have welcomed the Other into their midst. Problematically, though, as Rosello (2001, 18) has pointed out, this host/guest relationship is fraught with tension; to my mind, it is a tension that writes the Other out of the equation as an active participant in the cosmopolitan encounter: "Hospitality is often in flux: power comes and goes, and so do protection and respect, servitude and care. At the best of times, the host is the master (the owner of the house) and the servant of the guest. At the worst of times, the guest is the servant of the master, who is also the guest in his own house." In the case of hospitality toward the newcomer, it is presumed that the principles to which the Other adheres will over time become the same as the guest – in other words, that they will acculturate or assimilate to the dominant set of principles and no longer simply be guests. In either case, though, the Other remains silent; on their home turf, they may suffer the cosmopolitan gladly, while in the cosmopolitan's space, they are expected to take on the cosmopolitan's principles. One would hope, then, that the cosmopolitan's principles are truly open to the input of the Other. This cosmopolitan orientation presumes, of course, that all parties to the situation have the same intention and orientation: the fostering of human dignity, the creation of trust, the amelioration of past injustices, and the preservation or improvement of the degree of political agency held and experienced by each party. It, like other great ethical theories, also assumes that the good-in-itself of cosmopolitanism will carry the day, that when a cosmopolitan ethic is laid out, rational and well-meaning persons will come to live by its principles. We have not yet seen that day, however, in large part because conceptions of ethical cosmopolitanism formulated thus far fail us in the cosmopolitan encounter before these conceptions get a chance to get off the ground.

The Foundations of a Cosmopolitan Claims-Making Process

As many have pointed out, cosmopolitanism as generally conceived has a definite material basis, one that places its burdens on those in the economically developed world who have the economic capital and the ability to gain the cultural competencies to enable them to, in essence, consume the world. But what happens if this does not come to pass? What if the characteristics of the cosmopolitan condition are in place, as Szerszynski and Urry (2006, 115) identify them, but the ethic does not follow from the condition? Alternatively, extant formulations of normative cosmopolitanism demand hospitality to those who come into one's social space; *how is that demand for hospitality enforced?* As well, what happens if cosmopolitanism or some variant thereof is implemented as a policy, and *yet the ethic that the policy seeks to foster does not appear?* In other words, *what happens when a cosmopolitan ethic or a cosmopolitan encounter fails?* What is missing from normative cosmopolitanism as it has been formulated is a conception of accountability and responsibility as well as a claims-making process to enforce that accountability. That is, although normative cosmopolitanism has conceptualized itself as being ethically responsible to the Other as a virtue in its own right (in orienting to them on their own terms and in ensuring that their dignity is recognized and their agency is preserved), it has not yet thought of how such responsibility can be ensured or how the Others for whom cosmopolitans see themselves as being ethically responsible can challenge the cosmopolitans on their failings.

De Sousa Santos (2007, 10) gives us the foundations for dealing with this issue of accountability in discussing what he calls "insurgent cosmopolitanism," which, in giving "equal weight to the principle of equality and to the principle of the recognition of difference ... is no more than a global emergence resulting from the fusion of local, progressive struggles with the aim of maximizing their emancipatory potential *in loco* (however defined) through translocal/local linkages." By making a cosmopolitanism from below a core element of his concept of North-South relations, and by making it one that requires a transformation not only in the character of the relationship between North and South or Northerner and Southerner but also in *both* parties to the engagement, de Sousa Santos calls us to see one of the core ideas that should be present in any version of cosmopolitanism that lives up to its name: that the cosmopolitan encounter should be one in which a "fusion of horizons" occurs (Gadamer 1989, 305). There are five key elements of this form of cosmopolitanism: (1) the transcendence of the false dualism of universalism and cultural relativism, by seeing that what is needed are cross-cultural dialogues on concerns shared by each party that have similar or parallel forms; (2) that all cultures conceive of human dignity, but not in the same way; (3) that all cultures' conceptions of human dignity are "incomplete and problematic"; (4) that no culture is monolithic; and (5) that "not all equalities are identical and not all differences are unequal" (de Sousa Santos 2007, 14-15). De Sousa Santos then goes on to transform this into what I see as the basis for a cosmopolitan accountability – the idea of a diatopical hermeneutics (2007, 16):

Diatopical hermeneutics is based on the idea that the *topoi* of an individual culture, no matter how strong they may be, are as incomplete as the culture itself. Such incompleteness is not visible from inside the culture itself, since the aspiration to totality induces taking *pars pro toto*. The objective of diatopical hermeneutics is, therefore, not to achieve completeness – that being an unachievable goal – but, on the contrary, to raise the consciousness of reciprocal incompleteness to its possible maximum by engaging in the dialogue, as it were, with one foot in one culture and the other in another. Herein lies its *dia-topical* character.

While recognizing the dilemma associated with the recognition of one's cultural incompleteness entering into dialogue – namely, that those who think their culture is complete do not want to discuss their incompleteness, and those that are incomplete run the risk of being conquered – de Sousa Santos (2007, 21, 25) holds that it is the only possible tool for the mutually ethical engagement with an Other, especially in the historical situation of the post-imperial and postcolonial era. If the interest is in fostering a social order predicated on both equality and difference, then what de Sousa Santos (2001, 191) calls "the sociology of absences," the notion that our experience of the social world consists in what we have not yet experienced of that world, is the fundamental basis for fostering the cosmopolitan encounter. We must encounter one another based both on what we have experienced, and be aware that the encounter is predicated not on that experience but on the inexperience of Others that will become the experience of togetherness. For the fusion of horizons that cosmopolitan theorists want so badly to occur, it is only by understanding the absence and inexperience that characterizes us and undergirds the encounter.

This conception of a diatopical hermeneutics provides a preliminary solution to two crucial problems having to do with the nature of normative cosmopolitanisms thus far formulated, as well as the intellectual forebear to which nearly every cosmopolitan theorist must make reference.

The bulk of existing theories of normative cosmopolitanism, as has been alluded to above, operates as though it were a deontological or a virtue ethics, making it either a duty or a virtue for those in the North to act in a cosmopolitan manner. In formulating the principles of cosmopolitan ethics in an "it is right to" manner, many cosmopolitan theorists have in essence constructed a body of thought in which only the duty to act in a cosmopolitan manner is important.[4] The emphasis on the duty to act in a cosmopolitan manner or the claim of the virtue of taking the cosmopolitan high road leaves us with the first problem – a monological structure to normative cosmopolitanism. That is, normative cosmopolitanism makes demands on the cosmopolitan individual, almost always positioned as someone from the global North or a dominant group within a society, to seek out the core humanity of those typically classified as Other, to find common, humanistic ways of engaging with them on terms that can be mutually agreed on. Morgan (1995, 84) argues that the universalizing cosmopolitan, in seeking out the common characteristics of humanity in a quest to transcend difference, eliminates the very things that are to be sought; traditions, culture, epistemologies, and human difference all go by the wayside when the monological cosmopolitan is let loose in the world. And even in the case where it is precisely the difference that is to be sought out, experienced, consumed, or grappled with – that is, where cosmopolitan theory posits that the basis of a normative cosmopolitanism should be rational dialogue rather than monological consumption – there is still a failing that results in a retreat to monologism. Normative cosmopolitanism says little about what the Other should do when confronted by the well-meaning, duty-bound cosmopolitan.

To my mind – and this is the second problem a diatopical hermeneutics can help us address – this is in large part due to the intellectual progenitor of modern cosmopolitan thought, the Enlightenment, with its emphasis on the universality of human nature, rationality, and the construction of new modes of action that are predicated on non-religious (and therefore not culturally specific) bases. It would make sense that much of normative cosmopolitanism has a difficult time conceptualizing what happens when cosmopolitan ethics fail. In particular, this is because *the other is presumed to be the same as the self,* "enlightened" individuals all, motivated by the same human nature, the same reason, and the same fundamental bases of action. *Of course,* the rational individual, when confronted by an Other who is not known, would attempt to engage in dialogue, to sort out mutually acceptable principles for ways of acting detached from one's cultural contexts, and would interact in a way that is predicated on the reasonableness of truth claims each posits and the generation of reasoned principles for cohabitation in the world. And given the presumption of the universality of human nature, *of course* the person with whom one interacts would respond in kind. Unfortunately, though, as the late twentieth and early twenty-first centuries have shown us, not only can the Others in the world not be presumed to hold to the same Enlightenment values to which we claim to adhere, collectively we in the North can barely manage to adhere to those values ourselves.

If we conceptualize the cosmopolitan encounter in the way de Sousa Santos would want, however, then we have the material for developing an accountability mechanism to ensure that normative cosmopolitanism can be truly cosmopolitan. De Sousa Santos (2001, 192) calls on both parties to the cosmopolitan encounter to recognize the incompleteness of their cultures and to maintain a critical self-reflexivity with the possibility of gaining deeper insights into themselves and into their interlocutors by engaging in a procedure of translation of one's concerns into another's way of thinking (what he calls a procedure of "mutual intelligibility"). In this, he argues that the result allows "common ground to be identified in an indigenous struggle, a feminist struggle, an ecological struggle, etc., etc., without cancelling out in any of them the autonomy and difference that sustain them" (de Sousa Santos 2001, 192). Rather than the a priori assumption of cosmopolitan principles derived from the cultural traditions and precepts of Western Enlightenment occupying the place of ethical frame, yielding a monological encounter, or one in which dialogue occurs only to the extent that the perceived completeness of the cosmopolitan's cultural frame is preserved, this model of the cosmopolitan encounter prioritizes the mutual development of principles of conversation and cohabitation out of the encounter itself and the culturally determined ways of thinking, or epistemes, that are brought to bear in it. Also, because both parties are invested in the formulation of these principles, either party can call on the other to adhere to them if the other fails to, yielding a measure of accountability in which ethical failings can be addressed and, one would hope, redressed. Like the monological normative cosmopolitanisms discussed above, a model of the cosmopolitan encounter predicated on a diatopical hermeneutics assumes the good intentions of the parties to the encounter and their sense of obligation to the kind of hermeneutic interaction proposed by de Sousa Santos. However, this model – to which I adhere strongly – has the advantage of ensuring that those whom cosmopolitans encounter in their travels around the world, or in their neighbourhood when engaging with newcomers to their society, have an equal ability to make claims against cosmopolitans for failing to act in accordance with their ethics, or to ensure that cosmopolitans' openness to the Other moves beyond recognition and into reciprocity.

As Cheah (2006, 486) reminds us, a theory of cosmopolitanism that goes beyond "an intellectual ethos of a select clerisy, a form of consciousness without a mass base" must contain two elements: a grappling with the existence of institutions able to foster or maintain a cosmopolitan condition, and a discussion of the ways in which those institutions can "be in a relation of mutual feedback" with a polity oriented to collective interests and the maximization of human freedom. Thus far, I have focused on the ways in which I would want to see the normativity of these institutions operate by highlighting the need for accountability mechanisms within any normative cosmopolitanism. What I have called for to this point is the conceptualization of a cosmopolitan claims-making process, that is, a procedure by which the cosmopolitan's Other can make claims against cosmopolitans in the event of their failure to adhere to their own principles, despite the duty or virtue they feel in claiming their adherence or in positing the ethic in the first place. This, however, would require the institutional context that Cheah claims is necessary to move cosmopolitanism from the realm of theory into the world. To my mind, the complex of interculturalism and the "accommodations crisis" in Quebec, as explored by the Bouchard-Taylor Report, provides the perfect opportunity to observe the nascent possibilities of a cosmopolitan claims-making process in action.

L'interculturalisme, Cosmopolitanism, and the "Accommodations Crisis"

The demographic makeup of Canadian society has changed significantly since Confederation. From a country based on the founding "three nations" (English, French, and First Nations/Inuit/Métis), Canada has become a nation of immigrants from around the world. Although for much of its history Canada determined its membership in line with British imperial models of citizenship, since the repatriation of the Constitution in 1982 new conceptions of Canadian national identity have had to be developed. In line with changing immigration trends, which from the 1970s have seen increasing numbers of persons from developing countries come to Canada, conceptions of how to manage the balance between national identity and particular ethnic, cultural, or religious identities have changed. Thus, federal conceptions of multiculturalism have changed since the 1970s, roughly in four stages. In the 1970s, the celebration of cultural differences through *ethnicity multiculturalism* was the dominant model for intergroup relations, focusing on cultural sensitivity and the cultural mosaic. The 1980s saw a move toward *equity multiculturalism,* recognizing the need to address issues of systemic discrimination against visible minority groups and to create a level playing field for all groups in Canadian society. *Civic multiculturalism,* focusing on citizenship and belonging, became the dominant model in the 1990s, and with it a move toward dealing with issues of constructive engagement in Canadian social life. In the 2000s, *integrative multiculturalism,* with its attention to integration, dialogue, and mutual understanding, became the primary model of multiculturalism, and began to introduce a discourse of rights and responsibilities on the part of all Canadians, whether mainstream or members of visible minority groups (Helfer 2007, 8-9; cf. Rocher et al. 2007).

Because of its unique history – its position as a "subjugated people," the historic underdevelopment of the province, and its place as the largest francophone community in North America – Quebec identified a number of problems with federal conceptions of multiculturalism. Ranging from the critiques made by François Roche and colleagues (2007, 30-42) of the failure of the federal government to preserve both bilingualism and biculturalism in its early formulations of multicultural policy (which required learning at least one of the two official languages), to the argument that the treatment of all non-English cultural groups as equivalent would result in the competition among them for resources and access to power, the province worked to develop its own model for handling cultural diversity – interculturalism. Generally speaking, interculturalism is defined in the following manner:

> L'interculturalisme, c'est l'interaction entre les cultures, l'échange et la communication où une personne accepte la réciprocité de la culture de l'autre ... En autres termes, on peut voir l'interculturalité comme une manière d'être, une vision du monde et des autres, une sorte de relation égalitaire entre les êtres humains et les peuples ... L'interculturalité, c'est pousser plus loin le multiculturalisme. (INCP-RIPC n.d., para. 13)

This model of interculturalism emphasizes a self-reflexive examination of one's cultural position, the "penetration of the system by the other," negotiation and compromise, intercultural training, and the formation of exchanges between members of the host country and newcomers

(INCP-RIPC n.d., para. 20-21). Put another way, the core difference posited between multiculturalism and interculturalism in the general, more global sense is that multiculturalism focuses more on the integration of newcomers into the national or majority culture, whereas intercultural policies represent a way of living together (INCP-RIPC n.d., para. 26). In the context of Quebec, these general characteristics of interculturalism have been modified in certain respects to ensure the continued particularity of Québécois culture and institutions, while at the same time making efforts to ensure that the particularities of the cultural communities that make up Québécois society are preserved. As Rocher and colleagues (2007, 40), discussing CCPARDC (2007, 20), put it:

> En contraste, la politique québécoise, plus soucieuse de la survie culturelle de la minorité francophone, se préoccupe davantage de l'intégration: "l'interculturalisme québécois continue d'affirmer son originalité comme variété de pluralisme. Il contient l'idée qu'à la longue et au gré d'une dynamique transculturelle, chaque culture empruntera quelque chose aux autres et contribuera à l'évolution de la culture québécoise, tout en préservant sa spécificité."

Quebec's model of interculturalism is theorized to work by developing a societal infrastructure so that all members of the cultural communities are, through their membership, able to participate in the common public culture of the host community (Rocher et al. 2007, 44). It can be argued that there is a level-of-analysis issue operating between the two doctrines; whereas multiculturalism is primarily seen as operating at the level of state institutions, interculturalism appears to represent an interpersonal ethic demonstrated as "the principles of a multicultural state, but also exhibit[ing] a range of more positive personal attitudes toward diversity" (Kymlicka 2003, 157). Also, in a multicultural society it is entirely possible to have peace and harmony without intergroup contact or conversation; however, interculturalism's operation at the level of the citizen is posited as making possible a broader and richer conception of the positive contributions of diverse communities (Kymlicka 2003, 154-57). Ultimately, it is the tension between "citizenship" and "membership," with their concomitant levels of analysis, as well as the tension between official bilingualism (though unofficial mononationalism) and the privileging of the French language as one of the common cores of Québécois society that characterizes the difference between Canadian multiculturalism and Québécois interculturalism.

As part of the development of interculturalism in Quebec, the provincial government developed an additional part of the core societal identity that revolved around what it called the "moral contract," those shared values to which each member of Quebec society, whether *pure laine* or newcomer, would adhere. First and foremost, Quebec is posited as a francophone society, one in which the common language provides the basis for intercultural communication. Following this, Quebec constitutes itself as a free and democratic society, one in which diversity is seen as an asset, the rule of law obtains over all else, political and religious authorities are separate (the principle of *laïcité*), women and men have equal rights, and the exercise of one's rights must take place in respect of the rights of others and the general well-being of the society (MICC 2009, para. 4). Other conceptions that have been proposed include additional criteria such as the favouring of "the reconciliation and acceptance of differences in mutual respect, between citizens of diverse origins" and an obligation to eliminate "every form of direct and systemic discrimination" (Rocher et al. 2007, 49). In each variant of this *contrat moral,* the delimiting factor is limits imposed by "democratic values and inter-community exchange" (Sévigny 2008, para. 9); that is, the bottomline principle all Quebecers are expected to uphold is the respect for the core elements of a democratic society as posited in the Canadian Charter of Rights and Freedoms (1982) and the Quebec Charter of Human Rights and Freedoms (1975).

The legal mechanism by which this respect is supposed to be manifested, both in Quebec and the rest of Canada, is the accommodations process. Accommodations processes are intended to rectify situations of either indirect discrimination, defined as "the application of a seemingly neutral, universally applicable practice that nonetheless adversely affects groups defined on the basis of the grounds for discrimination prohibited by the Charter," or systemic discrimination, "when various practices, decisions or behaviours combine with other practices within an organization or those of other social institutions to produce discrimination" (MICC 2008, 5). In Quebec, there are thirteen specific grounds for discrimination that are prohibited in Chapter 10 of the Charter of Human Rights and Freedoms that form the legitimate basis for accommodations requests, including discrimination on the basis of race, colour, sex, pregnancy, sexual orientation, civil status, age, religion, political affiliations, language, ethnic or national origin, social condition, or disability; Chapters 15 to 19 specifically lay the groundwork for accommodations requests with regard to access to public transportation, public places, hiring or termination of employment, and unions and professional association membership. This process, as noted by Bouchard and Taylor (2008, 63n2), has the logic of "what accommodates some people without inconveniencing other people." Legally speaking, the Supreme Court of Canada and the Quebec Charter of Human Rights and Freedoms have created a duty to accommodate on the part of federally and provincially regulated employers, in which employers and other public institutions are required to ensure that "a category of people who display a trait for which the statute or norm makes no provision" (Bouchard and Taylor 2008, 63) can be included in the processes of society to the extent that this inclusion does not cause an undue hardship on the employer or institution in terms of its ability to accommodate the request.

The Bouchard-Taylor Commission identified two models for the accommodations process: the legal route, in which the accommodations request is taken to court and subjected to the normal adversarial process and imposition of a decision by the court; and what they call the "citizen route," which emphasizes its basis in the negotiation between members of the general public, the responsibility of each of the parties to the negotiation to one another and to respecting the Charter rights, and the values of interculturalism that are embodied in this negotiation process, specifically "exchanges, negotiation, agreement and reciprocity, rather than confrontation and division" (Bouchard and Taylor 2008, 64). In preparing *Building the Future: A Time for Reconciliation,* Bouchard and Taylor (2008, 48-62) tracked the prevalence of accommodations cases that had been pursued through the legal route, finding that only seventy-two cases involved legal adjudication between 1985 and 2007, whereas a countless number (since they are handled in a more informal manner, their numbers are not officially tracked) were resolved through the citizen route that they privilege in their report.

Given the number of "legal route" accommodation cases that Bouchard and Taylor found, it is surprising that there was the perception of an "accommodations crisis" at all. The commission was convened, after all, amid a wide-scale perception that the influx of newcomers, particularly from Muslim countries, had resulted in a rapid increase in the number of accommodations that were being granted, particularly on religious grounds, and would ultimately result not only in a backpedalling from the gains made in *la Révolution tranquille* but also in a fundamental transformation of Quebec society (Bouchard and Taylor 2008, chs. 3, 4, 10). Coming in the wake of the events of 11 September 2001, and combined with the media attention being given to such accommodations processes as the hearings over the wearing of a *kirpan* (a Sikh ceremonial knife) in a *Collège d'enseignement général et professionel,* the so-called tempest in a teapot of the accommodations problem seemed to reach critical mass. Additional factors cited by Bouchard and Taylor (2008, 185-86) that contributed to the perception of an accommodations crisis in the province include the ongoing and historically rooted fragility of the identity of Quebecers, given their minority status within Canada; economic issues; the decline in support for Québécois sovereignty; and the manifestation of what were seen as religious accommodations as Quebec completed the process of laicization, all contributing to the societal anxiety that latched on to prominent accommodations cases as an indication of the "crisis." And it is this anxiety that Bouchard and Taylor identify as being a significant part of the problem with regard to social integration in Quebec. Because Quebecers have long seen themselves as a minority culture with regard to the Canadian frame of reference, and because their cultural definition has historically been "French Canadian" (ethno-nationally based) rather than "Quebecer" (based on the civic nation), the perception of many Quebecers with regard to accommodations has been that it is a contest between minority groups rather than a more typical "host/newcomer" relationship (Bouchard and Taylor 2008, 189-91, 212-14).

One way in which the majority/minority anxiety problem might be addressed, the commission held, is to emphasize the citizen route of harmonization practices as opposed to involving the judicial system, as in the legal route. The notion of the "concerted adjustment," which "covers requests stemming from an obligation that is sometimes of a legal nature and sometimes of a non-legal nature" (Bouchard and Taylor 2008, 64-65), is one that takes account of the process by which most accommodation requests are addressed: a claimant requests accommodation on some basis guaranteed by the Charters; a determination of the barriers that impact on the person requesting accommodation is made; options for eliminating these barriers are explored; and accommodation is made to the point of "undue hardship," the contextual limit point at which an employer or social institution can be expected to accommodate the claimant (Bouchard and Taylor 2008, 162-65; CHRC 2005, 3). In this model, the accommodations request is handled through negotiation and compromise rather than through the adversarial approach taken in the legal route. As Bouchard and Taylor point out (2008, ch. 4), major public institutions such as the educational and health care systems in Quebec already utilize the citizen route quite successfully; and in at least one of the *kirpan* cases that was seen to be part of the accommodations crisis, when the case made its way to the Supreme Court of Canada, the decision that was imposed at the conclusion of the legal route was identical to the negotiated compromise reached through the citizen route (Bouchard and Taylor 2008, 281).

Two core reasons why Bouchard and Taylor privilege the citizen route as an accommodations mechanism include the reality of its existence as the primary mode of handling accommodations, particularly with regard to front-line managers, and what they see as "the advantage or the necessity of encouraging citizens to resolve their own conflicts" (Bouchard and Taylor 2008, 64). The latter justification represents one aspect of their commitment to seeing accommodations processes and harmonization practices in a pedagogical and not a strictly bureaucratic sense. By compelling citizens to negotiate with one another in an attempt to solve their differences, regardless of the basis for those differences (whether property lines or examination schedules in CEGEPs), the responsibility of each citizen to make the claim for her own position, to hear out the other party to the dispute, and to figure out a way in which the situation can be resolved amicably is one that would be consonant with the norms of a democratic society, particularly one whose polity is geared toward "peace, order, and good government."

There is a deeper reason, however, why Bouchard and Taylor privilege the citizen route for managing accommodations requests, one that is predicated on the very norms and practices of interculturalism. By arguing that the best way to address issues of systemic and indirect discrimination is through interaction, interpersonal negotiation, and the mutual education of one another, whether *pure laine* Québécois or new Quebecer, Bouchard and Taylor (2008, 114) prioritize elements of Quebec's model for integration of the body politic: the development of consensus on horizons; the participation of the citizenry in public debates and decision making; equality; reciprocity (which demands the interaction of members of the society); social mobility; the fostering of solidarity through respect; and the protection of rights. As well, they focus on the integration process at both the macro and the micro levels of social life, arguing that the same processes of integration are required on the part of both individuals and the institutions that structure a society. Within their sketch of the integration process, though, they insert what to my mind is the key linkage with interculturalism and, as I will show below, with normative cosmopolitanism – namely, the ideal of an integrative pluralism, one that encourages and respects diversity and recognizes the "interdependence of all the dimensions considered" in the process of fostering and maintaining social solidarity (Bouchard and Taylor 2008, 115). This interdependence leads them to conclude that the crucial conception of Quebec interculturalism includes French as the common language, a "pluralistic orientation that is concerned with the protection of rights," maintains a "creative tension" between diversity and the continuity of Québécois social life, and prioritizes integration, participation, and interaction (Bouchard and Taylor 2008, 121). Their notion of how the accommodations process should proceed through the citizen route serves to support these very notions.

The emphasis on an integrative pluralism in concert with the more elaborated version of interculturalism offered by Bouchard and Taylor thereby provides a possible solution to the anxiety characterized by the majority/minority problem discussed above. Bouchard and Taylor (2008, 217) do not go so far as to suggest that intercultural interactions will assuage French Canadian Québécois anxiety about their status both in Quebec and with regard to the rest of Canada; in fact, they seem to walk away from that opportunity in a number of places in the report, merely leaving the possible benefits in solving this crucial issue to statements such as that "they scarcely have a choice but to get involved, on pain of enormous impoverishment," or that a retreat into the *pure laine* ethnic identity would "mean making concrete one of the most criticized features of Canadian multiculturalism," or that careful readers should intuit from between the lines. The authors do go so far as to say that "the identity inherited from the French-Canadian past is perfectly legitimate and it must survive because it is a source of diversity, but it cannot alone define the Quebec identity and must take into account the other identities present, in a spirit of interculturalism" (189), and to state that once it is made clear that newcomers to the province are not out to remake their home countries in Quebec but simply to integrate, it will be possible for all Quebecers to be reconciled to harmonization processes.

To my mind, the fostering of interculturalist interactions and an integrative pluralism can help assuage the primordial anxiety at the heart of the Quebec identity in three key ways. First, these types of interactions and the accommodations requests that are to be addressed through them can serve, as the Bouchard-Taylor Commission showed, to foster and reinforce the trust that all Quebecers share a commitment to the same essential public values (Bouchard and Taylor 2008, 208). Second, they can serve to demonstrate that despite the pressures that Bouchard and Taylor (2008, 215-16) see cultural communities putting on the majority group in Quebec (and rightfully so), the type of integration that is being sought through the accommodations process is a two-way street, where the majority group recognizes the need for adjustments to historical ways of doing things but also where requesters show their commitment to being fully participating and contributing members of Quebec society. Finally, and this goes to the "minority" element of the majority/minority position, it would demonstrate that Quebec interculturalism is a more ethical and successful model for the integration of newcomers precisely because it balances the duty to accommodate with the responsibility of all involved in the situation to adjust their orientations to their Others so that the social distance between them is reduced.

Accommodations as a Form of Cosmopolitan Claims Making

It is in this way that I see the analysis of the state of interculturalism and the accommodations process in Quebec presented by Bouchard and Taylor as providing the basis of a solution to the core problem I have identified with normative cosmopolitan theories developed to date, namely, the lack of a claims-making process in which parties to the cosmopolitan encounter can hold one another accountable vis-à-vis their stated ethical position.

Taking an all-too-brief phenomenological look at the accommodations process described by Bouchard and Taylor, we would find two parties to the process, one of whom is making a claim against the other. Rather than this claim being predicated on some kind of pure self-interest or on the basis of some type of rational truth-claim, in this case the claim is being made against an already existing body of ethical and legal principles that are supposed to be brought to bear by the first party in dealing with the claimant. Shared by both parties is a trust that each is committed to these principles, foremost among them democratic values (or, as Bouchard and Taylor [2008, 164] call them, "common public values," ones that "are expressed through public institutions, i.e., those that have successfully passed the test of public deliberation and political decision-making"), to at least the ideas of interculturalism and the integration of newcomers into society in a spirit of reciprocity and equality in difference, and the concomitant duty to accommodate institutions to those who are unfairly disadvantaged despite the best efforts of those institutions. If there were perfect synchronicity between both parties on these matters, then it would follow that the handling of any accommodations request would be an easy matter, one that might resemble the stereotypical Habermasian ideal speech situation. And this is the situation I argued above that extant notions of normative cosmopolitanism posit as the "cosmopolitan encounter."

But what happens if the commitments of one party to this encounter are less strong with regard to one or more of these principles than those of the other? Bouchard and Taylor (2008, 67-68, 283) report that a number of speakers before the commission claimed they were committed to the idea of interculturalism, but still insisted on the absolute duty of newcomers to accommodate themselves to Quebec society without recognizing any reciprocal obligation. How does this impact on the situation? In this case, there are two elements of societal discourse that come to bear. The first is the duty to accommodate, which requires that, barring any undue hardship on the accommodating institution, a situation of discrimination, even when systemic or indirect, must be addressed to ensure the equality of rights for all. In the case of accommodations requests, as Carastathis (2009) rightly points out, what is being requested is not some type of special treatment but merely a recourse to a right that is already given in the law, that is, requesters' legal rights to equality in difference, to have the infrastructural supports necessary to facilitate their integration into Quebec society, and to participate fully in all aspects of life in Quebec. The second element of public discourse, and in some ways the more important for our purposes, has to do with the expectation and obligation of reciprocity given in Quebec interculturalism. Under the interculturalism model, all Quebecers are expected to interact with one another within a shared public language, with respect, and with an eye toward developing a consensus on "horizons, basic orientations and reference points that nurture the collective imagination" (Bouchard and Taylor 2008, 114). This mode of interaction, as Bouchard and Taylor highlight, *is assumed to go in both directions.* That is, it is assumed that through the process of intercultural interaction, both newcomer and host, both majority group and minority group, change as a result of the interaction; or, to put it another way, "the immigrant, for example, must accept certain changes in relation to his culture of origin and the host society must agree to change in response to its contact with the immigrant. As we heard during our hearings, the mechanism must operate both ways" (114).

It is this last element that brings us back to the idea of cosmopolitan claims making. If we claim that a normative model of cosmopolitanism is one that should result in a kind of fusion of horizons, that both cosmopolitan and Other are changed (hopefully for the better) by the cosmopolitan encounter, then we need to identify models of accountability that can be brought to bear by either party to the encounter. The citizen route of the accommodations process proposed in the Bouchard-Taylor Report provides us with the foundations for developing such a mechanism. Even though their concern was with intercultural relations within Quebec – a situation in which newcomers arrive of their own accord, and in most cases voluntarily arrive in Quebec knowing what will be expected of them – the general procedure and principles they propose for fostering an intercultural ethic can still be brought to bear on the global level.

Cosmopolitanizing Cosmopolitanism

Taken together, the notion of a diatopical hermeneutics and the basis for the accommodation of newcomers outlined by Bouchard and Taylor give us the infrastructure for a cosmopolitan claims-making process. A diatopical hermeneutics requires that both parties to the cosmopolitan encounter recognize their cultural incompleteness and be open to their own transformation through the collaborative construction of modes of cohabitation. This occurs through the occasion in which intercultural and interpersonal dialogue occurs "with one foot in one culture and the other in another" (de Sousa Santos 2007, 16). The fusion of horizons that theorists of hermeneutic models of normative cosmopolitanism, myself included, would want to see happen as the result of these kinds of encounters is greatly fostered when this type of encounter occurs. And as Bouchard and Taylor point out, newcomers to Quebec – and I would argue, immigrants and refugees in any country around the world – already engage in this kind of process, learning to accommodate themselves to the dominant culture in their new place of residence, balancing between the poles of what becomes a hybridized identity. What I, along with de Sousa Santos, and Bouchard and Taylor, would want to see is a greater prevalence of this kind of openness and the transformation of dominant cultures through their interactions with newcomers. And when this situation fails to occur, when the dominant group fails to adhere to its clearly stated ethical principles of equality and inclusiveness, policies such as the duty to accommodate and the accommodations processes outlined in the Bouchard-Taylor Report provide newcomers a voice to hold the host society accountable to those principles.

So far, this pertains only to those cosmopolitan encounters that take place on the cosmopolitan's home turf, and if we stay within the remit of the Bouchard-Taylor Commission, we would not be able to say much beyond the borders of Quebec. Recognizing the isomorphism of social relations in a globalized world, however, we are able to translate the lessons learned here from the locality of the home turf to moments when the cosmopolitan is "away." The openness to the Other demanded when the cosmopolitan is on his or her turf can now be invoked when the cosmopolitan encounter fails. Rather than consuming or viewing the world and the culture of the inhabitants within it, cosmopolitans are now compelled to engage with the Other on mutually agreed terms, recognizing that they do not know what they will find on the Other's turf, that they do not yet have the experience of the world that will enable them to know the Other, and allow for their own cultural incompleteness to recoil on them in the course of developing a basis for communication and engagement. In other words, it should be a core characteristic of a normative cosmopolitanism that cosmopolitans are always ready to be compelled by their Others to be open to engaging with them, to be prepared to be held accountable to their principles, and to be called on to give up the epistemic privilege that comes with the ability to travel the world.[5]

An examination of the accommodations crisis in Quebec, then, brings into relief a larger number of issues than simply those brought about by the increase in immigration to a province whose core identity includes anxiety over being the "majority minority." Rather, without specifically intending it, the Bouchard-Taylor Commission has demonstrated for us the importance of ensuring that the linkage between ethics, social relations, and public policy – namely, the issue of accountability to one's stated ethical principles in interpersonal relations or in the realm of the law – is in place. I have argued here that this gives us the basis for thinking more broadly about a cosmopolitan claims-making mechanism that can be brought to bear on interpersonal, intercultural, and intersocietal interactions in the twenty-first century. If it is going to be a core tenet of normative cosmopolitanism that cosmopolitans be truly open to the Other and want genuinely to be able to live well with and toward others, then it is imperative that that openness transcend simply being willing to try an Other's food. To really bring about such an ethics, we need to foster a cosmopolitan claims-making process that results in the transformation of both parties to the encounter. My argument here has been that the combination of a duty to accommodate, a specified infrastructure for holding people accountable to cosmopolitan principles, and a diatopical hermeneutics that forms the conceptual foundation for such an infrastructure provides us with the tools to conceptualize and actualize such a claims-making process. In essence, I believe we now have the tools to actually make cosmopolitanism *cosmopolitan*.

Notes

1 From the Bouchard-Taylor Report (2008, 259): "One observation that emerges strongly from our consultations is that it is pointless to talk about interculturalism if we do not act with respect to labour market integration and the fight

against discrimination. This explains the importance of a vigorous campaign in this regard, otherwise, intercultural discourse risks losing a great deal of its effectiveness." And: "The theme of integration seems pivotal in more than one respect. It centres, first of all, on the recognition of immigrants' skills and diplomas, then their francization, followed by a broader effort to regionalize immigration and, finally, better coordination between government departments (recommendations C1 to C9)" (265). Taken with other statements throughout the report, it is clear that Bouchard and Taylor see a clear linkage between what I would call questions of recognition and redistribution, though their faithfulness to liberalism as a political and political-economic stance would necessarily prevent them from seeing the redistribution problem in Quebec as a structural problem à la Fraser and Honneth, and would instead lead them to see it as a recognition issue, i.e., as an issue of Quebec's failure to recognize foreign professional and educational credentials as equivalent to North American qualifications.

2   In addition to the works in this volume, see also Attfield 2006; Calhoun 1999, 2002, 2004; Chhachhi 2006; Erskine 2002; Hall 2002; Held 2002, 2003; Kennedy 2006; Kurasawa 2004; Kwok-Bun 2002; Lemert 2004; Nash 2003; Pollock et al. 2000; Rundell 2004; Roudometof 2005; Skrbis and Woodward 2007; Skrbis et al. 2004; Szerszynski and Urry 2006; Turner 2006; Zubaida 2002.

3   On the spatiality of ethics, see Appiah 2004; Calhoun 2002; Held 2003; Molz 2006; Turner 2006. On the hermeneutics of the Other, see, *inter alia,* Appiah 2004; Cheah 2006; Derrida 2001; Held 2003; Lemert 2004; Molz 2006; Rundell 2004; Skrbis et al. 2004; Turner 2006. On the metaprinciples of autonomy and impartialist reasoning, see Held 2003. On the issues of dignity, mutual recognition, and trust, see Honneth 2007, in addition to the authors listed here.

4   Held's metaprinciples, for example, dictate only that the cosmopolitan must act so as to preserve another's autonomy, and insist on the use of impartialist reasoning as the basis for any discussion on common principles to which parties to the conversation should refer in their action (Held 2003). It is in holding to these metaprinciples that rightness inheres. Szerszynski and Urry's discussion (2006) of the cosmopolitan condition, in insisting that the cosmopolitan maintain an "openness to other people and cultures," leads us to a virtue ethics, one in which the *intention* to be open to Others carries the day, even when our efforts are rebuffed by the Others to whom we are open.

5   Of course, this could and should be extended to the realm of international relations. It is beyond the remit of this chapter, however, to discuss how an insurgent cosmopolitanism along the lines that de Sousa Santos (2007) develops would change the nature of international political structures.

References

Appadurai, Arjun. 1992. "Global Ethnoscapes: Notes and Queries for a Transnational Anthropology." In *Recapturing Anthropology: Working in the Present,* ed. by Richard G. Fox, 191-210. Santa Fe: School of American Research Press.

–. 1996. *Modernity at Large: Cultural Dimensions of Globalization.* Minneapolis: University of Minnesota Press.

Appiah, Kwame Anthony. 2004. *The Ethics of Identity.* Princeton, NJ: Princeton University Press.

Attfield, Robin. 2006. "The Shape of a Global Ethic." *Philosophy and Social Criticism* 32 (1): 5-19.

Bouchard, Gérard, and Charles Taylor. 2008. *Building the Future: A Time for Reconciliation.* Report to the Consultation Commission on Accommodation Practices Related to Cultural Differences. Quebec: Government of Quebec.

Calhoun, Craig. 1999. "Nationalism, Political Community and the Representation of Society: Or, Why Feeling at Home Is Not a Substitute for Public Space." *European Journal of Social Theory* 2 (2): 217-31.

–. 2002. "The Class Consciousness of Frequent Travelers: Toward a Critique of Actually Existing Cosmopolitanism." *South Atlantic Quarterly* 101 (4): 869-97.

–. 2004. "A World of Emergencies: Fear, Intervention, and the Limits of Cosmopolitan Order." Thirty-fifth Annual Sorokin Lecture, University of Saskatchewan.

Carastathis, Anna. 2009. "Synthèse." Presentation at the Colloque sur la rapport Bouchard-Taylor, un an plus tard: perspectives internationales conference, Université de Montréal, Québec.

Cheah, Pheng. 2006. "Cosmopolitanism." *Theory, Culture and Society* 23 (2-3): 486-96.

Chhachhi, Amrita. 2006. "Postscript: Tensions and Absences in the Debate on Global Justice and Cosmopolitanism." *Development and Change* 37 (6): 1329-34.

CHRC (Canadian Human Rights Commission). 2005. *Duty to Accommodate: Frequently Asked Questions and Answers.* Ottawa: Government of Canada.

de Sousa Santos, Boaventura. 2001. "*Nuestra América:* Reinventing a Subaltern Paradigm of Recognition and Redistribution." *Theory, Culture and Society* 18 (2-3): 185-217.

–. 2007. "Human Rights as an Emancipatory Script? Cultural and Political Conditions." In *Another Knowledge Is Possible: Beyond Northern Epistemologies,* ed. by Boaventura de Sousa Santos, 3-40. London and New York: Verso.

Derrida, Jacques. 2001. *On Cosmopolitanism and Forgiveness.* New York and London: Routledge.

Erskine, Toni. 2002. "'Citizen of Nowhere' or 'the Point Where Circles Intersect?' Impartialist and Embedded Cosmopolitanisms." *Review of International Studies* 28: 457-78.

Gadamer, Hans-Georg. 1989. *Truth and Method.* London and New York: Continuum Books.

Fraser, Nancy. 1997. *Justice Interruptus: Critical Reflections on the "Postsocialist" Condition.* New York: Routledge.

Fraser, Nancy, and Axel Honneth. 2003. *Redistribution or Recognition? A Political-Philosophical Exchange.* London: Verso.

Genestier, Philippe. 2010. "La mixité: mot d'ordre, vœu pieux ou simple argument?" *Espaces et sociétés* 140-41: 21-35.

Hall, Stuart. 2002. "Political Belonging in a World of Multiple Identities." In *Conceiving Cosmopolitanism: Theory, Context, and Practice,* ed. by Steven Vertovec and Robin Cohen, 25-33. Oxford: Oxford University Press.

Hannerz, Ulf. 1992. *Cultural Complexity: Studies in the Organization of Meaning.* New York: Columbia University Press.

Held, David. 2002. "Culture and Political Community: National, Global, and Cosmopolitan." In *Conceiving Cosmopolitanism: Theory, Context, and Practice,* ed. by Steven Vertovec and Robin Cohen, 48-59. Oxford: Oxford University Press.

–. 2003. "Cosmopolitanism: Globalisation Tamed?" *Review of International Studies* 29: 465-80.

Helfer, S. Gubbay. 2007. *Usage and Meanings of "Common Values" and "Shared Values."* Report presented to la Commission de consultation sur les pratiques d'accommodement reliées aux différences culturelles (CCPARDC), Montréal, Québec.

Honneth, Axel. 2007. *Disrespect: The Normative Foundations of Critical Theory.* London: Polity Press.

INCP-RIPC (International Network on Cultural Policy – Réseau international sur la politique culturelle). n.d. "Questions nouvelles et émergentes: le concept d'interculturalité et la création d'observatoires culturels." http://www.incp-ripc. org/meetings/2002/newissues_f.shtml.

Kennedy, Michael D. 2006. "Calhoun's Critical Sociology of Cosmopolitanism, Solidarity and Public Space." *Thesis Eleven* 84: 73-89.

Kurasawa, Fuyuki. 2004. "A Cosmopolitanism from Below: Alternative Globalization and the Creation of a Solidarity without Bounds." *Archives of European Sociology* 45 (2): 233-55.

Kwok-Bun, C. 2002. "Both Sides, Now: Culture Contact, Hybridization, and Cosmopolitanism." In *Conceiving Cosmopolitanism: Theory, Context, and Practice,* ed. by Steven Vertovec and Robin Cohen, 190-208. Oxford: Oxford University Press.

Kymlicka, Will. 2000. "Nation-Building and Minority Rights: Comparing West and East." *Journal of Ethnic and Migration Studies* 26 (2): 183-212.

–. 2003. "Multicultural States and Intercultural Citizens." *Theory and Research in Education* 1 (2): 147-69.

Lemert, Charles. 2004. "Can the Worlds Be Changed? On Ethics and the Multicultural Dream." *Thesis Eleven* 78: 46-60.

Malcomson, Scott L. 1998. "The Varieties of Cosmopolitan Experience." In *Cosmopolitics: Thinking and Feeling Beyond the Nation,* ed. by Pheng Cheah and Bruce Robbins, 233-45. Minneapolis: University of Minnesota Press.

MICC (Ministère de l'Immigration et des Communautés culturelles). 2008. *Diversity: An Added Value. Government Policy to Promote Participation of All in Québec's Development. Summary.* Quebec: Government of Quebec.

–. 2009. "Fondements de la société québécoise: Valeurs communes de la société québécoise." http://www.quebecinterculturel.gouv.qc.ca/.

Molz, Jennie Germann. 2006. "Cosmopolitan Bodies: Fit to Travel and Travelling to Fit." *Body and Society* 12 (3): 1-21.

Morgan, William J. 1995. "Cosmopolitanism, Olympism, and Nationalism: A Critical Interpretation of Coubertin's Ideal of International Sporting Life." *OLYMPIKA: The International Journal of Olympic Studies* 4: 79-92.

Nash, Kate. 2003. "Cosmopolitan Political Community: Why Does It Feel So Right?" *Constellations* 10 (4): 506-18.

Pollock, Sheldon, Homi K. Bhabha, Carol A. Breckenridge, and Dipesh Chakrabarty. 2000. "Cosmopolitanisms." *Public Culture* 12 (3): 577-89.

Portes, Alejandro. 2000. "Globalization from Below: The Rise of Transnational Communities." In *The Ends of Globalization: Bringing Society Back in,* ed. by Don Kalb, 253-72. New York: Rowman and Littlefield.

Robbins, Bruce. 1998. "Actually Existing Cosmopolitanism." In *Cosmopolitics: Thinking and Feeling Beyond the Nation,* ed. by Pheng Cheah and Bruce Robbins, 1-19. Minneapolis: University of Minnesota Press.

Rocher, François, Micheline Labelle, Ann-Marie Field, and Jean-Claude Icart. 2007. *Le concept d'interculturalisme en contexte Québécois: Généalogie d'un néologisme.* Rapport présenté à la Commission de consultation sur les pratiques d'accommodement reliées aux différences culturelles (CCPARDC). Montréal and Ottawa: Université du Québec à Montréal and Université d'Ottawa.

Rosello, Mireille. 2001. *Postcolonial Hospitality: The Immigrant as Guest.* Stanford, CA: Stanford University Press.

Roudometof, Victor. 2005. "Transnationalism, Cosmopolitanism and Glocalization." *Current Sociology* 53 (1): 113-35.

Rundell, John. 2004. "Strangers, Citizens and Outsiders: Otherness, Multiculturalism and the Cosmopolitan Imaginary in Mobile Societies." *Thesis Eleven* 78: 85-101.

Sévigny, Charles-Antoine. 2008. "Multiculturalisme – Vers un renouvellement de l'interculturalisme québécois." *Le Devoir,* 9 May 2009. http://www.ledevoir.com/.

Skrbis, Zlatko, Gavin Kendall, and Ian Woodward. 2004. "Locating Cosmopolitanism: Between Humanist Ideal and Grounded Social Category." *Theory, Culture and Society* 21 (6): 115-36.

Skrbis, Zlatko, and Ian Woodward. 2007. "The Ambivalence of Ordinary Cosmopolitanism: Investigating the Limits of Cosmopolitan Openness." *Sociological Review* 55 (4): 730-47.

Szerszynski, Bronislaw, and John Urry. 2006. "Visuality, Mobility, and the Cosmopolitan: Inhabiting the World from Afar." *British Journal of Sociology* 57 (1): 113-31.

Turner, Bryan S. 2006. "Classical Sociology and Cosmopolitanism: In Defence of the Social." *British Journal of Sociology* 57 (1): 133-51.

Werbner, Pnina. 1997. "Introduction: The Dialectics of Cultural Hybridity." In *Debating Cultural Hybridity: Multi-Cultural Identities and the Politics of Anti-Racism,* ed. by Pnina Werbner and Tariq Modood, 1-28. London: Zed Books.

Zubaida, Sami. 2002. "Middle Eastern Experiences of Cosmopolitanism." In *Conceiving Cosmopolitanism: Theory, Context, and Practice,* ed. by Steven Vertovec and Robin Cohen, 33-47. Oxford: Oxford University Press.

8

A World of Strangers or a World of Relationships? The Value of Care Ethics in Migration Research and Policy

Yasmeen Abu-Laban

Liberal democracies have demonstrated evolving and varied responses to sojourners, immigrants, and refugees since the end of the Second World War, and particularly since the end of the Cold War. Despite the increased political salience of migration, however, as well as growing numbers of scholars addressing the policy consequences of migration and integration practices, relatively little attention has been paid to the ethical issues surrounding human migration. As a pertinent example, consider the work that has been done through the international Metropolis project since the mid-1990s. The Canadian government, Canadian academics, and Canadian non-governmental organizations have played a key role in the evolution of this project, which focuses on issues of immigration and integration in urban settings. It is evident that by and large Metropolis has favoured empirical studies over those that are normative.[1] Since Metropolis aims to be "policy-relevant," this means that its scholarly as well as policy discussions have been skewed toward dealing with "what is" as opposed to "what ought to be."

Building on Joseph Carens's helpful invocation (1996, 2000) to better link the "realistic" and the "idealistic" in the study of migration ethics, as well as to ground justice considerations in relation to context, I set out in this chapter to reconsider the Canadian case. Canada is a relevant choice in light of its foundation as an immigrant-receiving settler colony as well as its continued use of immigration. I suggest that in order to be attuned to a full range of perspectives that might develop from explicit consideration of ethics in migration, it is critical to give simultaneous attention to a portrayal of "what is." This is because ethical considerations have not been the only area where there has been a discernible silence in migration research: significantly, the migration experience of women has traditionally also been ignored in much empirical work.

Only since the late 1980s have scholars even begun paying attention to gender and the migration experience. In the process, they have uncovered the fact that despite prevailing images that associate migration with men (or men bringing in wives and children), women in fact do move, and they sometimes move on their own, independently of men. For example, in Canada, since at least the 1930s women have moved in numbers equivalent to men, if not more (Boyd 2006, 1). Recent Canadian and comparative work also challenges the image of the passive female migrant. For example, the collection of works edited by Alexandra Dobrowolsky and Evangelia Tastsoglou (2006) utilize careful empirical analyses to show that female migrants express their agency in a number of spheres – economic, social, and political. Since these more recent empirical insights that pay explicit attention to gender are critically important to coming up with more *realistic* portrayals of migration and migration policy, it is relevant to ask whether more explicit attention to gender – and by extension other relations of inequality – may also serve our *idealistic* portrayals of migration and migration policy.

In work linking migration and ethics, cosmopolitanism serves as one of the most important entry points into contemporary debates and appropriate policy responses, as shown, for example, by the favourable reception given to Seyla Benhabib's significant intervention *The Rights of Others* (2004). I will argue, however, that the cosmopolitan perspective (whether explicitly rooted or not) shares with traditional empirical accounts to varying degrees a tendency toward "gender blindness," when in fact a more comprehensive consideration of the ethical issues surrounding the migration of men and women today requires that gender be explicitly considered. By way of contrast, a potentiated "ethics-of-care" perspective holds considerable promise for dealing with the challenges that gender – and other unequal relations of power such as "race" and class – pose to our understanding of both social reality and global justice. This is because an ethics-of-care perspective is attuned to relationships and contextual details, as well as power, obligations, and policy.

In making this argument, I will take a threefold approach. First, I will highlight some of the existing work dealing with migration and ethics to illustrate the silence on gender in many different traditions, including cosmopolitanism and some of its variants. Second, I will give an overview of some of the key interventions made in the work of proponents of feminist care ethics that may enable us to move from consideration of a "world of strangers" to a "world of relationships." Finally, since the care perspective has just begun to be applied to migration – mainly through consideration of care workers in the American and global context (see, for example, Robinson 2006; Tronto 2005) – I will outline how some of the insights of care ethics can sensitize us to other issues that emerge in relation to Canadian immigration practices. The case of Canada is useful for showing how the feminist ethics of care can embolden us in terms of what we look at as researchers and policy makers, as well as potentially how we act as global citizens.

A World of Strangers

> In a world of cosmopolitan patriots, people would accept the citizen's responsibility to nurture the culture and politics of their homes. Many would, no doubt, spend their lives in the places that shaped them; and this is one of the reasons local cultural practices would be sustained and transmitted. But many would move, and that would mean that cultural practices would travel also (as they have always traveled). The result would be a world in which each local form of human life was the result of long term and persistent processes of cultural hybridization: a world, in that respect, much like the world we live in now.
>
> – Kwame Anthony Appiah (1996, 22)

Bruce Robbins (1998, 1) noted that "something has happened to cosmopolitanism." For Robbins, what had happened was that cosmopolitanism had gone from being a term of derision to one with a certain cachet. Indeed, the proliferation of late twentieth-century discussions of cosmopolitanism might be seen as an element of the *fin de siècle* zeitgeist that – often optimistically – embraced the idea of a world without borders, and a world where the nation-state was not the primary source of allegiance (Abu-Laban 2008, 1). The uncertainties for the future of national identities introduced by consideration of globalization were part of the best analyses. As summarized by Stuart Hall (1995), there were three distinct possibilities in response to the globalization predicted for the twenty-first century: (1) national identity may actually be strengthened; (2) national identity may be weakened; and (3) new, shifting, and even hybrid forms of identity may emerge to challenge a singular national identity.

In many ways the articulation of a rooted cosmopolitanism, as propounded by Kwame Anthony Appiah and others, offers a way of acknowledging (dealing with, covering off) all these ambiguities and eventualities. This is because rooted cosmopolitanism holds out the possibility of citizens' responsibilities toward national (local) practices as well as the retention or possible strengthening of the same, while also speaking of a hybridization of culture/identity as a consequence of movement across national boundaries. In a recent rearticulation, Toni Erskine (2008) draws on feminist ethics to argue for an "embedded cosmopolitanism" that gives recognition to a range of "dislocated communities" that go beyond place/space/territory. At the heart of Erskine's formulation (2008, 5-6) lies the idea that we are "constituted by multiple, multifarious, overlapping, and often transnational, territorially and non-territorially defined communities."

From the vantage point of territorially based identities, the continuing ambiguities of real-world politics in the early years of the twenty-first century still make rooted cosmopolitanism a potent way of accounting for the deepening processes of cultural, technological, and economic globalization that coexist alongside countless examples that speak to the continued relevance of states, nationalism, and a singular national citizenship. On the one hand, as Craig Calhoun (2004, 233) notes, "cosmopolitans suffered September 11 as an especially severe shock, and the continuing prominence of national security agendas and both religious and ethnic identities as a gloomy regression from what had seemed clear progress." Indeed, the growing fortification and strengthening of state border controls and surveillance practices, although in evidence long before 11 September 2001, reached unprecedented heights in the context of the "war on terror" (Abu-Laban 2004; Donaldson 2005; van Selm 2005). Civilizational discourses feed nationalisms in which the threat of terrorism is seen to reside in both non-citizens and racialized citizens, who, in turn, may be treated in "exceptional" ways when it comes to the rule of law and due process rights (Razack 2008). In Canada and internationally, the disadvantage of holding Canadian citizenship along with birthright Syrian citizenship was captured in the media coverage of the case of Maher Arar, the dual citizen who was erroneously accused by American officials of being a member of al-Qaeda and subjected to rendition for torture in his country of birth (Abu-Laban and Nath 2007).

And yet, on the other hand, in the very same post-9/11 period when state borders, national identities, and a single national citizenship seemed to matter most, the United Nations Educational, Scientific and Cultural Organization (UNESCO) launched a research project designed to investigate "migration without borders" (Pécoud and de Guchteneire 2007). To consider migration without borders is to begin to ask why citizens alone hold the right to legally enter and stay in a country. In the words of UNESCO Assistant Director-General for Social and Human Sciences Pierre Sané, immigration needs to be thought of as a human right connected to emigration:

> According to Article 13-2 of the Universal Declaration of Human Rights, "Everyone has the right to leave any country, including his own, and to return to his country." But the right to leave is not complemented by a right to enter: one may emigrate, but not immigrate. From a human rights point of view, we are faced with an incomplete situation that sees many people being deprived of their right to emigrate by an absence of possibilities to immigrate. It is therefore worth envisaging a right to mobility: in a world of flows, mobility is a resource to which everyone should have access. (Sané 2007)

The idea of rooted cosmopolitanism, when applied to the question of whether there should be borders, may at least be seen to offer a bridge between two competing perspectives that have dominated much of the current discussion on immigration and ethics. These perspectives revolve around a debate between communitarianism, or nationalism, and the right to exclude others on the one hand (Walzer 1998 and, at the extreme, Masters 2001), and liberalism, or cosmopolitanism, and the call for (semi) open borders, on the other (Benhabib 2004; Carens 1998). From a standpoint that takes equal moral worth seriously, it is hard to justify the fact that citizens from Organization for Economic Co-operation and Development (OECD) countries have generally open (visa-free) access to the globe, while those from countries of the global South face so many restrictions, particularly those erected by OECD countries (for an overview of barriers, see Steiner 2009). Free movement and greater global justice may even be argued to trump welfarist arguments of exclusion (Carens 1988), and cosmopolitan theorists have identified responsibilities on the part of "developed states" to ensure greater global justice (Pogge 2001). Ways in which the communitarian/ cosmopolitan divide may be bridged can be seen in calls for the free movement of people in global civil society (civilianship) even as national citizenship is maintained (see Frost 2004). Or they might be seen in calls to allow for more open borders, with, however, differential social (welfare) rights as well as other differential citizenship rights (Pécoud and de Guchteneire 2007, 20).

Even such imagined bridging schemes that might be in keeping with a rooted cosmopolitanism are not premised on alleviating all inequalities, however. In particular, the unequal distribution of wealth means that the ability to enjoy the possibility of movement, even if the right is there, is not assured. In actual practice, cosmopolitanism (rooted or not) may indeed be "the class consciousness of frequent travelers" (Calhoun 2004, 245). Thus, attention needs to be paid to the very specific contexts in which people may experience privilege and/or harm. This is all the more so because "global civil society" is characterized by inequalities between countries as well as nuanced unequal relations of power that turn on class, "race," ethnicity, gender, and other social divides (see also Abu-Laban 2000).

Arguably, it is the starting point of cosmopolitanism that may make consideration of these social relations easier to place as a backdrop rather than as central to ethical considerations. In particular, it is interesting to note that the thinking in connection with how "the stranger," "the foreigner," or "the other" ought to be treated has deep traditions that reverberate in today's discussions of rooted cosmopolitanism. This is graphically illustrated by Kwame Anthony Appiah's notable subtitle to his book *Cosmopolitanism: Ethics in a World of Strangers* (2006). Likewise, despite her express attention to articulating a cosmopolitan position that is mindful of the "embedded" character of moral experience, Toni Erskine's subtitle to her *Embedded Cosmopolitanism: Duties to Strangers and Enemies in a World of "Dislocated Communities"* (2008) also employs the trope of the stranger. At first glance, this may appear to be explained by the fact that all communities – including apparently "dislocated communities" – exclude non-members, strangers, and especially enemies. But the reappearance of the figure of the stranger may also be linked to the manner in which "community" is employed by Erskine.

Erskine (2008, 6) is concerned with broadening the definition of "community" beyond the conventional focus in international relations, in which it is synonymous with "the state." This is a worthwhile undertaking, and indeed its relevance extends beyond the field of international relations to the inherent methodological nationalism underpinning the modern human sciences as a whole. As Nisbet (1973) observed many years ago, although the idea of community has been central to the Western philosophical tradition, it has also been one of the most contested terms in the human sciences. While Erskine (2008, 254) emphasizes that individuals may have overlapping memberships across different communities (with overlapping memberships becoming challenged under conditions of rigid definition against "another," or challenged by a "totalizing" community, which limits a person's participation in another community), she does not attend to all the ways in which community has been a contested concept. In particular, many feminist and critical scholars who employ the concept of community explicitly reject the idea of homogeneity from the outset; in this view, any community is defined by heterogeneity, sometimes conflict, sometimes cooperation, and always fluidity owing to its socially constructed character (Yuval-Davis 1991, 59). Put differently, the idea that politics is about the construction of strangers/enemies/others and the ongoing struggle of how the community is (morally) constituted is a starting point in certain conceptions (see Yuval-Davis 1997, 46-73), whereas for Erskine (2008, 242-43) it is, quite literally, an ending point. As an ending point, the trope of the stranger lingers. As a starting point, the discussion might be different because the stranger would not dominate the script.

Similar to the character of the stranger in cosmopolitan accounts (whether rooted or embedded or not), guideposts for the treatment of the stranger may be identified in many religious traditions, with particular implications for immigrants. For example, Islam, Christianity, and Judaism all view hospitality as a virtue, which suggests certain readings that might be given for how to respond to immigrants (Mazrui 2006; O'Neill and Spohn 1998; Plaut 1996). Philosophical writings on the question of how the stranger or the foreigner ought to be treated are also evident in the foundational work of Immanuel Kant, whose understanding of hospitality as the right not to be treated as an enemy in another land provides the basis for a cosmopolitan citizenship that is central to contemporary discussions (see Benhabib as cited in Post 2006), including in relation to immigrants and refugees (Benhabib 2004). What I want to suggest is that across the liberal and communitarian divide, and across works emerging from various traditions, whether sacred or secular, a common problem emerges: in many of these discussions, the stranger, the foreigner, the other, or the immigrant/refugee is treated as an abstract and ungendered subject. This is significant, for as Elaine Scarry (1996, 98) notes, "the way we act towards 'others' is shaped by the way we imagine them."

In other words, gender is not always an explicit component of long-standing cosmopolitan frameworks, and not always a sustained consideration in relation to how it may guide action. An outright silence, or an absence of sustained articulation, matters because the actual lived, and typically varied, experiences of men and women who migrate can sensitize us to different normative considerations, as well as quite different policy responses. The possibilities and enriched analytical utility may become clearer if we contrast envisioning a "world of strangers" (or even a "world of dislocated communities") with envisioning a "world of relationships." It is relationships that are at the heart of an ethics-of-care perspective.

A World of Relationships

Although ideas of responsibility and social interconnections may be addressed outside an explicit ethics-of-care perspective (see Young 2007, 159-86), an immediate advantage of such a perspective has to do with the fact that gender and other social relations of power are placed front and centre in care ethics. This has to do with the origins of care ethics. Additionally, although gender is taken into consideration, it does not, and indeed ought not, lead to essentialism, or treating all men and all women as inherently, always, categorically different in either experience or needs.

Care ethics stems from the work of social psychologist Carol Gilligan, who addressed the implications of boys and girls appearing to reason their way out of ethical dilemmas differently. According to Gilligan, whose critical book *In a Different Voice* was published in 1982, the moral reasoning of females (with a tendency to emphasize relationships and care) differed from that of males (with a tendency to emphasize rules and justice). In the years since Gilligan published *In a Different Voice*, the scholarly work on care ethics has proliferated, as have critiques and variant articulations.

Olena Hankivsky (2004) usefully identifies two distinct "generations" of work. On the one hand, Carol Gilligan's work and other earlier interventions were problematic in tending to link an ethics of care to one's gender. This perspective was criticized as essentialist, for suggesting absolutist views on "male behaviour" versus "female behaviour." More contemporary scholarship, which is less open to critique on grounds of essentialism, tends to link an ethics of care to understanding and even re-envisioning connections between people regardless of gender (Hankivsky 2004, 11). It is this second generation of work that illuminates in distinctive ways themes of "citizenship," "community," and "responsibility." This more recent scholarship stresses the importance of care in relation to moral obligations, arguing that all human life is embedded in relations of interdependency and care (Engster 2005, 61).

In light of the expanding literature embracing a care ethics perspective, a brief overview of the emergent themes suggests its rich potential for strengthening migration research and policy. In this regard, the work of Fiona Williams (2001) and Virginia Held (2004) is useful for highlighting at least five significant areas in considering the principles, issues, and policy implications of an ethics of care (see also Adkin and Abu-Laban

2008). First, an ethics of care "demands that interdependence be seen as the basis of human interaction; in these terms, autonomy and independence are about the capacity for self-determination rather than the expectation of individual self-sufficiency" (Williams 2001, 487). As such, vulnerability is viewed as a human condition that varies across time and space (Williams 2001, 487). Put differently, whereas many existing Kantian moral theories (such as the work of Pogge on cosmopolitanism) tend to focus on rational decisions by independent autonomous individuals, care ethics views people as relational and interdependent, with social ties relating to both our varied histories and who we are (Held 2004, 143). (Although some proponents of feminist ethics may reject the idea of community as being of intrinsic moral value [Erskine 2008, 151], such a critique does not rule out conceptualizing community in ways that are attuned to heterogeneity and interrelationships.)

Second, an ethics of care attributes moral worth to positive caring relationships, "whether based upon blood, kinship, sexual intimacy, friendship, collegiality, contract or service" (Williams 2001, 487). The human quality of care is not strictly measurable in precise economic terms because there is a limit to the ability of human services such as nursing, teaching, or caring for the young or the old to achieve "economic efficiencies" without sacrificing the quality of care (Adkin and Abu-Laban 2008, 55).

Third, an ethics of care is alert to historical and contemporary power inequalities. It is alert in particular to power inequalities in giving and receiving care, which may be constituted through relations of gender, disability, age, ethnicity, "race," nationality, class, religion, and sexuality, among others (Williams 2001, 487). More broadly, by being attuned to power differentials, care ethics can guide us to consider "what we ought to do" not simply by superficial acceptance of highly abstract rules and principles about "all humans" but also in relation to utilizing empathy, sensitivity, and responsiveness to needs in order to consider what we ought to do for particular others (Held 2004, 144-45). In this case, the "oughts" do not come from designated sources of moral authority but from a deeper analytical understanding of the particularistic limitations subsumed under purportedly universalistic principles.

Fourth, and importantly, the implications of care ethics are not simply confined to the private sphere or to the local, but like cosmopolitanism (and its rooted and embedded variants) it can have a global dimension. As such, caring relations are not just about family, friends, and co-citizens but can extend beyond – to persons who suffer, who are denied justice and an approximation of equality of condition in distant parts of the globe (Held 2004, 144).

Fifth, and not least, care ethics work brings with it new tools for analyzing and re-envisioning public and social policies at national and global levels. For example, in examining a range of social policy areas in Canada, Olena Hankivsky (2004, 7) has argued that care ethics compels us "to examine the far-reaching consequences of not prioritizing care and its values in the construction of our polity, its institutions, and in the content of our policies." Ongoing discussion of an ethics of care in social policy has necessitated attention to such ideas as the restructuring of work/life time, financial and practical support to caregivers as well as those requiring care, meaningful choices, equal access to public space and transport, and anti-discrimination and anti-poverty policies (Williams 2001, 487-88). At a global level, Fiona Robinson (2009) suggests that human rights are "hollow without recognizing the need for networks and relations of care that are equitable, well resourced, and that underpin and give shape and meaning to rights." Basically then, an energized focus on the meaning of care relationships may be one avenue to a national as well as global debate about human needs and the kinds of institutions and practices that are necessary to meet those needs.

Taking these ideas about interdependence, the value of care, power and inequality, and obligations to others globally, and re-envisioning policy, we can now address Canadian immigration practices when it comes to legal permanent immigration.

The Case of Canada Reconsidered
As a country founded on settler colonization, the Canadian state's policies and practices in relation to indigenous peoples, as well as the policies and practices relating to the entry and residence of immigrants, reveal a complex legacy of racial, ethnic, gender, and class exclusions (Abu-Laban 1998). A full consideration of Canada would consider the thorny challenges that emerge in relation to its colonial past and its colonial present, since these inegalitarian features raise profound questions about the viability of cosmopolitanism, given its emphasis on equal moral worth. As well, despite its status in comparative immigration studies as a "traditional" country of immigration (that is, a settler colony) as distinct from European polities that employed "guest worker" schemas, it is misleading to address only permanent immigration and settlement in Canada. This is because chronic labour shortages are being dealt with

today – as in many other periods in the twentieth century – through the importation of temporary migrants who are denied citizenship rights and for the most part any hope of achieving Canadian citizenship (Stasiulis 2008, 104). The migration picture is further complicated if human trafficking and so-called illegal immigration are considered. In light of space limitations, in what follows I will leave the historical and current realities of colonialism, temporary migration, and human trafficking aside and focus only on contemporary policies and practices concerning licit (permanent) entry. Specifically, the policies and practices concerning licit permanent entry will be considered in relation to five specific themes emerging from consideration of gender and care ethics: (1) interdependency, (2) the moral value of care and caring relationships, (3) power and vulnerability, (4) globality, and (5) policy implications. Each theme will be addressed in relation to immigration.

Interdependency

First, the attention given to interdependency and interrelationships by care ethics raises the question of whether Canada's immigration policy also recognizes this or whether it rests on the false assumption of self-sufficient/autonomous individuals. The answer is mixed, although overall the emphasis is on self-sufficiency/autonomy. As Monica Boyd (2006, 2) has pointed out, legal permanent entry has different modes that are closely related to gender. In Canada, males usually outnumber females in refugee flows; women are more likely to be admitted as family members rather than as independent or economic immigrants; and women are also much more likely than men to enter Canada under the Live-In Caregiver Program. Although Canada's Immigration and Refugee Protection Act makes reference to reunification of families, it is really conceptions of dependence and independence that are woven into the language of the policy itself. Thus, it is independent immigrants who are assessed on the formal, economically based, and skill-based criteria of the point system, and spouses (typically women) and other family members (such as children or grandparents) are treated as dependent. They are dependent because they must be supported by the sponsor for a varying number of years, and their work (whether paid or not) is unacknowledged and made invisible. In this way, Canadian immigration policy is not premised primarily on viewing people relationally. The policy is embedded in expectations of individual self-sufficiency in terms of both selection and sponsorship. The willingness to countenance the separation of families is also seen in the introduction in 1995 of a right-of-landing fee on all adults (and until 2000 this even included refugees) prior to the issuance of permanent residence. This is another way in which expectations of self-sufficiency have increased since the 1990s. Consequently, independent immigrants represent the largest stream of immigrants in the past decade (Abu-Laban 2009).

Moral Value of Care and Caring Relationships

A second question that emerges from a consideration of care ethics and immigration is whether moral worth is accorded to care and caring relationships in Canada's policy. Here again the answer is mixed, but tending toward the negative. In keeping with the idea that kinship is regulated by the state (Stevens 1999), the Canadian state carefully articulates a definition of the family. On the positive side, it is worth noting that the definition of family class has expanded in recent years to include a spouse, a common-law or a "conjugal" (same-sex) partner, and certain orphaned relatives if they are under twenty-two years of age.[2] The overall definition of the family, however, brings with it limitations in terms of the kinds of interdependent and caring relations that may develop between people in extended families and as a consequence of disaster or war. In other words, in terms of policy, the family is defined in ways that are insensitive to varied lived experiences and contexts that may be part of people's collective and individual histories, and even perhaps the relationships that may motivate a desire to emigrate to seek better opportunities in the first place.

Additionally, flowing from the emphasis on individual self-sufficiency, which is a paradigmatic hallmark of neoliberal citizenship, the valorization of the economic class of immigrants and the point system itself serve to downplay the value of caring labour.

As noted, men are more likely than women to make use of the point system for entry into Canada. Tellingly, the one area of immigration in which care is expressly desired is the separate Live-In Caregiver Program, which offers dramatically weaker opportunities for citizenship than the point system used with so-called economic immigrants. As Daiva Stasiulis and Abigail Bakan (2005) have pointed out in their book *Negotiating Citizenship*, those coming in under the Live-In Caregiver Program are primarily women and primarily from countries of the Third World (especially the Philippines); located in the isolation of an employer's home, they face considerable risk of abuse. Moreover, despite the fact that live-in caregivers provide indispensable care to children, seniors, and people with disabilities in Canada, it is hard to say that this labour is valued when the Live-In Caregiver Program's avenue to citizenship is measured against the more secure route for independent immigrants.

Moreover, it is important to note that many immigrants not entering through the Live-In Caregiver Program, particularly immigrant women to Canada, end up doing caring labour (Brodie 2008). Of course, what constitutes "care," and therefore "caring labour," is hotly contested because there are considerable variations across time, space, and cultures. In terms of contemporary Canada, however, it is fair to highlight the labour involved in the care work of parents, the work of caregivers for aging and sick family members, and some really concrete areas of the paid labour force: daycare workers and nannies, as well as much work in hospitals and in the service sector. The low wages and often difficult adverse conditions associated with much caring work in Canada does not suggest that this is valued, even though all of us, at one point or another (often daily), need care in order to survive and thrive, and even though immigration has become one very visible means through which care is provided to many Canadian-born citizens.

Power and Vulnerability
A third feature of care ethics is that it draws attention to issues of power and inequality and may attune us to what we ought to do for particular groups. Hence, it can be asked whether Canadian policy has paid special attention to the most vulnerable. Here again, while mixed, the record basically suggests that Canadian policy does not do this. It is true that Canada has been in many ways at the forefront in developing means and responses to be attuned to gender when it comes to the ability to make refugee claims, since it is frequently women who are in refugee camps. For example, in the late 1980s Canada developed a "Women at Risk" program to assist vulnerable women in United Nations High Commissioner for Refugees (UNHCR) camps (this is now called the Urgent Protection Program). In 1993, Canada was the first country to introduce gender-based persecution in relation to refugee assessments, thereby somewhat widening the definition of refugees established in the United Nations Convention Relating to the Status of Refugees. More broadly, within Citizenship and Immigration Canada (as in other departments) since the late 1990s there has been sensitivity to gender-based analysis. Overall, however, special programs are small. Women at Risk targeted a total of only 2,500 women and their dependents through the 1990s, and from 1993 to 2002 a total of only 1,345 refugee claims were accepted on the basis of gender discrimination (Boyd 2006, 3-4). (In this same time span of a decade or so, Canada accepted in the neighbourhood of 225,000 to 250,000 immigrants annually, with the smallest component being refugees – around 30,000 annually.)

Much has been written by Canadian immigration scholars looking at gender regarding how the terms of sponsorship can render migrant women vulnerable in relationships, or in relation to accessing social services (such as language training prior to the 1990s) (Abu-Laban 2009). Under the Conservative government of Stephen Harper, however, resources for gender-based analysis have been dwindling (Bakker 2009, 234-35). In addition, gender mainstreaming is not equivalent to what has been termed diversity mainstreaming, where a wide range of possible points of inequality might be assessed in conjunction with gender, with the goal of social justice in mind (Hankivsky 2005). In short, then, the policy is not attuned to the most vulnerable, and is becoming less so.

Globality
A fourth feature that care ethics may attune analysts to is the global level. It can therefore be asked whether the policy supports caring relations in other societies or whether it pursues local (that is, Canadian-based) caring relations at the expense of global ones. The answer is that there is more emphasis on the local. Many people may seek to migrate because of care. For instance, a primary motivation for West Indian and Filipino domestic workers to immigrate to Canada is to assist in their own families' financial and social welfare (Stasiulis and Bakan 2005, 102); that is, the desire to immigrate is motivated by relationships to others and a feeling of responsibility. At the same time, the importance of these interdependent relationships in the "sending state" is not recognized by Canadian state policies. This may be seen as contradictory in light of the value placed on recruiting domestic workers to help some (Canadian) families, and it may also be seen as discriminatory/racist. As Bakan and Stasiulis (1997, 17) observe:

> The denial of entry to the children and partners of foreign domestics, and the forced separation of families through Canadian immigration programs like the LCP [Live-In Caregiver Program], expose dramatically the racism of official state discourses that speak of the "sanctity of families." The "family" that is to be protected from unnecessary state intervention is the middle class white family. The same state shows no hesitation in disrupting the family lives of usually poor, rural women from developing countries.

Turning to the question of the international human rights regime, Canada, as a signatory to the United Nations Convention Relating to the Status of Refugees, has agreed, along with many other countries, that it must assist those fleeing persecution as a result of state violations of rights. In relation to immigration policy, it is notable that giving assistance to refugees and others in need of protection is the only area of immigration that is specifically framed in relation to humanitarianism. Family class immigrants are formally chosen on the basis of helping families to reunite with some of their members. Independent immigrants assessed through the point system are formally chosen based on their ability to compete and succeed in the economy. While Canadians have tended to use the term "brain drain" to speak about educated Canadians going south to the United States, a brain drain might be seen from the global South to Canada, which is no small point when we are thinking about the global system (Steiner 2009, 53-55).

If we look at the way refugee selection has worked in practice, the record is also mixed. On the one hand, in 1986 Canada was the first country (and so far the only one) to receive the UNHCR Nansen Medal (now called the Nansen Refugee Award) for its response to Indochinese and other refugees, and, as noted, Canada has been at the forefront in dealing with issues relating to the particular circumstances that confront refugees if they are female, whether in terms of their inability to move to make claims at the borders of another state, or in terms of the distinct patterns of persecution they may face. At the same time, however, it is important to note that in terms of the three permanent flows, refugees have always been the smallest. Moreover, the vast majority of the world's refugees are not located in countries of the industrialized West, like Canada, but rather in developing countries (Steiner 2009, 76). The varied costs and benefits associated with refugees are therefore unevenly borne globally.

In addition, Canada has in recent years embarked on a path that may make it more difficult to meet its international obligations when it comes to refugees. Specifically, the 2004 Safe Third Country Agreement between Canada and the United States has been extensively critiqued by immigration law scholar Audrey Macklin (2003) for this very reason. The Canadian Council for Refugees (2007) has also repeatedly drawn attention to dwindling numbers of claims, which it attributes to the agreement.

Policy Implications
Lastly, care ethics links to policy, so this is an appropriate point to pause to ask what might be gleaned from care ethics in relation to immigration policy. Clearly, when it comes to Canada's approach to legal permanent

migration, the policy record is mixed, and mostly out of step with the values and principles that inspire a care ethic. As such, current policy may be seen as not attuned to gender and other markers of difference, and therefore to human needs. Thus, there is room for creative thinking and policy improvement when it comes to how we envision people on the move (or in Canada), how we value care, how we think about power differentials and responses, how we think about human interdependencies, and how we conceptualize and respond to international obligations.

Although policy change may involve incremental adjustments (such as slightly redistributing the numbers among different categories while maintaining the overall levels, or providing a quicker route to citizenship for domestic workers), these are essentially what Joseph Carens (1996) might call "realistic" approaches. The real promise of care ethics, however, lies in its potential for re-envisioning policy. This re-envisioning process is linked more explicitly with what Carens calls "idealistic" considerations.

Idealistic considerations might suggest that the very categories used in immigration (such as "independent" and "dependent") fail to recognize the reality of human interdependency and should be dismantled in favour of categories that do give value to a wider array of positive caring relationships. The lack of value attached to care and caring relationships (and the difficulty of measuring the value of care) suggests that the point system ought to be abandoned, and indeed that the family be defined in more inclusive ways. The fleeting attention given to those that are the most vulnerable in Canadian policy might be rethought in more critical terms to address issues relating to the radical inequities between countries of the global North and global South – all the more since the benefits that flow to many Canadian-born citizens from immigrant care connect Canada directly to the places and conditions that foster global chains of care in the first place. Here immigration itself might be seen to be linked to a broader responsibility for the conditions of development (and de-development), human security (and insecurity), as well as histories and legacies of colonialism (and postcolonialism) in the international political economy. A care perspective also compels policy makers to attend to these concerns in ways that are attuned to power differences (as a result of gender, class, and other divides) *within* countries of the global North and global South. It therefore compels a way of seeing context and our interconnectedness at multiple levels. In other words, a care perspective demands that attention be paid to the most vulnerable, and that the care of the Canadian-born not be addressed without consideration of the care of those born outside Canada.

Ultimately, a care perspective also brings with it attention to not only a right to emigrate/immigrate but also the conditions that might enable people to choose to move (or not move, even if a right is there). Put differently, a care perspective asks more of us than simply to imagine a world without borders (Sané 2007). A care perspective asks us to imagine a world in which movement and non-movement are undifferentiated by class, gender, and other forms of difference. It is notable that the UNESCO-sponsored discussion of "migration without borders," for all of its new thinking, does not invite academics, publics, or policy makers to imagine how a right of movement would be undifferentiated, perhaps owing to the fact that neither gender nor care are prominent in the empirical and normative framings of the research (see Pécoud and de Guchteneire 2007).

Conclusion

My aim in this chapter was to reconsider the case of Canada with the understanding that context is important for thinking about some of the ethical issues stemming from migration, and that migration research and policy has tended to focus on "what is" rather than "what ought to be." By also weaving in consideration of gender (a consideration ignored in much contemporary empirical work on immigration), this chapter has shown how care ethics can direct analysts to the varied individual and collective contexts that confront those who would like to move, who do move, or who cannot move.

Theories of rooted cosmopolitanism invite us to consider the relationship between local/national attachments and more global obligations; in some variants, it might even be argued that those same local/national commitments sustain global ones. In liberal democracies like Canada, a contemporary national emphasis on individual rights, and to a lesser extent group recognition, reflects the larger human rights revolution (Kymlicka 2007a). To the extent that individual rights, and more recently multiculturalism, are reflected through the United Nations (Kymlicka 2007b), Canada's evolving national commitments and discourses may mesh with this larger level. It is cosmopolitan approaches to migration that have alerted us to the incomplete nature of the post-Second World War articulation of human rights in the United Nations insofar as fundamental issues concerning borders and the question of whether there should be a human right to move were left unaddressed. Still, Canadian policy makers (and even Canadian citizens) are not necessarily more at the forefront of this call than others (see Sharma 2006). Undoubtedly the call for "open borders" may seem a utopian or preposterous proposition, depending on one's perspective, and yet it is a rooted cosmopolitan perspective that may temper this call, for example, by serving to theorize a bridge between more open borders and national commitments to mostly citizens alone, like the social rights associated with the welfare state.

Viewed in this light, in many ways the policy implications of a care ethics perspective in relation to migration may be more radical than rooted cosmopolitanism. Care ethics goes further than saying that national and global commitments may coexist, or perhaps at times even fuel each other. This is because addressing the migration experience of women and men in ethical terms is not simply an end in itself but also a potential means of beginning to address a host of power differentials, and thereby reimagining the nature of citizenship, action, and how we continually reconstruct "communities," including the local/national and global communities. It is relevant to address, in both realistic and idealistic considerations of "what ought to be," the contribution that a potentiated feminist ethic of care may bring to issues surrounding the terms of entry and settlement of refugees and migrants, as well as government treatment of non-citizens. In this endeavour, the time-worn gender-blind framing of "the stranger" in policy and political discussions that is so central to cosmopolitanism, and that may creep into rooted cosmopolitan discussions, may be hindering the development of nuanced understandings of the conditions that propel men and women to move or not to move, as well as of their varied needs.

Acknowledgments
For constructive comments on an earlier draft of this chapter, I thank the anonymous reviewers, as well as the editors of this volume, Will Kymlicka and Kathryn Walker.

Notes
1 For both the Canadian and international sites, see http://www.metropolis.net/. *Epigraph:* Appiah 1996, 22-23.
2 Specifically, a family class applicant must be the sponsor's spouse, common-law, or conjugal partner; dependent child, including a child adopted abroad; child under eighteen to be adopted in Canada; parents or grandparents; or an orphaned child under eighteen who is a brother, sister, niece, nephew, or grandchild and is not a spouse or common-law partner.

References

Abu-Laban, Yasmeen. 1998. "Keeping 'em Out: Gender, Race and Class Biases in Canadian Immigration Policy." In *Painting the Maple: Essays on Race, Gender and the Construction of Canada,* ed. by Joan Anderson, Avigail Eisenberg, Sherrill Grace, and Veronica Strong-Boag, 69-82. Vancouver: UBC Press.

–. 2000. "Reconstructing an Inclusive Citizenship for a New Millennium: Globalization, Migration and Difference." *International Politics* 37 (4): 509-26.

–. 2004. "The New North America and the Segmentation of Canadian Citizenship." *International Journal of Canadian Studies* 29: 17-40.

–. 2008. "Gendering the Nation-State: An Introduction." In *Gendering the Nation-State: Canadian and Comparative Perspectives,* ed. by Yasmeen Abu-Laban, 1-18. Vancouver: UBC Press.

–. 2009. "The Welfare State under Siege? Neo-Liberalism, Immigration and Multiculturalism." In *Women and Public Policy in Canada: Neo-Liberalism and After?* ed. by Alexandra Dobrowolsky, 146-65. Don Mills, ON: Oxford University Press.

Abu-Laban, Yasmeen, and Nisha Nath. 2007. "From Deportation to Apology: The Case of Maher Arar and the Canadian State." *Canadian Ethnic Studies* 39 (3): 71-98.

Adkin, Laurie, and Yasmeen Abu-Laban. 2008. "The Challenge of Care: Early Childhood Education and Care in Canada and Quebec." *Studies in Political Economy* 81 (Spring): 49-76.

Appiah, Kwame Anthony. 1996. "Cosmopolitan Patriots." In *For Love of Country: Debating the Limits of Patriotism,* ed. by Joshua Cohen, 21-29. Boston: Beacon Press.

–. 2006. *Cosmopolitanism: Ethics in a World of Strangers.* New York: W.W. Norton.

Bakan, Abigail B., and Daiva Stasiulis. 1997. "Introduction." In *Not One of the Family: Foreign Domestic Workers in Canada,* ed. by Abigail B. Bakan and Daiva Stasiulis, 3-28. Toronto: University of Toronto Press.

Bakker, Isabella. 2009. "'Show Us the Money': Tracking Gender-Equality Commitments and the 'Constraints' of Canadian Budgeting." In *Women and Public Policy in Canada: Neo-Liberalism and After?* ed. by Alexandra Dobrowolsky, 226-43. Don Mills, ON: Oxford University Press.

Benhabib, Seyla. 2004. *The Rights of Others: Aliens, Residents and Citizens.* Cambridge: Cambridge University Press.

Boyd, Monica. 2006. "Gender Aspects of International Migration to Canada and the United States." Paper presented at the International Symposium on International Migration and Development, Turin, Italy, 28-30 June.

Brodie, Janine. 2008. "Putting Gender Back in: Women and Social Policy in Canada." In *Gendering the Nation-State: Canadian and Comparative Perspectives,* ed. by Yasmeen Abu-Laban, 165-84. Vancouver: UBC Press.

Calhoun, Craig. 2004. "Is It Time to be Postnational?" In *Ethnicity, Nationalism and Minority Rights,* ed. by Stephen May, Tariq Modood, and Judith Squires, 231-56. Cambridge: Cambridge University Press.

Canadian Council for Refugees. 2007. "Supplementary Submission to Cabinet in Respect to the Designation of the US as a Safe Third Country for Refugees." http://www.ccrweb.ca/.

Carens, Joseph H. 1988. "Immigration and the Welfare State." In *Democracy and the Welfare State,* ed. by Amy Gutmann, 207-30. Princeton, NJ: Princeton University Press.

–. 1996. "Realistic and Idealistic Approaches to the Ethics of Migration." *International Migration Review* 30 (1): 156-70.

–. 1998. "Aliens and Citizens: The Case for Open Borders." In *The Immigration Reader: America in a Multidisciplinary Perspective,* ed. by David Jacobson, 365-87. Malden, MA: Blackwell.

–. 2000. *Culture, Citizenship and Community: A Contextual Exploration of Justice as Evenhandedness.* Oxford: Oxford University Press.

Dobrowolsky, Alexandra, and Evangelia Tastsoglou. 2006. "Crossing Boundaries and Making Connections." In *Women, Migration and Citizenship,* ed. by Alexandra Dobrowolsky and Evangelia Tastsoglou, 1-35. Aldershot, UK: Ashgate.

Donaldson, John W. 2005. "Fencing the Line: Analysis of the Recent Rise in Security Measures along Disputed and Undisputed Boundaries." In *Global Surveillance and Policing,* ed. by Elia Zureik and Mark B. Salter, 173-93. Cullompton, UK: Willan Publishing.

Engster, Daniel. 2005. "Rethinking Care Theory: The Practice of Caring and the Obligation to Care." *Hypatia* 20 (3): 50-74.

Erskine, Toni. 2008. *Embedded Cosmopolitanism: Duties to Strangers and Enemies in a World of "Dislocated Communities."* Oxford: Oxford University Press.

Frost, Mervyn. 2004. "Thinking Ethically about Refugees: A Case for the Transformation of Global Governance." In *Refugees and Forced Displacement,* ed. by Edward Newman and Joanne van Selm, 109-29. New Delhi and Tokyo: Manas Publications and United Nations University Press.

Gilligan, Carol. 1982. *In a Different Voice: Psychological Theory and Women's Development.* Cambridge, MA: Harvard University Press.

Hall, Stuart. 1995. "The Question of Cultural Identity." In *Modernity: An Introduction to Modern Societies,* ed. by Stuart Hall et al., 596-634. Cambridge: Polity Press.

Hankivsky, Olena. 2004. *Social Policy and the Ethic of Care.* Vancouver: UBC Press.

–. 2005. "Gender vs. Diversity Mainstreaming: A Preliminary Examination of the Role and Transformative Potential of Feminist Theory." *Canadian Journal of Political Science* 38 (4): 977-1001.

Held, Virginia. 2004. "Care and Justice in the Global Context." *Ratio Juris* 17 (2): 141-55.

Kymlicka, Will. 2007a. "Ethnocultural Diversity in a Liberal State: Making Sense of the Canadian Models." In *Belonging? Diversity, Recognition, and Shared Citizenship in Canada,* ed. by Keith Banting, Thomas J. Courchene, and F. Leslie Seidle, 39-104. Montreal: Institute for Research on Public Policy.

–. 2007b. *Multicultural Odysseys: Navigating the New International Politics of Diversity.* Oxford: Oxford University Press.

Macklin, Audrey. 2003. "The Value(s) of the Canada-US Safe Third Country Agreement." Caledon Institute of Social Policy. http://www.caledoninst.org/.

Masters, Michael W. 2001. "Ecology, Ethics and Immigration: The Writings of Biologist Garrett Hardin." *Social Contract* (Fall): 5-12.

Mazrui, Ali A. 2006. "Strangers in Our Midst: In Search of Seven Pillars of Wisdom." In *Displacement, Asylum, Migration: The Oxford Amnesty Lectures 2004,* ed. by Kate E. Tunstall, 92-126. Oxford: Oxford University Press.

Nisbet, Robert. 1973. *The Social Philosophers: Community and Conflict in Western Thought.* New York: Thomas Y. Crowell.

O'Neill, William R., and William C. Spohn. 1998. "Rights of Passage: The Ethics of Immigration and Refugee Policy." *Theological Studies* 59: 84-106.

Pécoud, Antoine, and Paul de Guchteneire. 2007. "Introduction: The Migration without Borders Scenario." In *Migration without Borders: Essays on the Free Movement of People,* ed. by Antoine Pécoud and Paul de Guchteneire, 1-30. Paris and New York: UNESCO and Berghahn Books.

Plaut, W. Gunther. 1996. "Jewish Ethics and International Migrations." *International Migration Review* 30 (1): 18-26.

Pogge, Thomas W. 2001. "Priorities of Global Justice." In *Global Justice,* ed. by Thomas Pogge, 6-23. Oxford: Blackwell.

Post, Robert, ed. 2006. *Another Cosmopolitanism: Seyla Benhabib with Jeremy Waldron, Bonnie Honig and Will Kymlicka.* Oxford: Oxford University Press.

Razack, Sherene H. 2008. *Casting Out: The Eviction of Muslims from Western Law and Politics.* Toronto: University of Toronto Press.

Robbins, Bruce. 1998. "Actually Existing Cosmopolitanism." In *Cosmopolitics: Thinking and Feeling Beyond the Nation,* ed. by Pheng Cheah and Bruce Robbins, 1-19. Minneapolis: University of Minnesota Press.

Robinson, Fiona. 2006. "Care, Gender and Global Social Justice: Rethinking Ethical Globalization." *Journal of Global Ethics* 2 (1): 5-25.

–. 2009. "EAI Interview: Fiona Robinson on the Ethics of Care," interviewed by John Tessitore. *Carnegie Council: The Voice for Ethics in International Affairs,* 16 February. http://www.cceia.org/.

Sané, Pierre. 2007. "Foreword." In *Migration without Borders: Essays on the Free Movement of People,* ed. by Antoine Pécoud and Paul de Guchteneire, ix-x. Paris and New York: UNESCO and Berghahn Books.

Scarry, Elaine. 1996. "The Difficulty of Imagining Other People." In *For Love of Country: Debating the Limits of Patriotism: Martha C. Nussbaum with Respondents,* ed. by Joshua Cohen, 98-110. Boston: Beacon Press.

Sharma, Nandita. 2006. *Home Economics: Nationalism and the Making of "Migrant Workers" in Canada.* Toronto: University of Toronto Press.

Stasiulis, Daiva. 2008. "Revisiting the Permanent-Temporary Labour Migration Dichotomy." In *Governing International Labour Migration: Current Issues, Challenges and Dilemmas,* ed. by Christina Gabriel and Hélène Pellerin, 95-111. London and New York: Routledge.

Stasiulis, Daiva K., and Abigail B. Bakan. 2005. *Negotiating Citizenship: Migrant Women in Canada and the Global System.* Toronto: University of Toronto Press.

Steiner, Niklaus. 2009. *International Migration and Citizenship Today.* London and New York: Routledge.

Stevens, Jacqueline. 1999. *Reproducing the State.* Princeton, NJ: Princeton University Press.

Tronto, Joan. 2005. "Care as the Work of Citizens: A Modest Proposal." In *Women and Citizenship,* ed. by Marilyn Friedman, 130-47. Oxford and New York: Oxford University Press:

van Selm, Joanne. 2005. "Immigration and Regional Security." In *International Migration and Security: Opportunities and Challenges,* ed. by Elspeth Guilde and Joanne van Selm, 11-27. London and New York: Routledge.

Walzer, Michael. 1998. "Membership." In *The Immigration Reader: America in a Multidisciplinary Perspective,* ed. by David Jacobson, 341-64. Malden, MA: Blackwell.

Williams, Fiona. 2001. "In and beyond New Labour: Towards a New Political Ethics of Care." *Critical Social Policy* 21 (4): 467-93.

Young, Iris Marion. 2007. *Global Challenges: War, Self-Determination and Responsibility for Justice.* Cambridge: Polity Press.

Yuval-Davis, Nira. 1991. "The Citizenship Debate: Women, Ethnic Processes and the State." *Feminist Review* 39 (Autumn): 58-68.

–. 1997. *Gender and Nation.* London: Sage.

9

The Doctrine of the Responsibility to Protect: A Failed Expression of Cosmopolitanism

Howard Adelman

Alison Brysk has characterized Canada as a "Global Good Samaritan" given its doctrine of the Responsibility to Protect (R2P)[1] that linked an activist human security doctrine with the promotion of humanitarian intervention to enforce human rights. R2P was "animated by *cosmopolitan* values and a benign form of liberal nationalism" (Brysk 2009, 93; emphasis added). The human security doctrine provided the *political* theoretical basis for R2P. Rooted moral cosmopolitanism (in its Canadian version) provided the *ethical* theoretical foundation for the use of force to intervene in the domestic affairs of other states for humanitarian purposes.[2] Fundamental weaknesses of R2P can be traced to flaws in that ethical theoretical foundation.

There are three supporting principles of R2P. A society of states is *not* defined by the power and control each state exercises over its own citizens, but by the responsibility each of those states assumes for protecting the rights and well-being of those citizens. When states have a weak capacity to protect their citizens, other states have obligations to help – the second leg of the ethical tripod underpinning R2P. This leads to the third leg. When non-coercive assistance fails, then the international community is obliged to intervene militarily and assume responsibility. Obligations to others do not proceed from our interests or connections or even from the way that the course of action in a faraway country plays on our heartstrings, but are based on the abstract principle of the universal duty to protect. That obligation to protect is delegated by the cosmopolitan community to the individual state, the government of which can be pushed aside if it fails to fulfill its obligations.

This version of cosmopolitan moral duties can be directly correlated with the rooted cosmopolitanism of Will Kymlicka. Kymlicka's version of rooted cosmopolitanism is expressed in Canada's stance in the United

Nations, where rhetorical debates over R2P and its application are conducted. This ideology has had no effect on the ground in Darfur, the prime case claimed as the testing ground for R2P. That failure in application and the rhetorical contradictions behind it can be linked to the faulty premises and theoretical weaknesses of rooted cosmopolitanism.

R2P as an Emergent Cosmopolitan Norm

In liberal internationalist theory, states transfer sovereignty to an international body in some areas of interstate relations, such as the governance of air traffic. In cosmopolitan theory, power is delegated from the cosmopolis to individual states that exercise delegated responsibilities. The primary responsibility of a state is to care for the well-being and rights of its citizens. When a state defaults on its responsibilities to its citizens, the international body can assume domestic sovereignty.[3] The cosmopolitan super-state entity has not only the right but also the duty to step into the breach by using coercive force when the government commits or allows mass atrocities such as genocide, ethnic cleansing, or massive crimes against humanity (Bellamy 2006).[4]

Thus, state sovereignty is no longer, if it ever was, absolute; rather, it is conditional on the state's fulfillment of its responsibilities. When state authorities dramatically fail to meet their obligations, the political leaders are also held responsible and can be tried by the international community. The newly created International Criminal Court (ICC) makes perpetrators of mass rape, ethnic cleansing, and genocide subject to trial by an international criminal court not only for acts of commission but also in cases where political authorities fail to prevent these heinous acts. The United Nations retains a residual right to authorize intervention to protect citizens of a state when a sovereign state fails to do so. A coalition of the willing cannot take up the slack as it did in Kosovo (Evans et al. 2001, 13, 55).

This is the minimal moral obligation we owe to others, according to the most cosmopolitan-lite theorists, even when the victims are unknown strangers with whom we have no contact. We are obliged to do what we can to reduce this inhumane treatment. This does not mean we are *necessarily* obliged to protect them or to send in military forces to confront their government. In some cases, we may be unable to do so if intervention is unrealistic. Nevertheless, if we can successfully act, coercive intervention becomes a universal obligation. If it is unrealistic to bring coercive force to bear and to provide protection through the deployment of military force, then we are *not* obligated to intervene any more than a doctor's obligation to help a suffering patient requires intervention in every case. It is not hypocrisy to have an obligation in theory that in the real world we are sometimes unable to meet. If, however, we are reduced to being an ineffective moral superego on the world stage in virtually every case, then the moral obligation to intervene to prevent or mitigate genocide or mass human rights violations is undercut.

R2P received overwhelming United Nations rhetorical backing by both the General Assembly and the Security Council.[5] Not only has this theatrical flourish been without teeth or bite but it does not even possess a political tongue, for R2P as it is currently utilized and interpreted is conditional on approval of the sovereign state that has failed in its duties of protection, thus eviscerating the concept's cosmopolitan aspirations and the central tenet of R2P. Does this gutting and inversion of the doctrine have anything to do with the link between R2P and rooted cosmopolitanism? This has to be established. But R2P does upend the principle of self-determination of a people. The power of the people within a state to choose its representatives is usurped by an international institution. The usurpation is carried out in the name of an international popular will. So if an individual loses his or her voice as part of the national will, that voice is regained presumably as part of an international popular will that displaces any national popular will. Finally, this international will determines that protection of individuals in a state – rather than national glory, peace, equity, the exhibition of excellence by the few, or a myriad of other possible priorities – should be the most important objective.

In the effort to promote an obligation on the part of Canada to protect everyone subjected to mass atrocities,[6] proponents have also claimed that this is an emerging norm. Except as an exercise in salesmanship, it does not help to misrepresent the historical status of the norm being championed and dub it as "emerging" if there is no evidence for its applicability and if empirical reality and actual practice appear to undercut its validity. The principle of state sovereignty and the obligation not to interfere in the domestic affairs of states, although indeed a social construct (Biersteker and Weber 1996), trumps R2P every time. Further, R2P is also a construct, but one made out of willow branches rather than steel.

R2P is a misleading and mistaken construct. We do not have a universal and equal obligation to protect everyone. Such an obligation is not emerging; there is no sign that it is about to grab the world in its embrace. Nor should it! For it misrepresents the order of our moral obligations to others and how we can and should act to ensure that each individual is treated humanely and with respect. That which is an ideal does not translate into a present responsibility. Utopian visions are not the same as moral obligations.

Further, there is also the claim that R2P, in emerging as a predominant norm, is displacing or, at the very least, qualifying what has heretofore purportedly been the absolute norm of non-intervention in the domestic affairs of other states. The principle of non-intervention has never been absolute (cf. Hurrell 1996). There were always qualifiers; they have expanded and grown. Some would make the qualifiers subject to and trumped by a higher, and not just a competing, principle. R2P would set aside the principle of non-intervention in favour of an obligation of the United Nations to intervene militarily to protect the citizens of a state when those citizens are being severely abused or when they are in dire need. Rather than the sovereign-state paradigm receding into obscurity, both as a theoretical construct and as a reference point for practical policy, the principle of non-intervention remains strong even if weakened by the emerging globalized economic order and the interpenetration of the international into the domestic sphere. Instead of simply adding additional qualifiers in adjudicating between competing principles when intervening in states, R2P redescribes intervention as a right based on a redefined conditional sovereignty, one rooted in moral responsibility itself rather than power. In the process, a presumably powerful doctrine of R2P is constructed that is theoretically weak, that is practically unworkable, and that undermines rather than reinforces responsibility. Cosmopolitans believe that abstract norms should dictate practice, whereas norms are embedded in and abstracted from actual practice (cf. Frost 2003).[7]

Some of those practices involve cosmopolitan believers acting as individuals playing a crucial role through non-governmental organizations to combat poverty and inhumanity. Other than serving as moral super-egos, however, these individuals and NGOs have been decidedly ineffective in combating state oppression and injustice, and have had no significant role in humanitarian intervention involving the use of coercive military force.[8] When there has been intervention, states have been the key players.

States are no longer exclusively, and perhaps not even largely, self-sustaining as in the nineteenth-century vision, but this does not mean that they are not central. The major wars have become intra-state wars. They are primarily wars of identity and wars of criminality where the general wills existing within a state are multiple rather than unified. These changes in historical actuality require corresponding changes in ethical theory appropriate to changing historical circumstances. The dialectic of history produces a very different ethics of international relations, and hence of humanitarian intervention, but it does not try to impose an abstract universal principle on a recalcitrant historical reality. That is why R2P, although unanimously endorsed, was stillborn and plays no effective role in its first and central case, Darfur.

Practices on the Ground in Darfur

Although the Kosovo intervention appeared to be based in a European outlook and the Iraqi intervention in an American outlook, both challenged R2P as the basis for confronting crimes against humanity. The Darfur case was the first one to put R2P (and rooted cosmopolitanism) to the test. Although the advocates of R2P have been outstandingly successful in obtaining endorsement and institutional support for the doctrine,[9] they have been singularly impotent in making the doctrine effective. The states that make up the international community are so rooted in past practices and so wedded to their national interests that even though they adopt a "universal" doctrine, they proffer an interpretation that undercuts the universality by making the doctrine subordinate to national interests. Overriding state sovereignty is eschewed even in cases of mass atrocities.

Intended to help construct a better world, Canada's humanitarian initiatives (elimination of landmines, attempts to control the export of small arms to regions of violence, demobilization of child soldiers) have been part of Canadian foreign policy under the conceptual rubric of "human security," which stresses the security of people rather than states.[10] Development and redefinition of international norms to govern humanitarian intervention have been part of this thrust. With direct engagement in the development of normative theory and not just altered practices, however, the central dilemmas of abstract cosmopolitan theorizing came to the fore, especially when such theorizing clashed with international initiatives governed by self-interested states rooted in realism.

Practices are more revealing than the quest to formulate abstract principles, and ethics works in conjunction with interests interpreted broadly. Thus, there has been no intervention per se in Darfur in spite of the gross violations of human rights that Americans dubbed genocide. Nevertheless, there is an African Union force present in Darfur, based as much on interest in regional stability as on concern with humanitarian factors. The Khartoum government vetoes non-African troops as part of the force. For a while, the presence of this force corresponded with a sharp reduction in organized violence. The force has significant backing in terms of cash, training, and equipment from Canada. An international community with a shared sense of duty and direction was not a prerequisite to that contribution. This is a significant accomplishment in an area with competing national interests and rivalries concerning resources, but it is not a manifestation of R2P.

Those rivalries offer a partial explanation. In R2P, the international order ideally depends on each state respecting free and equal citizenship and, at the very least, not making groups of its citizens targets of violent state actions. Further, in the Canadian version, respect must be given to the different cultural traditions of the Fur, Masalit, and Zaghawa settled "African" agriculturalists as well as the nomadic Arab herder populations. The interests of the nomads and the settled agriculturalists cannot be easily reconciled, however, given the creeping desertification southward that has led to a rivalry for water and land, offsetting their previous interdependence. As a result, respect for cultural norms within a universal system of rights is of little help. Moreover, economic globalization exacerbates the problems. The presence of oil in Darfur attracts outside interests, especially Chinese. Desperate to control this resource, China supports those in power in order to secure its future access to the oil.

Given these different interests, cultures, and constellation of forces, translating moral cosmopolitanism into constraints on state actions by upholding the universality of human rights, the moral equality of all individuals, and the quest for global justice, and institutionalizing these goals through international law or legal cosmopolitanism, is a chimera. Re-establishing the Fur, Masalit, and Zaghawa on their lands, rebuilding their homes, and reversing domestic ethnic cleansing will prove to be impossible. The minimal protections for those domestically cleansed from their lands is difficult enough to achieve given the realpolitik of China, the caution of the Europeans based on their gradualist cosmopolitanism, and the distinctive rooted cosmopolitanism of the United States, which vests little authority in an international body like the UN and prefers instead to work bilaterally, as it did in southern Sudan.

So while all parties are willing to pay lip service to R2P, no concrete action follows. There is no intervention. The insistence that Khartoum live up to its responsibility as a state, as defined by R2P, remains rhetorical. The ICC may go after President Omar al-Bashir, but this has only a marginal effect on him personally and no effect on the millions forcefully displaced.

But didn't pursuing Bashir through the International Criminal Court (ICC) demonstrate at least some effectiveness in translating moral theory into cosmopolitan legal practice? President Bashir's indictment by the ICC in March 2009 for war crimes and crimes against humanity occurred five years after a unanimous declaration by the US Congress that the Khartoum government was committing genocide in Darfur. In response to the indictment, Bashir expelled thirteen international and three national humanitarian NGOs for allegedly providing information to the ICC. The expulsion resulted in a drastic decline in food and health care for the 2.7 million internally displaced persons in Darfur.[11] Four years after the UN's unanimous endorsement of the doctrine of R2P, which insists that when sovereign states fail to protect their own citizens the international community has a responsibility to step in, the legal initiative made the humanitarian situation much worse without any corresponding threat of effective intervention.

Problems of Rooted Cosmopolitanism in General

The reality is that rooted cosmopolitanism acknowledges the importance and value of a fixed territorial base in determining norms but does not acknowledge that the rivalry over a fixed territorial base undercuts any possibility of imposing universal norms. Further, rooted cosmopolitanism, while acknowledging the malleability of culture over time, still calls for the return of the forcibly displaced African agriculturalists when in reality Arab nomadic culture, in the face of lack of water for the herds, is dramatically changing as the nomads settle into the agricultural areas once occupied by the Africans. At the same time, many of the latter are becoming urbanized. No vision of the good life drives the change. The vision of a feasible life under the circumstances predominates. R2P has no relevance. Nevertheless, Canada calls futilely for the repatriation of those internally displaced to homes that have been destroyed or occupied. There will be little realistic effort to dislodge the usurpers, let alone the government in Sudan.

This may simply be a problem of applying moral theory in the real world and may not reflect any theoretical weaknesses, but the weaknesses in practical application are rooted in the theory itself in general and in each of its multiple versions, although I focus on only two: the rooted cosmopolitanism of Kwame Anthony Appiah, which underpins the American approach to R2P, and that of Will Kymlicka, which underpins Canadian approaches to R2P.

Cosmopolitanism in General

Except for an increasingly common globalized consumer culture, we no longer envision a common homogeneous culture of language and history that was once viewed as the Holy Grail of cosmopolitanism.[12] Few cosmopolitans even push *political* cosmopolitan *citizenship*, where everyone from a myriad of cultures belongs to a common global polity under a world government (even one with only residual powers) that supersedes the power of nation-states.[13] All forms of political cosmopolitanism, however, endorse global or international institutions as the final arbiter and the culmination of modernity's move from local to universal governance.[14] Many also insist that we are advancing toward *legal* cosmopolitanism.[15] Aspirational legal cosmopolitans espouse the development of universal legal norms based on human rights codified in international law; these norms go beyond both positive domestic law and interstate law, although few claim that this is anything more than a beachhead in the aspiration toward cosmopolitan law – an aspiration that reached its zenith with the Manhattan School (MS).[16] The creation of the ICC on 1 July 2002 can be cited as an important advance in this direction following the pioneering work of the European Court of Human Rights (cf. Cali 2007).

The shift in emphasis from international law per se to cosmopolitan moral principles underpinning that law, to *moral* rather than *legal* cosmopolitanism, may indicate that legal cosmopolitanism has passed its zenith.[17] Those cosmopolitan moral principles are rooted in a liberal culture of individual rights legitimated by a popular will that demands the right to democratic governance based on the principle of fairness, no longer as a second-order rule but as a principle of substantive redistribution. Moral cosmopolitanism reached its apogee with the universal acceptance of R2P. This, I suggest, may turn out to be the Little Bighorn of cosmopolitanism rather than its apogee.

The conviction that each person is a member of a common humanity with responsibilities toward the cosmic human order is common to all articulations of cosmopolitanism.[18] In moral cosmopolitanism, "each person has a *moral* responsibility toward every other person no matter where that person lives, no matter what the national or cultural context in which the person is located" (Van Hooft 2007, 303; emphasis added).

Rooted Cosmopolitanism as a Version of Moral Cosmopolitanism
A growing school of thought argues that political cosmopolitanism not only has not advanced but should not; politics is inherently practised in the vernacular and needs to be rooted in particular cultures and nationalities (Kymlicka 2001, especially ch. 10). Moral cosmopolitanism's aspiration must be disaggregated from the goal of political

cosmopolitanism and need not be embedded in any presumptions of a common human nature or the universal rationality of all humans. To succeed, moral cosmopolitanism must be rooted in the development of communities, societies, and nations that increasingly adhere to an over-arching moral doctrine, one that accepts the principles that all humans are equal and enjoy a set of universal rights that receive their legitimacy and can be protected and enhanced only in a democratic polity. In this view, moral cosmopolitanism is an emerging aspirational vision of an ethical commons rather than inherent in nature or reason itself.[19]

The following are common premises and characteristics of rooted cosmopolitanism:

- Globalization has made some form of cosmopolitanism inevitable.
- A cosmopolitan order, if it is realistic, must build on democratic sover-eign polities that share the principle of free and equal citizenship because the national societies in those states are committed to the values of freedom and democracy, and therefore provide the best context for nursing these cosmopolitan values.
- Any cosmopolitan order must eschew global cultural homogenization and the goal of emancipating individuals from their inherited identi-ties, although these identities are not considered unchangeable since individuals retain the right to continue or alter those identities along with the ascribed norms with which they are associated.
- If economic globalization has made *some* form of cosmopolitanism inevitable and necessary (although "economic cosmopolitanism" is an erroneous label), and if political cosmopolitanism is unreal and cultural cosmopolitanism is imperialistic, if legal cosmopolitanism is a will-o'-the-wisp, then the only form of authentic cosmopolitanism remaining is moral cosmopolitanism.
- Rooted cosmopolitanism is committed to moral cosmopolitanism, but without being conjoined with a quest for world moral homogeneity.
- Although accepting the reality of the nation-state, moral cosmopol-itanism constrains the actions of that state both domestically and in foreign policy by upholding the universality of human rights, the moral equality of all individuals, the quest for global justice, and the institutionalization of these goals through legal cosmopolitanism when possible.
- An other-regarding cosmopolitanism does not transcend its roots but expresses them.

Various expressions of rooted cosmopolitanism have in common a territorial base and a linguistic mode of expression as a foundation, and the positive value of autonomy and the role of the inner critical self-consciousness and conscience in determining what is preserved and what is discarded have proven themselves to be the best vision and *telos* of the good life.[20]

American Rooted Cosmopolitanism: Kwame Anthony Appiah

Credited with originating the concept of rooted cosmopolitanism[21] (as opposed to Martha Nussbaum's classical universal moral cosmopolitanism [2006], which insists that all human beings are entitled to equal concern and respect[22]), Kwame Anthony Appiah (1994, 1996, 2005; Taylor 2008) disdains "the hard-core cosmopolitan who regards her friends and fellow citizens with icy impartiality"[23] in which principles of distributive justice demand *no* exclusions of persons and peoples. In contrast, Appiah celebrates the vernacular and the local, family and religion, heritage and history, and patriotic feeling against the anti-nationalism of abstract universal cosmopolitanism. While rejecting any notion of a reified cultural identity, Appiah would marry our cultural differences to a common humanity. Appiah takes both the universal rights of individuals and identity politics seriously, but rejects any "extreme" obligations for an autonomous individual to respond to others. At the same time, he follows his father's injunction never to forget that his children should be "citizens of the world."[24] Appiah is not a communitarian,[25] however, for his family values propelled him outward toward the universal and the love of all humanity. Further, rooted cosmopolitanism confronts the status quo with the aspirational. It relies on public mobilization to undermine the actuality of power without the institutionalized organization to provide a replacement for that power.

The resulting cosmopolitanism is very flaccid since one need act only "if you are the person in the best position to prevent something really awful, and if it won't cost you much to do so" (Appiah 2008, 161). Individual opportunity and convenience at minimal cost cosmopolitanism! Save the child if you happen to be nearby and if the child is drowning in a wading pool with little risk to yourself. No sacrifice of possessions or career or even of the opportunity and chance to attend an opera is required.[26] "The final responsibility for each life is always the responsibility of the person whose life it is" (Appiah 2007, 35), even though that life is shaped by communal practices. A deeply felt commitment to the local provides the foundation for the commitment to the global, but not at the cost of family and friends to whom we are and must continue to be partial even as we regard all humans as deserving of equal respect. We simply need to do our share in helping the global poor. On the collective level, our responsibility is not unlimited but extends only to preventing these populations from starving (or drowning) by donating modestly to the international poor.

Appiah is a cosmopolitan-lite (what he calls "partial cosmopolitanism"), lacking a capacious view of the duties we owe strangers in need in foreign lands. He is also a strong liberal who emphasizes the category of the individual.[27] Appiah does not spell out the mechanism of sentiment's journey into cosmopolitan space. He makes clear that his cosmopolitan space does not entail a sense of an equal duty to all, although the respect for and obligations to all others purportedly arise in everyone and are therefore universal both in those to whom the obligations are directed as well as those who bear the duties. Our cosmopolitan obligations are not to humanity in general but to specific groups of that humanity that attract our compassionate responses. Humanity is not itself an identity. For Appiah, we carry *no* responsibility for the preservation of their cultures lest we end up reinforcing reification rather than change. Forced change on cultures is not tolerable either, however. Cosmopolitans are obligated to intervene in cases of genocide because *their* own core values are violated, but not if great sacrifice is involved.

This pretty well characterizes the American response to Darfur. Enormous public mobilization is linked to patriotism and the universal rights of individuals rather than the collective rights of the Fur, Masalit, and Zaghawa. It is minimal-cost cosmopolitanism with very loud support for the plight of the Darfurians but little evidence of any willingness to incur any significant sacrifice.

Canadian Rooted Cosmopolitanism: Will Kymlicka

I love cosmopolitanism. Some of my best friends are cosmopolitans, but not when they look down on the longings for identity that captive nations may have ... that's where Canadians are world leaders. (Ignatieff cited in Gopnik 2009, 32)

Adam Gopnik (2009) went on to write that "the belief that the rights of the community can trump the rights of the individual – and that this is not incompatible with liberalism but exactly what humanizes it – really is a distinctly Canadian intuition ... argued in different ways, and with different emphasis, by the influential McGill philosopher Charles Taylor ... the essayist John Robert Saul and the Queen's University philosopher Will Kymlicka" (cf. Kymlicka 2001, ch. 10).

Canadian rooted cosmopolitanism is specifically contrasted with the view that individuals do and *should* be able to move freely between and among particular cultures. Versus Appiah, minority cultures should be given state support to enable the preservation of minority cultural membership (cf. Waldron 1995).[28] Preservation of culture is a public good and a precondition for the good life just as much as civil and personal liberties, democracy, and the rule of law. Canadian rooted cosmopolitanism endorses state support for minority cultures, not just as a public good but to help preserve an intergenerational continuity of a community occupying a more or less demarcated territory where the members of that community share a specific language and history (Kymlicka 1995, 18), what Dworkin (1985, 231) characterized as a "shared vocabulary of tradition and convention." For Kymlicka (2001, 212), "language is increasingly important in defining the boundaries of political communities, and the identities of political actors,"[29] for debate in public requires a common verbal and body language in which individual citizens feel comfortable. In contrast to a particular culture, modern civilization is uniform and globally linked by science and technology, an interwoven transportation and communication system characterized by an urban and secular global economy that supports and is supported by an educated population, a professional bureaucracy, and a democratically elected legislative and executive body (Kymlicka 2001, 207).

Minorities should be given a degree of support to preserve their culture relative to its cohesiveness, but minority national cultures are to be distinguished from minority immigrant cultures. Aboriginal nations have the right to make their own language and educational policies and even restrict land sales in their own territories subject to other preconditions of the good life. Given Kymlicka's radical divide between nations within a larger society and ethnic groups that cohere following immigration, immigrants cannot claim rights to national self-government, cultural autonomy, or state support for preservation of their language.[30]

Canadian versus American Rooted Cosmopolitanism

The United States is preoccupied by the enormous abuse of the individual human rights of agriculturalists in Darfur. Canadians focus on the threat to the continuity of the culture and way of life of the Fur, Masalit, and Zaghawa. In contrast to the absence of any American sacrifice on the ground because of minimal US national interests in western Sudan (unlike in the south), Canada, although unable to deploy troops to the peacekeeping force in Darfur because of the veto power of Khartoum, does what it can to provide trainers and equipment. Further, American rooted cosmopolitanism (ARC) is still tied to abstract, detached universal principles and the rhetoric of a haunting conscience. In the Canadian version (CRC), the principles are embodied in sets of practices as the individual struggles to reconcile competing voices of tradition and change. Further, while ARC retains the ideological underpinnings of cosmopolitanism in its aspiration toward universality and homogeneity, CRC comprehends the variety of motivating factors of human beings and is more wedded to constructivism, where, at the highest level, sovereignty is treated as a variable in which historical context and actual practices reveal the mode in which abstract contradictions are mediated.

There are other differences beside stressing practices versus rhetoric and abstract principles, protecting minority cultures versus championing self-determination and individual human rights, exhibiting a more self-sacrificial versus a more frugal approach except when interests are involved, and conceiving of a world with wider rather than narrower variations in the spectrum of legitimate democratic sovereign polities. Perhaps the most important difference is the commitment of CRC to institutional and United Nations mechanisms fostered by diplomacy to advance its ethical convictions, compared with the ARC propensity to stress American initiatives that often eschew reliance on UN diplomatic channels, although the latter are employed when they are congruent with the prior American position.

CRC privileges protection and equality of treatment over robust participation and empowerment of the citizens of those states to take charge. In the CRC schizophrenic view of popular will rooted, on the one hand, in the nation and, on the other hand, in a cosmopolitan view of the international community, the latter is emphasized, thereby undermining the popular will of the local nation. Further, nations exhibiting a preference for the rule of law and democracy to preserve and enhance as well as reflect a national culture are favoured. The rule of law is best able to facilitate self-determination and self-government. Thus, order and good government take priority over popular participation and the right to rebel when politicians usurp the sovereignty of the people. On the one hand, this leads to the political cosmopolitan conclusion that "democracy can and must become the method of global governance" (Archibugi 2008, xiv; Held 2001, 2010). On the other hand, when it is not and there are gross violations of human rights, a paternalistic takeover of sovereignty vitiates the potency of the people to rebel.[31]

For Appiah, sovereignty is singular and absolute rather than malleable as it mediates among competing principles. Unlike the good as defined by Kymlicka, which is ultimately individual, although not the fundamentalist individualism of Canada's neighbour to the south, a basic good is the well-being and continuity of the community. The nation does not have inherent value simply because it serves the well-being of the individual, whereas for Appiah the individual is the ultimate end.[32]

Without trying to establish definitively that these two very different articulations of rooted cosmopolitanism are but reflections and reinforcements of the different cultural climates of the two countries, and recognizing at the same time the generalization and simplification involved, the comparison does suggest that the ethical theories are more rooted than cosmopolitan. Rooted cosmopolitanism is inherently at odds with a vision of cosmopolitanism free of historical and national ties. It is particular to the culture of a society, and thus a very unlikely foundation for forging a universal and coherent practical approach to dealing with gross violations of human rights. If cosmopolitanism has different national traditions giving it different meanings, and if some cultures are by tradition anti-cosmopolitan, how can rooted cosmopolitanism develop a cosmopolitan approach? Further, since different interpretations are permitted, how can any doctrine or policy arising from such premises be expected to have any uniformity of interpretation? Each vernacular is bound to give any cosmopolitan policy iteration its own twist – precisely what happened to R2P, which first claimed to subordinate sovereign state responsibilities to a cosmopolitan vision and ended up defining R2P implementation as conditional on the sovereign consent of the alleged perpetrator of the atrocities.

Rooted cosmopolitanism claims to overcome the dichotomy between local culture and universal civilization, between the everyday life and abstract universal principles, but if each culture has its own way of overcoming the dichotomy, where is the universal residue of cosmopolitanism? If ARC is rooted in a family legacy stressing individualism and self-reliance, and CRC in a community legacy of mutual care, where can we find unity when it comes to means and policies for achieving cosmopolitan ends? The responsibility for ensuring individual initiative on the one hand, and the duty to protect deprived others on the other, are radically different founding principles. If such close neighbours as the United States and Canada, with their enormous affinities, are so far apart on the founding ethics of any collective responsibility for intervening in cases of mass atrocities, how can one expect a coherent doctrine to emerge from the UN when half the states are not even democracies? How is it possible to get any coherent policy with respect to military intervention in a state that fails to protect its citizens on a massive scale? If each country views others and their needs and rights through its own historical lenses, then how can these countries even agree on what is happening? And since coercive intervention requires coordinated control in decision making, how could such an intervention possibly be effective?

The Implications for Practice

The conundrums are manifested in actual practices. All forms of political cosmopolitanism endorse global institutions as the final arbiter and the culmination of modernity's move from local to universal governance, from norms rooted in particular traditions to norms embedded in abstract rationality and principle, and from a concern with opportunity, crises, and timely behaviour to a concern with the timeless foundations of behaviour (Toulmin 1990, especially ch. 1; see also Rengger 1995, 48-52). However, the *political* cosmopolitanism of Canada puts far greater emphasis on ceding aspects of sovereignty to global institutions that need to be developed in order for each individual to be guaranteed freedom and to be treated equally under the law. In contrast, the United States supports Uganda in its fight against the Lord's Resistance Army and uses its proxy, Ethiopia, to intervene in Somalia. Canadians support the African Union's efforts to provide protection in Darfur. Each country does its own thing consistent with its own cultural propensities and economic and political interests. This is more akin to realism than cosmopolitanism.

Although ARC and CRC are fundamentally ethical doctrines, they follow different political processes to connect universal norms to the real world.[33] The political goal, however, remains identical – to create a world in which all humans identify with one another and respect one another as humans enjoying a common humanity and mutual dependence. This also involves allegiance to a worldwide community of human beings in which each and every individual enjoys the same rights and freedoms and participates in a form of government, however varied its expressions, that represents its members and acts to serve and protect them. A utopian version places the ethical obligation on the individual;[34] CRC and ARC articulate the ethical obligations of states.

ARC traces its origins to Hobbes and Locke as well as American exceptionalism (Kaufmann 1999), and back to Roman cosmopolitanism and St. Augustine, who differentiated between the citizens of the City of God and the vast majority who live in the earthly city (Dyson 1998). American ideologically driven imperial moral cosmopolitanism is married currently to a neoconservative ideology and reinforced by the US's superpower status in the world and its own perceived victory over its rival cosmopolitan enemy, Communism. American imperial cosmopolitanism now defines global terrorists and their supporters as the enemies of the new cosmopolitan order.[35] In this view, cosmopolitanism in the form of free trade, democracy, and human rights requires at least the threat of force to counter reactionary and authoritarian tendencies, and, if necessary, the imposition of democracy and the protection of human rights by force when the ideological premises of the West are threatened in the real world.

In contrast to ARC (as well as a European version [Kaufmann 2003]), the Canadian view stands out for its reliance on multilateral institutions and for its tendency to want to make sovereign state institutions subservient to global norms and, if possible, global institutions. Eschewing the language of the civilized versus the barbarians and championing inclusiveness while targeting those who prey on their own people, this version of liberal cosmopolitanism traces its origins to Hugo Grotius and Immanuel Kant.[36] Although much more ambitious than that of Kant (1997) as expressed in *Perpetual Peace,* the fifth preliminary article of the envisioned League of Nations forbade interference in the internal affairs of one state by another state. In the political process of CRC, the international body would have legal authority, could use coercive measures, and could operate domestically to assume responsibility for the well-being and rights of the citizens of that state. In effect, individuals would be protected by an extension of Grotius's idea (1925) of what Kant called cosmopolitan law, a form of law that was distinct from, but combined elements of, both international law governing the relations between states and domestic law governing the relations between a state and its citizens. For Kant, universal human rights were presupposed in and expressed through law.[37]

Political cosmopolitanism is different from moral cosmopolitanism in that the former installs a political, legal, and military authority that goes well beyond the voluntary ethical responsibility that serves to facilitate the provision of the needs of foreigners in need and the protection of their rights. The International Committee of the Red Cross

(ICRC)[38] and NGO relief and human rights organizations operate under a principle of moral cosmopolitanism and the duties we bear toward our fellow humans on this planet, based usually on serving basic needs, sometimes on universal rights, at other times on a primary allegiance to bring about the morally good,[39] and in still other contexts reducing the amount of fear and destruction in this world (cf. Shklar 1984). In all versions, people ought to be taught first and foremost that they are above all citizens of the world.[40] Education, policy advocacy, and action through witnessing become the means to achieve that idealistic goal as well as to understand ourselves better and to solve the problems of poverty, disease, and violent conflict that plague this world, while being inherently superior in serving the highest aspects of humankind.[41]

The American and Canadian versions of moral cosmopolitanism require political action by nation-states, however. Based on a populist interpretation of Kant, the Canadian version of *political* cosmopolitanism linking the system of sovereign states to a global order of responsibility envisions working through a moral ideal, using norms as guidelines and the United Nations as the institution for increasingly enhancing the role of global governance under the rule of universal law. The unilateral imperial view of cosmopolitanism of the US linked with realism[42] (as well as the gradualist regional institutional step-by-step approach to cosmopolitanism of Europe) can offer lip service to such a vision, but without concrete political implications. Thus, the doctrine of R2P can be unanimously endorsed but it will mean different things to different states, with virtually no chance of having a coherent impact.

Conclusion

Kymlicka can go further than Appiah in his cultural sympathies, but neither is relevant when people face the loss of their way of life – something even more fundamental than loss of language. Kymlicka, and Canadians in general, may be more sympathetic to the Darfurian minority cultures, but this is of little help in countering the overwhelming threat. Actual practices of Canadians in Sudan count infinitely more than the rhetoric at the UN. The *res publica* may proceed within the Security Council, but it will reveal more a discourse smacking of obfuscation and equivocation than a dialogical analysis of the issues. In the end, decisions only reflect the compromises among radically different perspectives, none of which will provide adequate protection to the forcibly displaced. So, whether the emphasis is on protection (Canadian) or empowerment and self-determination (American), neither stand will have any impact in Darfur.

Conversely, incoherence and over-ambition in the international arena,[43] and the attempt by the well-intentioned to insist on military intervention, very likely contributed to delays in the deployment of protection officers. The lack of coherence carries an enormous cost. A significant share of the responsibility for that incoherence can be ascribed to the rooted cosmopolitan moralists. Policies must not only correspond with reality but develop from coherent principles that define priorities. The practices in Darfur are the result of reconciling competing principles in the context of a particular situation. The continuing championship of R2P by Canadians was matched by the inability to advance any agenda for providing physical security and a long-term policy for the settlement of all Darfurians.

Not only has rooted moral cosmopolitanism, as the most eviscerated form of the doctrine of cosmopolitanism in general, been ineffective in bringing morality to bear in international crises but it has even undermined moral practices and priorities that would better protect affected civilians as well as support national popular will rather than an ethereal global community as the basis for political action. R2P, with its foundation in rooted moral cosmopolitanism, distorts reality. The situation in Darfur is misidentified as genocide and not domestic ethnic cleansing and a crime against humanity. R2P is also internally inconsistent between the essence of its doctrine and its interpretation when the doctrine is cited and supposedly put into practice. Flawed in both its theoretical underpinnings and the efforts to apply R2P, rooted moral cosmopolitanism and its offshoot, R2P, are a distraction that undermines more than it reinforces the local and regional good Samaritans carrying the bulk of the responsibilities. Thus, this critique argues not simply that abstract principles are difficult to apply but also that the aspiration, rooted as it is in contradictions and incoherence, causes significant harm and provides no benefit. Moral principles may be thought to be valid independent of any benefit that results, but if their application leads to increased harm, then surely their validity must be questioned.

What about the claim that, even if in the short run more harm might result, in the long term such an ethical regime will be of inestimable value to mankind? The theoretical analysis points out the reasons why this will not be the case; incoherence is built into the foundations so that the application will end up being reduced to the lowest common denominator of minimal effort. Does this mean that we give up the quest for a categorical principle, in this case one to govern the relations between and among states? This chapter cannot make that case, but it does point to the benefits of an ethics rooted in context and sets of

practices rather than in abstract principles.[44] Positing an ethical responsibility for states to intervene militarily to prevent or mitigate genocide,
as distinct from their right to do so, is a recipe for raising international
hypocrisy to a whole new level. R2P undercuts authenticity and integrity
in the conduct of our affairs.

Notes

1 Cf. International Commission on Intervention and State Sovereignty 2001.
2 A moral doctrine prescribes how we are obligated to treat others. However, an
   ethical set of rules is not used in Ronald Dworkin's idiosyncratic sense (2011, 41)
   of how we ought to live ourselves but in the sense of rules according to which
   we ought to govern our conduct or, in this case, rules by which our states should
   be governed in dealing with mass atrocities.
3 Deng and colleagues (1996, 6-10) first depicted this doctrine as the fulfillment
   of a growing resolve of the international community to override sovereignty in
   defence of human rights rather than intervening within the purview of the
   sovereign state. R2P as eventually articulated claimed that the international
   community would be *fulfilling* the sovereign obligations that the state failed to
   fulfill. See also Annan 1999, 49-50.
4 Bellamy tried to shift the emphasis from coercive intervention to prevention,
   but Weiss (2007, 104) found the effort to be irresponsible and unrealistic since
   intervention, not prevention, was the key problem.
5 In paragraphs 138 and 139 of the Outcome Document of the World Summit of
   the United Nations General Assembly in 2005, all UN heads of state and governments endorsed R2P by consensus. On 28 April 2006, the UN Security Council
   unanimously adopted Resolution 1674 on the Protection of Civilians in Armed
   Conflict.
6 This includes mass starvation. Thus, intervention should have been considered
   in the mass famine caused by Mao Zedong's Great Leap Forward in China in the
   period 1958-62 (Dikötter 2010).
7 Frost reconciles the apparent contradiction between the principle of state sovereignty and humanitarian norms without putting cosmopolitan norms in an
   absolute trump position through a "constitutive theory of individuality," in
   which, as in the Scottish Enlightenment tradition, ethics are central to what it
   is to be human. He stresses that sovereign-state theory is increasingly tied to
   democratic theory, thus bringing the two sets of norms into a complementary
   role without setting aside the principle of state sovereignty. Further, whether or
   not a norm is settled or emerging is determined by whether an action requires
   special justification to overrule a norm. State sovereignty, then, is the settled
   norm, not humanitarian intervention.
8 A number of civil society organizations advocated developing mechanisms to
   facilitate the implementation of R2P, such as the Will to Intervene (W2I). W2I
   proposed action plans to reinforce R2P, in part because of the recognition of the
   gap between rhetoric and action. There is little evidence that all this effort advanced the cause of genocide prevention and mitigation of mass atrocities.

9 Gareth Evans (2007), who headed the International Crisis Group, proposed that R2P advocates organize. He proposed creating a Global Centre and regional offices to champion R2P by setting boundaries around R2P (restricting its use to mass atrocities), determining when non-consensual force can be used, building capacity to make R2P operational, and developing effective strategies. See also Bellamy 2009, 93.

10 From a human security perspective, violent conflict is approached in terms of preventive diplomacy and other initiatives that focus on people-centred conflict resolution and peace-building activities. Intervention to protect populations at risk is viewed as part of the spectrum of these initiatives, albeit an extreme one.

11 "Humanitarian workers say the supply of medicine, clean water and food has already been significantly affected, and could worsen in coming weeks," *Guardian*, Nairobi, 24 March 2009. USAID's 3 April 2009 Situation Report 7 stated: "The expulsions have resulted in a significant reduction in humanitarian capacity" (USAID 2010).

12 Pure cosmopolitanism dreams of an ethereal polis and world order in which humans live free of the factionalism of any earthly polis – hence *cosmo-polis* (κοσμοπολιτής).

13 Zeno's well-ordered cosmopolitan commonwealth, first described by Posidonius in his school in Rhodes, envisioned a world state. In Dante, "mankind should be ruled by one supreme prince and directed toward peace by a common law issuing from him and applied to those characteristics that are common to all men" (Shaw et al. 1996: *De Monarchia* I: XIV, 4-5).

14 They also coalesce on the historical trajectory from an oral to a written culture, from norms rooted in particular traditions to norms embedded in abstract rationality and principle, from the concern with opportunity and timely behaviour to a concern with the timeless foundations of behaviour (Toulmin 1990, esp. ch. 1; see also Rengger 1995, 48-52).

15 The nineteenth-century Italian foreign minister P.S. Mancini based his legal cosmopolitanism on the premise that "human beings are born cosmopolitans" (cf. Mancini 1874, as cited in Koskenniemi 2007a). See also Koskenniemi (2007b).

16 The Canadian-born legal theorist Thomas M. Franck (1999), one of the founders of the Manhattan School of international law, was a proponent. In Franck's view, there was no need to promote an essentialist thesis that we all have a common nature or all share in a common rationality. The emphasis was on an emerging set of norms that were about to set aside the existing dysfunctional legal order by embracing and codifying universal principles of fairness that articulate the highest sense of values as viewed collaboratively by the keenest sensibilities of our human conscience. See Koskenniemi 2002. The Manhattan School envisioned the transformation of interstate into cosmopolitan international law by a series of shifts: (1) from formal law to case law through the analysis of adjudication; (2) from interstate positive law to a cosmopolitan vision of law as an instrument of social engineering; (3) from a second-order norm of consistency to functional adaptation; (4) from sovereign-state self-determination to individual human rights; (5) from a study of interstate treaties to an analysis of second-order universal rules of process to ensure fairness; and (6) from an emphasis on laws to stress on practices recognized as normative.

17 Cultural, political, legal, and moral cosmopolitanism are increasingly weak ver-
    sions of cosmopolitanism. Moral cosmopolitanism, especially rooted cosmopol-
    itanism, is its most threadbare form.

18 Although many argue that we are well on the way to achieving economic cosmo-
    politanism, where the whole world is integrally knitted into a single economy
    of production, trade, and finance, economic cosmopolitanism is not a legitimate
    version of cosmopolitanism. Unlike moral cosmopolitanism, which is other-
    directed, the basic values of so-called economic cosmopolitanism are founded
    on self-interest. Economic globalization, in contrast to cosmopolitanism, is built
    on the premise of each individual pursuing his or her own *self-interest,* and
    through that pursuit a global economy has emerged. The universal norms merely
    set the rules of fair play in the pursuit of those interests by combining compara-
    tive advantage with an international division of labour and specialization to
    produce an economic world order built on principles of equal opportunity, open
    markets, and non-discrimination where we are all equal as consumers: Appiah
    2006, 97; Nussbaum 2006; Ryan 2006; Sen 2007. The belief in this supposedly
    inevitable and unstoppable trend may be valid, but economic globalization is
    not a cosmopolitan vision.

19 "The one world in which we live has a chance of survival only if there is no
    longer any room in it for spheres of differing, contradictory, and even antagonistic
    ethics. The world needs *one* basic ethic" (Dallmayr 2003, 424).

20 This is the irreducible "essentially Protestant" aspect to Kymlicka's thesis (Parekh
    2006, 106).

21 Berman (2001) credits Appiah with the origin of the phrase. Cohen (1992) offers
    an alternative account. There are many non-Canadian expressions of rooted
    cosmopolitanism. See Berman 2001; Cheah and Robbins 1998; Loss 2005; Pereira
    2003; Rajan and Sharma 2006; Robbins 1998; Walkowitz 2006.

22 Nussbaum (1994) asked two questions: Should you give preference to your own
    child's education over that of a stranger? Should you give benefits to your fellow
    nationals at the expense of others in the rest of the world?

23 Leib (2006, 89) offers insights into this tension between Nussbaum's abstract
    cosmopolitanism and Appiah's rooted cosmopolitanism.

24 Appiah grew up where the Asante empire was once dominant in what is now
    Ghana, as the son of a famous Ghanaian politician and a mother who was the
    daughter of Sir Stafford Cripps. He learned to live with multiple loyalties in many
    different countries where he experienced deep love and a variety of friendships.
    His family legacy demanded that he behave as a citizen of the world but without
    much self-sacrifice.

25 Communitarianism claims that any obligation to distant persons begins with
    one's family, extends to friends, the community, and the nation, and then to
    the rest of the world but *with decreasing intensity.*

26 Contrast this view with that of Singer, his utilitarian cosmopolitan colleague at
    Princeton, who has a much greater sense of individual self-sacrifice. He gives 25
    percent of his income to charity for, Singer argues, we have a moral duty to help
    others as long as our sacrifices do not outweigh the benefits to others as individ-
    uals. Sacrifices that jeopardize our own necessities (food, water, shelter, clothing,
    sanitation, health care, or education) do outweigh the benefit. "If it is in our

power to prevent something very bad from happening, without thereby sacrificing anything morally significant, we ought, morally, to do it" (Singer 1972).

27 Appiah (2005, ch. 1) celebrates individual initiative and responsibility. He cites Mill's letter to his friend David Barclay: "There is only one plain rule of life eternally binding, and independent of all variations in creeds, and in the interpretation of creeds, embracing equally the greatest moralities and the smallest; it is this: try thyself unweariedly till thou findest the highest thing thou art capable of doing, faculties and outward circumstances being both duly considered, and then DO IT" (26).

28 Kymlicka (1995, 85) directly challenged Waldron's views. Further, Kymlicka is not a communitarian like Michael Walzer. Though Walzer (1995, 153) supports some form of state support for minority cultures and ethnic activity on the basis that the character of ethnicity is a public good and would allow taxpayers' money "to seep through the state/ethnic group (state/church) barrier," he is opposed to state support to coercively protect rights, such as the language rights of francophones in Canada.

29 Kymlicka (2001, 212). Like Appiah, Kymlicka belongs to the school of philosophy shared by Jürgen Habermas and Paul Ricoeur in celebrating the *res publica,* the vision of liberalism and deliberative democracy where public debate is intended to engage people in the appreciation of differences while fostering a culture of respect based on a minimal cross-cultural set of values and enough of an overlap in their vocabulary of values to begin a conversation. While the point of a conversation may be to persuade, it is not to convert but to concede the inevitability of conflict and disagreement while celebrating the tolerance for pluralism that mutual understanding brings in the interchange between different cultures. In doing so, rooted cosmopolitanism embraces the equivocation of language rather than the positivist love of univocals and the clear and distinct ideas and concepts of abstract universalism. Rooted cosmopolitanism embraces ironic as opposed to direct speech, prizes ambiguity and indeterminacy rather than absolute clarity and predictability. Cosmopolitanism is reconceived as socially grounded rather than reflecting detachment from one's place of origin and a way in which to uphold loyalty to one's state simultaneously with a sense of obligation to the rest of the world.

30 For an excellent condensed but critical summary of Kymlicka's views, see Parekh 2006, 99-109.

31 The Canadian paternalistic view is akin to the liberal communitarian thesis of Avishai Margalit and Joseph Raz (1990, 439), who insist that self-government has only instrumental value insofar as it contributes to the well-being of a community and is not an end in itself. For a discussion of these differences, see Tesón 1998.

32 Appiah (2005, 22) is strongly sympathetic toward communitarian philosophers, particularly the Canadian philosopher Charles Taylor: "To be sure, an emphasis on how we make sense of our lives, our selves, through narrative is shared by a number of philosophers – Charles Taylor and Alasdair MacIntyre among them – who worry that conventional versions of liberal theory scant the social matrix in which our identities take shape. At the same time, the Millian language of life plans resonates with their insistence that to live our lives as agents requires that

we see our actions and experiences as belonging to something like a story. For Charles Taylor, it is 'a basic condition of making sense of ourselves' that 'we grasp our lives in a narrative'; narrative, then, is not 'an optional extra' ... So we should acknowledge how much our personal histories, the stories we tell of where we have been and where we are going, are constructed, like novels and movies, short stories and folktales, within narrative conventions. Indeed, one of the things that popular narratives (whether filmed or televised, spoken or written) do for us is to provide models for telling our lives. At the same time, part of the function of our collective identities – of the whole repertory of them that a society makes available to its members – is to structure possible narratives of the individual self."

33 Frank Vibert, director of the European Policy Forum, articulated the distinctive European view of cosmopolitanism with its roots in Alexandre Kojève, a key intellectual source behind the European Economic Community that evolved into the European Union. Kojève (2001, 115) sought to depoliticize and "mandarinize" the process through economic arrangements and the particularity of a situation (Waszek 1988, 196). As Frost (2008) put it, the real ethical norms that underpin ethical commitments are constituted by international actors in actual global social practices. Ethics is not then reduced to particular and relative expressions of specific cultural traditions, but is found in the case studies of the way purported universal norms are contaminated by and connected to the real world (Howse 2006). However, the European version of rooted cosmopolitanism envisions moving from a nation-state consciousness gradually and peacefully to larger and larger regional political and economic units with shared institutions and policies en route to a global and peaceful order. Gradually, the argument goes, "the power of states are being rearticulated in a much more complex way, involving the development of a world of multilayered power, multilayered authority and complex forms of governance" (Held 2001). For Held, contemporary Europe and the EU provide a prime example in which supranational bodies provide a check on states to ensure the enforcement of certain human rights and thus a gradual thickening of human rights law.

34 In the utopian view, each and every individual has the duty to act as if he or she were currently a citizen of the world whose most important task is to bring Utopia into being.

35 This hegemonic neo-imperialism has liberal roots as well (Ignatieff 1984, 1999a, 1999b, 2001a, 2001b, 2002, 2003a, 2003b, 2003c; Ignatieff et al. 2003). Morefield (2005, 227-30) offers a general critique of imperial cosmopolitanism and its liberal variation.

36 Franceschet 2002, ch. 4. Cf. Kant 1963, 11-26. Kant was convinced that the natural laws of history were teleological, carrying humans toward an ultimate destiny even if the means had been mutual human antagonism and violent conflict. The last precondition to be put in place is "a universal civil society which administers laws among men." As Kant depicted this final stage, a league of nations would be created, thus subjecting each nation to the rule of international law. As his eighth thesis states, "the history of mankind can be seen, in the large, as the realization of Nature's secret plan to bring forth a perfectly constitutional state as the only condition in which the capacities of mankind can be fully developed, and also bring forth that external relation among states which is perfectly adequate to this end."

37 Cf. Weinrib 1992, 15-69. In Kant, property law, the constitution of a state, inter-state laws, and the general will as the foundation of all law all "partake of a conceptual unity that integrates them into one comprehensive idea of reason," the unity under which the diversity of law is given order (Weinrib 1992, 17).

38 The objective of the ICRC is "to prevent and alleviate human suffering wherever it may be found," but the organization eschews the political and remains stead-fastly neutral.

39 "Only this stance asks us to give our first allegiance to what is morally good – and that which being good, I can commend as such to all human beings ... we should give our first allegiance to no mere form of government, no temporal power, but to the moral community made up by the humanity of all human beings" (Nussbaum 1996). See also Nussbaum 1997.

40 This was the answer of Greek Cynic Diogenes Laertius, when asked where he came from. Of course, if there truly were a cosmopolitan universal polity, why would one need "citizenship"?

41 For a more international institutional cosmopolitan approach to poverty and the application of the "responsibility to protect" doctrine, see McNeill and St. Clair 2005.

42 For the classical statement of realism, see Morgenthau 1951. Also see Morgenthau's articulation (1963) of an Augustinian cosmopolitan imperial responsibility. The American version is known as neo-realism or liberal internationalism. See, for example, the writings of Keohane (1989, 2003) and Buchanan and Keohane (2006).

43 For a detailed elaboration and defence of this incoherence with respect to R2P, see Brown 2003.

44 Thus, although I oppose the general principle of R2P, I argued that we should have intervened to prevent and mitigate the Rwandan genocide because of who we are as Canadians, who we want to be, our place in the world, our historical connection with Rwanda, the feasibility of the initiative, and the enormous costs of inaction (cf. Adelman and Suhrke 1996).

References

Adelman, Howard, and Astri Suhrke. 1996. *Early Warning and Conflict Management.* Vol. 2 of *The International Response to Conflict and Genocide: Lessons from the Rwanda Experience.* Copenhagen: DANIDA.

Annan, Kofi. 1999. "The Two Concepts of Responsibility." *Economist* 352 (8137): 49-50.

Appiah, Kwame Anthony. 1994. "Loyalty to Humanity" (reply to Martha Nussbaum's essay "Patriotism and Cosmopolitanism"). *Boston Review* 19 (5): 10.

–. 1996. "Cosmopolitan Patriots." In *For Love of Country: Debating the Limits of Patriotism,* ed. by Josh Cohen, 21-29. Boston: Beacon Press.

–. 2005. *The Ethics of Identity.* Princeton, NJ: Princeton University Press.

–. 2006. *Cosmopolitanism: Ethics in a World of Strangers.* New York: W.W. Norton.

–. 2007. *The Ethics of Identity.* Princeton, NJ: Princeton University Press.

Archibugi, Daniele. 2008. *The Global Commonwealth of Citizens: Toward Cosmo-politan Democracy.* Princeton, NJ: Princeton University Press.

Bellamy, Alex. 2006. "Whither the Responsibility to Protect: Humanitarian Intervention and the 2005 World Summit." *Ethics and Humanitarian Affairs* 20 (2): 143-69.

–. 2009. *Responsibility to Protect*. London: Polity Press.

Berman, Jessica. 2001. *Modernist Fiction, Cosmopolitanism, and the Politics of Community*. Cambridge: Cambridge University Press.

Biersteker, Thomas J., and Cynthia Weber, eds. 1996. *State Sovereignty as Social Construct*. Cambridge: Cambridge University Press.

Brown, Chris. 2003. "Selective Humanitarianism: In Defense of Inconsistency." In *Ethics and Foreign Intervention*, ed. by Deen Chatterjee and Don Scheid, 31-50. Cambridge: Cambridge University Press.

Brysk, Alison. 2009. *Global Good Samaritans: Human Rights as Foreign Policy*. New York: Oxford University Press.

Buchanan, A., and R.O. Keohane. 2006. "The Legitimacy of Global Governance Institutions." *Ethics and International Affairs* 20: 405.

Cali, Basak. 2007. "Between Legal Cosmopolitanism and a Society of States; International Justice at the European Court of Human Rights." In *Paths to International Justice: Social and Legal Perspectives*, ed. by M.B. Dearborn and T. Kelly, 111-33. Cambridge: Cambridge University Press.

Cheah, Pheng, and Bruce Robbins, eds. 1998. *Cosmopolitics: Thinking and Feeling beyond the Nation*. Minneapolis: University of Minnesota Press.

Cohen, Mitchell. 1992. "Rooted Cosmopolitanism." *Dissent* 39 (4): 483-87.

Dallmayr, Fred. 2003. "Cosmopolitanism Moral and Political." *Political Theory* 31 (3): 421-42.

Deng, Francis M., Sadikiel Kimaro, Terrence Lyons, Donald Rothchild, and I. William Zartman. 1996. *Sovereignty as Responsibility: Conflict Management in Africa*. Washington, DC: Brookings Institution.

Dikötter, Frank. 2010. *Mao's Great Famine: The History of China's Most Devastating Catastrophe, 1958-62*. New York: Walker.

Dworkin, Ronald. 1985. *A Matter of Principle*. Cambridge, MA: Harvard University Press.

–. 2011. "What Is a Good Life." *New York Review of Books*, 10 February, 41-43.

Dyson, R.W., ed. and trans. 1998. *Augustine: The City of God against the Pagans*. Cambridge: Cambridge University Press.

Evans, Gareth. 2007. "Creating and Implementing a New International Norm." International Coalition for the Responsibility to Protect, 12 September. http://www.responsibilitytoprotect.org/index.php/crises/37-the-crisis-in-darfur/1386-12-september-2007-news-update.

Evans, Gareth, et al. 2001. "The Responsibility to Protect." Background Note, The International Commission on Intervention and State Sovereignty, Ottawa.

Franceschet, Antonio. 2002. *Kant and Liberal Internationalism: Sovereignty, Justice, and Global Reform*. New York: Palgrave Macmillan.

Franck, Thomas M. 1999. *The Empowered Self: Law and Society in the Age of Individualism*. Oxford: Oxford University Press.

Frost, Mervyn. 2003. "Constitutive Theory and Moral Accountability: Individuals, Institutions and Dispersed Practices." In *Can Institutions Have Responsibilities? Collective Moral Agency and International Relations*, ed. by Tony Erskine, 84-99. London: Palgrave Macmillan.

–. 2008. *Global Ethics: Anarchy, Freedom and International Relations*. Cambridge and London: Routledge.

Gopnik, Adam. 2009. "The Return of the Native: A Public Intellectual Remakes Himself as a Public Servant." *New Yorker,* 30 September, 26-32.

Grotius, Hugo. 1925 (1625). *The Law of War and Peace (De jure belli ac pacis),* trans. by Francis W. Kelsey, *The Classics of International Law,* vol. 2, ed. by James Brown Scott. Oxford: Oxford University Press.

Held, David. 2001. "Globalization, Cosmopolitanism and Democracy: Interview with Montserrat Guibernau." *Constellations* 8 (4): 427-41.

–. 2010. *Cosmopolitanism: Ideals and Realities.* London: Polity Press.

Hurrell, Andrew. 1996. "Vattel: Pluralism and Its Limits." In *Classical Theories of International Relations,* ed. by Ian Clark and Iver Neumann. New York: St. Martin's Press.

Ignatieff, Michael. 1984. *The Needs of Strangers: An Essay on Privacy, Solidarity, and the Politics of Being Human.* New York: Viking.

–. 1999a. *Whose Universal Values? The Crisis in Human Rights.* Amsterdam: Praemium Erasmianium.

–. 1999b. "Human Rights: The Midlife Crisis." *New York Review of Books* 46 (20 May): 9, 58-62.

–. 2001a. "The Rights Revolution." *Massey Lectures.* Toronto: House of Anansi Press.

–. 2001b. *Human Rights as Politics and Idolatry.* Princeton, NJ: Princeton University Press.

–. 2002. "Human Rights, the Laws of War, and Terrorism." *Social Research* 69 (4): 1137-58.

–. 2003a. *Empire Lite: Nation-Building in Bosnia, Kosovo and Afghanistan.* London: Vintage.

–. 2003b. "America's Empire Is an Empire Lite." *New York Times Magazine,* 10 January.

–. 2003c. *The Lesser Evil: Political Ethics in an Age of Terror.* Princeton, NJ: Princeton University Press.

Ignatieff, Michael, Kwame Anthony Appiah, and Amy Gutman. 2003. *Human Rights as Politics and Idolatry.* Princeton, NJ: Princeton University Press.

International Commission on Intervention and State Sovereignty. 2001. *The Responsibility to Protect.* Ottawa: International Development Research Centre.

Kant, Immanuel. 1963. "Idea for a Universal History with a Cosmopolitan Point of View." In *On History,* trans. and ed. by Lewis White Beck, 11-26. New York: Bobbs-Merrill.

–. 1997 (1795). *Perpetual Peace: Essays on Kant's Cosmopolitan Ideal.* Cambridge, MA: MIT Press.

Kaufmann, Eric. 1999. "American Exceptionalism Reconsidered: Anglo-Saxon Ethnogenesis in the 'Universal' Nation, 1776-1850." *Journal of American Studies* 33 (3): 437-57.

–. 2003. "The Rise of Cosmopolitanism in the Twentieth Century West: A Comparative and Historical Perspective on the United States and European Union." *Global Society* 17 (4): 359-83.

Keohane, R.O. 1989. *International Institutions and State Power: Essays in International Relations Theory.* Boulder, CO: Westview Press.

–. 2003. "Global Governance and Democratic Accountability." In *Taming Globalization: Frontiers of Governance,* ed. by David Held and Mathias Koenig-Archibugi. Cambridge: Polity Press.

Kojève, Alexandre. 2001. "Colonialism from a European Perspective." *Interpretation* 29: 115-30.

Koskenniemi, Martti. 2002. "Legal Cosmopolitanism: Tom Franck's Messianic World." *Journal of International Law and Policy* 35: 471-86.

–. 2007a. "Report of the Study Group of the International Law Commission." Erik Castrén Institute Research Reports, 21 (2).

–. 2007b. "The Ideology of International Adjudication." Paper presented at the 100th Anniversary of the Second Hague Peace Conference of 1907, The Hague, 7-8 September. http://www.helsinki.fi/eci/Publications/.

Kymlicka, Will. 1995. *Multicultural Citizenship.* Oxford: Clarendon Press.

–. 2001. *Politics in the Vernacular: Nationalism, Multiculturalism and Citizenship.* New York: Oxford University Press.

Leib, Ethan J. 2006. "Rooted Cosmopolitans." *Policy Review* 137 (June/July).

Loss, Jacqueline. 2005. *Cosmopolitanisms and Latin America: Against the Destiny of Place.* New York: Palgrave Macmillan.

Margalit, Avishai, and Joseph Raz. 1990. "National Self-Determination." *Journal of Philosophy* 87: 439-61.

McNeill, Desmond, and Asuncion St. Clair. 2005. "Development Ethics and Human Rights as the Basis for Global Poverty Reduction: The Case for the World Bank." Workshop for Researchers of the World Bank, Budapest, 1-2 April.

Morefield, Jeanne. 2005. *Covenants without Swords: Idealism, Liberalism and the Spirit of Empire.* Princeton, NJ: Princeton University Press.

Morgenthau, Hans. 1951. *Defense of the National Interest: A Critical Examination of American Foreign Policy.* New York: Alfred Knopf.

–. 1963. "The Political Conditions for an International Police Force." *International Organization* 17 (2): 393-403.

Nussbaum, Martha. 1994. "Patriotism and Cosmopolitanism." *Boston Review* 19 (5): 3-6.

–. 1996. "Patriotism and Cosmopolitanism." In *For Love of Country: Debating the Limits of Patriotism,* ed. by Joshua Cohen. Boston: Beacon Press.

–. 1997. "Kant and Cosmopolitanism." In *Perpetual Peace: Essays on Kant's Cosmopolitan Ideal,* ed. by James Bohman and Matthias Lutz-Bachmann. Cambridge, MA: MIT Press.

–. 2006. *Frontiers of Justice: Disability, Nationality, Species Membership.* Cambridge, MA: Harvard University Press.

Parekh, Bhikhu. 2006. *Rethinking Multiculturalism: Cultural Diversity and Political Theory.* New York: Palgrave Macmillan.

Pereira, Malin. 2003. *Rita Dove's Cosmopolitanism.* Urbana: University of Illinois Press.

Rajan, Gita, and Shailja Sharma, eds. 2006. *New Cosmopolitanisms: South Asians in the US.* Palo Alto, CA: Stanford University Press.

Rengger, Nicholas J. 1995. *Political Theory, Modernity and Postmodernity.* Oxford: Blackwell.

Robbins, Bruce. 1998. *Feeling Global: Internationalism in Distress.* New York: New York University Press.

Ryan, Alan. 2006. "Cosmopolitans." *New York Review of Books,* 22 June, 48-49.
Sen, Amartya. 2007. *Identity and Violence: The Illusion of Destiny.* London: Penguin.
Shaw, Prue, Raymond Geuss, and Quentin Skinner. 1996. *Dante: Monarchy.* Cambridge: Cambridge University Press.
Shklar, Judith. 1984. *Ordinary Vices.* Cambridge, MA: Harvard University Press.
Singer, Peter. 1972. "Famine, Affluence and Morality." *Philosophy and Public Affairs* 1 (1): 229-43.
Taylor, Astra. 2008. *Examined Life,* Zeitgeist Films: a documentary film of interviews with contemporary philosophers.
Tesón, Fernando R. 1998. "Ethnicity, Human Rights, and Self-Determination." In *International Law and Ethnic Conflict,* ed. by David Wippman. Ithaca, NY: Cornell University Press.
Toulmin, Stephen. 1990. *Cosmopolis: The Hidden Agenda of Modernity.* Chicago: Chicago University Press.
USAID (United States Agency for International Development). 2010. "Kenya – Food Insecurity." Situation Report #7, Fiscal Year 2010, 14 May. http://www.usaid.gov/.
Van Hooft, Stan. 2007. "Cosmopolitanism as Virtue." *Journal of Global Ethics* 3 (3): 303-15.
Waldron, Jeremy. 1995. "Minority Cultures and the Cosmopolitan Alternative." In *The Rights of Minority Cultures,* ed. by Will Kymlicka, 93-119. Oxford: Oxford University Press.
Walkowitz, Rebecca. 2006. *Cosmopolitan Style: Modernism Beyond the Nation.* New York: Columbia University Press.
Walzer, Michael. 1995. "Pluralism: A Political Perspective." In *The Rights of Minority Cultures,* ed. by Will Kymlicka, 139-54. Oxford: Oxford University Press.
Waszek, Norbert. 1988. *The Scottish Enlightenment and Hegel's Account of "Civil Society."* Dordrecht, Netherlands: Kluwer Academic Publishers.
Weinrib, Ernie. 1992. "Law as Idea of Reason." In *Kant's Political Philosophy,* ed. by Howard Lloyd Williams, 15-69. Chicago: University of Chicago Press.
Weiss, Thomas. 2007. *Humanitarian Intervention: Ideas in Action.* New York: Polity Press.

10

Climate Change and the Challenge of Canadian Global Citizenship

Robert Paehlke

Over the past forty years, the locus of environmental issues has gradually moved from local, regional, and national to global in scale and scope. Media and policy attention has shifted from pollution in local rivers or lakes to concerns such as the overfishing of the world's oceans, rainforest protection throughout tropical regions, and the inter-jurisdictional movement of pollutants such as acid deposition and persistent organic pollutants (POPs) from industrialized regions, in the latter case into the Arctic.

As well, for several decades now solutions have increasingly been attempted at the global scale. By the early 1990s, dozens of major environmental treaties had been signed, and more have followed since (Hurrell and Kingsbury 1992, xi-xiv). Even those issues that have a decidedly local character, such as the movement to encourage the consumption of local foods, are inspired by resistance to the lack of control over, and non-sustainability of, global-scale food systems.

Perhaps the most global of all environmental issues is, of course, climate change. Climate change is an excellent test for any theory of rooted cosmopolitanism. There can be little progress on this issue without concerted global action, yet each nation's contribution by itself (save perhaps for those of the largest and most energy-intensive nations) is arguably of limited significance. Every small and poor country can claim that their national actions make little difference. Even wealthy nations like Canada, Australia, Sweden, or Switzerland can claim that they contribute only a small share of the problem and therefore cannot provide a large share of the solution no matter what they do.

A truly cosmopolitan nation would see that this argument goes nowhere because almost every nation can make this too-small-to-matter claim. Moreover, the claims of low historical emissions advanced by China, India, Brazil, and other rapidly expanding economies will also doom the outcome if their emissions are rising faster than the rest of the world's emissions are falling. If these arguments prevail, only a very short list of nations would be obliged to do anything and clearly could not, on their own, do enough. Those with a cosmopolitan perspective, whether national leaders or ordinary citizens, would see this, and see that their nation is obliged to participate in a global effort and to press for the resolution of the many legitimate disagreements about which nation should accept what level of obligation.

Climate change is clearly a collective problem requiring a collective solution because greenhouse gases (GHGs) have the same effect regardless of where on the planet they are emitted. On the one hand, reductions may be easier to achieve because any and every reduction anywhere is equally effective. As well, emitting jurisdictions cannot easily imagine that they can avoid the effects of their actions. In contrast, many environmental issues have pronounced upstream-downstream dimensions. In the case of acid precipitation, for example, emissions from the United States Midwest had negative effects in Canada, New York, and New England, but few impacts within the emitting jurisdictions, making effective control more politically difficult.

On the other hand, action on climate change may be hard to achieve because nearly every nation assumes, or can pretend to assume, that someone else is obliged to go first or to cut emissions more deeply. During the administration of President George W. Bush, even the United States, which was and is responsible for a massive and disproportionate share of global emissions, seemed to imagine that it was being asked to do more than anyone else even when it had done next to nothing.

Global action on climate change involves other problems. First, the impacts are still to some extent uncertain, especially in terms of where and when they will hit hardest. Moreover, many of the places likely to experience significant impacts are nations or regions with minimal global influence. Small island states and Bangladesh will at some future date be inundated by the sea, and parts of North and East Africa will likely continue to experience severe drought. Those who depend on glacier runoff for fresh water (such as areas of Pakistan) are also threatened, and the Arctic has already warmed to the point where habitats are at risk and human settlements must be moved. None of these places or peoples has a very large share of geopolitical influence.

Second, the costs of avoiding climate change are immediate, whereas the worst impacts are in the future, often well beyond the likely terms of current political leaders. Politicians may be punished for imposing costs on industries and citizens, but inaction does not expose them to a deeply negative public reaction – a reaction that will occur only a generation or so in the future. On the other hand, it has recently become more widely understood that carbon taxes or cap-and-trade regimes can help to promote new industries, and so-called green infrastructure spending was implemented in many nations during 2008 and 2009 as an economic stimulus at a time of financial crisis.

Third, remedies are very expensive, will affect almost every economic sector, and are not equally available to all nations. That is, some nations have technological advantages in terms of energy efficiency and alternative energy, and other nations have significant natural advantages in terms of hydro, geothermal, wind, and solar energy availability. That said, these energy sources are more evenly distributed than oil, and once developed cannot easily be hoarded to artificially drive up prices: electricity must for the most part be used as it is produced.

Fourth, participation in climate change action must be near-universal to be sufficient. At the very least, all of the major emitters, including all industrialized nations and rapidly growing large economies, must participate in order to halt and ultimately rapidly reverse overall emissions growth. Cooperation must be widespread for its own sake, but also to avoid unduly penalizing those nations that do take action and thereby discouraging them from continuing to move forward. Without near-universal participation, everyone will be pointing an accusing finger at everyone else as an excuse for their own inaction.

Fifth, the issue has complex ethical dimensions that have a geo-historical character. The wealthiest nations (Europe, Canada, the United States, Japan, Australia, and New Zealand) have been emitting GHGs at a high per capita rate for considerably longer than a century (especially since the middle of the twentieth century). Other large nations whose economies have grown rapidly in recent decades have seen their per capita emissions rise in parallel, and in recent years their emissions rates have come to account for a significant proportion of today's total global output. However, the historical total of their emissions is trivial relative to the emissions of Europe and the United States in particular.

Thus, the allocation of obligations with regard to emissions reduction is complex. China, India, and other nations can argue that most of the obligation, at least for the short term, falls on historical emitters and that it is unfair to ask developing countries to curtail their economic growth just as they are approaching reasonable levels of economic output per capita. The response to this view is also reasonable, however. For one thing, the West can reduce emissions only so fast and climate change will continue if total global emissions are not rapidly slowed – and that in turn is impossible if much of the world continues to *increase* emissions levels. For another, it is not certain that rapid acceleration of fossil fuel use in the face of limited oil supplies is the best long-term economic strategy in any case.

This combination of characteristics associated with the politics of climate change makes the issue as global and as politically challenging as issues get. Given these complexities, it is impossible to imagine that any cosmopolitan nation can avoid participating, or even taking a leadership role, in action on climate change. Arguably, given the historical-use argument, leadership is particularly obligatory for Western nations, especially North America, where per capita emissions are by far the highest. Despite its dreadful overall performance on this issue to date, Canada, I will argue, *should and could* be an effective climate change leader for a number of reasons.

Canada's Potential as Climate Change Leader

Apart from signing and ratifying the Kyoto Protocol to the United Nations Framework Convention on Climate Change in the face of US hesitation, Canada has to date not demonstrated a serious commitment to effective action on climate change. Since it hosted an important early international climate change conference in Toronto in 1988, Canada has seen its GHG emissions rise in each of the next twenty years; moreover, those emissions actually rose more rapidly following the 1997 Kyoto meeting (Paehlke 2008). The one recent year in which emissions declined may be 2009, influenced by the global financial meltdown and the ensuing recession. Despite this history of ineffective on-the-ground policy implementation, it can be argued that Canada has both an obligation and a capacity to assume an important role on climate change.

Canada's obligation to act is rooted in its wealth, its technological capabilities, its history of internationalism and multilateralism, and its very high per capita emissions. North Americans have emitted and continue to emit more GHGs per person than any other region, and thus cannot reasonably demand actions of others that we are not prepared to first take ourselves. In the past, when pushed to act in keeping with environmental principles, Canadians have responded. Household recycling has been widely adopted despite initial concern that individuals would simply not sort their garbage effectively. It was also expected that smokers would resist bans on smoking in public places, but significant resistance to change did not materialize.

More germane to the changes necessary for action on climate change, Canadians sharply reduced their gasoline consumption in the period from 1980 to 1985 in the face of price increases and a media-driven atmosphere of "energy crisis." Transit use increased and average car size decreased. Climate change action requires that such an atmosphere be re-created and public action be motivated not just by glib commercials but by active leadership at all levels of government and all sectors of society, price incentives, and tough regulations regarding industrial GHG emissions and the energy efficiency of houses, vehicles, and appliances. These things have not been forthcoming and are less likely to be advanced by a Conservative majority government.

Nonetheless, the potential *opportunity* for Canadians to take effective action on climate change remains strong for three reasons: (1) Canada has a dramatic array of non-fossil energy options and a very low population density; (2) Canada's high current emissions make reductions using existing technologies relatively easy compared with much of Europe, where many of those technologies are already in place; and (3) much of Canada's emissions problem is concentrated in one emissions source in one location: Alberta's tar sands, much of which is extracted for export.

On the other hand, Canada's low population density and vast distances pose an energy challenge, owing to greater cross-country transportation distances than would be the norm in most nations. This geographic reality is less significant than it might at first appear, however. Most travel occurs within cities not between them, especially between distant ones. As well, most Canadians live adjacent to the US border, and a good proportion live in the Windsor-to-Quebec City corridor; as a result, there is the potential for effective energy-efficient intercity travel, including high-speed rail. As well, the movement of goods is more often north-south, between the United States and Canada, than east-west, within Canada. Moreover, transportation energy is only part of the energy story.

Canada's low population density, long coastlines, and vast mountains, rivers, forests, and prairies mean that the potential for renewable energy development is enormous. We are one of a small number of nations, especially high-energy-use nations, that could produce most of the energy they need from renewable sources alone. Canada has an astounding 243,792 kilometres of coastline, almost all of it quite windy (Paehlke 2008, 9-16). That is almost a kilometre of coastline for every one hundred Canadians (admittedly not all likely to become prime residential real estate), more than enough to supply all of the electricity we could consume (especially when combined with other and better-located sources).

Electric cars, electric rail, plug-in hybrids, ground source heat pumps, and a little bit of natural gas, and in time we might well have little need for oil or coal.

The advantage of having done very little thus far is that Canada could bring down GHG emissions significantly just by doing what most nations in Europe have already done, adopting the technologies they have already adopted and proven at great expense. Studies by the National Round Table on the Environment and Economy (NRTEE) (2006) have demonstrated that Canada could reduce GHG emissions by more than half by 2050 by widely adopting existing technologies: improved public transit, new lighting, heating and cooling systems, rooftop solar panels, wind energy, and the like. Overall success, of course, also requires that there not be a simultaneous radical increase in emissions from other sectors, such as the tar sands.

The tar sands are Canada's largest single GHG emissions source, a source that has expanded rapidly since 1996. Tar sands oil production began to grow with the tax breaks offered by the Alberta and federal governments beginning in 1996.[1] Production of oil from that source grew especially after oil prices began to spike with the onset of the Iraq war in 2003. The problem is that every barrel of oil extracted from the tar sands using current methods releases about three times the GHGs of a barrel of conventional oil. If future tar sands production grows to the scale envisioned prior to the financial crisis of 2008, the emissions might well offset or even overwhelm everything else Canada might reasonably do to reduce emissions through incremental improvements in automobile efficiency, better home insulation, improved lighting, and all other options except possibly the elimination of coal-fired power generation in Alberta and Ontario.

The reason for this is that many still imagine that Canada can and should eventually produce five million or more barrels per day from this single source when all of Canada consumes only two, an amount that should and could be considerably reduced with efficiency gains and fuel switching. Only with a radically effective change in extraction and process technology could Canada produce anything like this much oil from this source without remaining a climate change outlier nation. The possible options include carbon sequestration and the use of nuclear power and/or geothermal sources to provide the heat and/or heated water necessary to extract and process extracted material. None of these options will be operating at the necessary scale for many years, in part because over a decade has passed since Kyoto without serious pressure on the industry from any level of government.

These are three distinctive dimensions of the climate change issue in Canada. Even with these challenges, given its historical internationalist, cosmopolitan stance on many issues, Canada could yet resolve to take a leadership role on climate change, although such a turnabout might well require a new national government. Canada does, as noted, have the capacity for effective action given its renewable energy options, vast wealth, and technological capacities. The question is whether it has the political will given the money to be made on tar sands extraction, the political and economic pressures militating against decisive action, and its constitutional structure and political institutions (matters to be discussed below).

There are reasons for Canada to act decisively if Canadians would only focus on them more than on hockey scores and shorter-term and everyday concerns. The impacts of climate change on Canada may be less devastating than on some other nations (such as low-lying islands or Sub-Saharan Africa), but they are already highly visible, especially in the Far North. When summer ice in the Arctic Ocean is thinning and may disappear within a few years, Canadians have no excuse to be unaware of or uninterested in the implications of these changes.[2] These changes are taking place within and adjacent to Canadian territory. The problem is not that some other nation's ships will pass through "our" waters, but that there is a threat to the viability of the permafrost. The thawing of the permafrost could contribute to a feedback process that releases methane and further accelerates climate change.[3]

Many Canadians, although probably not a majority, are interested in this issue and their concern is in keeping with cosmopolitan attitudes. Canada's self-image has long been bound up with playing a positive, internationalist, multilateral, and peaceful role in the world. The question is whether this self-image will translate into a demand for action that thus far has not emerged in any decisive way. As well, the world's image of Canada is bound up with pristine nature in a vast and spacious country. These views of Canada are very much at odds with the nation's inability to take a leadership role on climate change or even to act effectively. A large majority of Canadians state that they would prefer action, but neither Liberals nor Conservatives when in power have moved forward in a significant way beyond signing and ratifying the Kyoto Protocol.

The possibility of effective action on climate change remains an open question and presents an opportunity to assess the effects of rooted cosmopolitanism. Canada has long been said to be thoroughly cosmopolitan in outlook (Gwyn 1995; Martin and Fortmann 2001, 43-52).

With its economy disproportionately based on trade and its national self-image bound up with environmental protection and multilateral participation, one would think that effective action would long since have been forthcoming, but this has not been the case thus far. With physical and geographical realities making effective action on climate change a viable possibility, this country seems a natural for playing a leadership role. How is it, then, that for twenty years Canada has not significantly reduced GHG emissions?

Rooted Cosmopolitanism and Canada's Better Nature

According to a 2006 public opinion survey conducted for the Canadian Automobile Association, a majority of Canadians, and even a majority in Alberta, where support is weakest, favour action on climate change.[4] Rooted cosmopolitanism may contribute to this outlook, but majority support has not translated into decisive policy action at the federal level and only selectively at the provincial level. Climate change is an unambiguously cosmopolitan concern; the impacts of climate change are global and collective action is likely to be inadequate to the task without the participation of all large and/or wealthy nations. In order to act on the concern, however, Canada and Canadians assert that they and the nation must live up to the internationalist self-image that is the source of so much pride in being Canadian.

Canada's linguistic complexity (especially the ever-present reality of the First Nations and Quebec), high proportion of immigrants, hesitation regarding hyper-patriotism (not unrelated to our proximity to the United States), and middle power status conspire to deepen support for cooperative international action and reinforce cosmopolitanism. Canadians identify being Canadian with playing a positive role in the world – with advancing not so much global integration as multilateral cooperation and internationalism. Yet when this clear opportunity to play a notable participatory role emerges, little is done.

Canadians are determined to be distinct from the United States, in part because we are proximate, our economies are integrated, and our societies are similar in so many ways. Canadians, for example, love the nation's public health insurance system for its own sake, but also because it is unique in North America. Canadians also take pride in standing apart from at least some US military adventures. We actively participate in peacekeeping through the United Nations. It is our desire to be distinctive, in effect our rootedness in Canadian realities and attitudes, that drives our cosmopolitanism and that arguably pushed this country to sign and ratify the Kyoto Protocol despite the fact that Canada's being a major energy producer resulted in an excess of caution on the part of the Chrétien government (Paehlke 2008).

However, even though the Canadian public supports at least the appearance of action on climate change and Canada has the necessary technological capacity and natural endowment, these conditions have led only to our making commitments, not to seeing them through. Effective action has been stymied by several aspects of Canada's institutional and constitutional structure. Similarly, although a majority of Americans have desired some form of public health insurance for a very long time, the nation failed to act effectively for decades (largely for institutional reasons, especially the power of political donations from large insurance firms). In both countries, entrenched interests and institutional structures have prevented government from translating majority public opinion into policy.

A large proportion of Canadians want to see Canada live up to its international environmental and multilateral image and to meet the challenges of climate change. In a 2007 Environics poll, 80 percent of respondents thought that the federal government was doing "only a fair" or a "poor" job addressing environmental issues.[5] In 2005 and 2006, over 80 percent were somewhat concerned to extremely concerned about global warming (as in the Canadian Automobile Association poll cited earlier). This is roughly equivalent to 2009 attitudes in most European and several Latin American countries and well above the levels of concern and expectations of government in the United States.[6]

The leading institutional barriers to action on climate change in Canada are: (1) the dominant role that the Constitution gives to provinces regarding natural resources; (2) the long-standing resistance in Western Canada to federal domination; and (3) the more recent trend toward a national multi-party system even in the face of an electoral system that advantages majority governments. I will consider each of these factors in turn.

Article 92 of the British North America Act grants exclusive jurisdiction over natural resources to the provinces (the main exception is uranium, over which the federal government has jurisdiction due in large measure to uranium's weapons potential). This is not the same thing, however, as having exclusive provincial jurisdiction over environmental protection. It is highly relevant here that the federal government has jurisdiction over international affairs, international and interprovincial trade, and criminal law (including the protection of public health), as well as broad regulatory and taxation powers and the residual powers of the peace, order, and good government (POGG) clause. The latter is arguably especially important regarding environmental protection, as such concerns hardly existed at the time the country was founded (Paehlke 2001, 73-123).

In effect, the constitutional authority granted to the provinces regarding natural resources has been supplemented by a historical reluctance on the part of the federal government regarding environmental protection. Kathryn Harrison (1996, 45-46) has thoroughly documented this pattern of reluctance in her book *Passing the Buck*. For example, the federal government took decades to provide legislative authority for environmental assessment, and despite court rulings that might allow decisive federal action it "studiously avoided" relying on the POGG clause in drafting legislation such as the federal Clean Air Act. David R. Boyd (2003, 261) notes that both constitutional experts and the Supreme Court agree that the federal government could do more with regard to the environment and that "climate change, the loss of biological diversity, and safe drinking water could ... be subject to federal laws." Boyd argues that both the federal and provincial governments have used constitutional ambiguity as an excuse for limited action on environmental protection.

The provinces have been more assertive regarding jurisdiction over natural resources, most dramatically in the response to Prime Minister Pierre Trudeau's National Energy Program in the 1970s. Bitterness over the NEP still lingers in Alberta. Regarding climate change, the government of Alberta has strongly resisted federal assertiveness. Former Premier Ralph Klein opposed Canadian commitments on climate change action before, during, and after Kyoto. He was especially vociferous during the run-up to ratification of the treaty, when he actually kept a microphone from Prime Minister Jean Chrétien on a Moscow stage and proceeded to speak against the Kyoto accord as if he were a key voice on Canadian foreign policy. Klein had earlier asserted that Canada could deal with climate change without international agreements and did not need "a bunch of international theorists to tell us how to do it," also denouncing "U.N. bureaucrats telling us how to run our country" for those who were insufficiently doubtful about theorists.[7]

Klein's views on climate change stood in sharp contrast to those who would see Canada's future as in essence acting as a "model citizen" in the world of nations (Welsh 2005). This rejection of a cosmopolitan approach to climate change was also central to the perspective of Stephen Harper before he became prime minister. In 2002, Harper, as leader of the Canadian Alliance party, sent a fundraising letter that, regarding the possibility of ratifying the Kyoto accord, asserted: "We're gearing up for the biggest struggle our party has faced since you entrusted me with the leadership. I'm talking about the 'battle of Kyoto' – our campaign to block the job-killing, economy-destroying Kyoto Accord ... Kyoto is essentially a socialist scheme to suck money out of the wealth-producing Nations."[8]

The great irony, of course, is that in a few short years energy transformation, green stimulus, and green jobs would be widely seen as the best prospect for a world economy mired in recession. The United States, Great Britain, Japan, Germany, Korea, and many other nations have taken this approach, and even Canada, with Harper as prime minister, has taken some steps, especially regarding rail transportation. Clearly, though, Harper's heart is not in action on climate change or a cosmopolitan sensibility. He is focused on enhanced provincial autonomy and doubtful about most collective global undertakings.

It may be that Canadians must choose between enhanced provincial power and a cosmopolitan role for Canada in the wider world. Nowhere is this choice starker than with regard to climate change. In the run-up to Kyoto and for year after year afterwards, the government of Canada had to cajole, encourage, and negotiate with energy-rich provinces. It is challenge enough for the Canadian government to play an effective role in a global context without also having to keep a constant eye on how this will play with the governments and electorates of Alberta, Newfoundland, and Saskatchewan.

It appears to be the case that some provincial governments are even more prone than the federal government to being influenced by one particular industrial sector, especially if a single industry accounts for a disproportionate share of economic activity. Examples of such disproportionate economic power include the forest industry in British Columbia, the oil industry in Alberta, and the oil (and previously fishing) industry in Newfoundland. The federal government faces more diverse pressures because the Canada-wide political economy is more diverse. Regarding climate change, the government of Alberta in particular is faced with a provincial economy in which economic growth, jobs, and provincial revenues are all highly dependent on the oil industry; it is almost literally the case that what is good for that economic sector is good for Alberta. It is little wonder that Alberta and the federal government are frequently at odds regarding climate change.

Many provinces, however, have acted *more* effectively than the federal government. British Columbia established North America's first carbon tax. Ontario has adopted a feed-in tariff system for renewable energy sources that allows smaller producers and even homeowners to sell wind and solar energy to the grid at a premium. Quebec has established a diverse array of initiatives under its Climate Change Action Plan for 2006-12. Numerous Canadian municipalities have also taken action on climate change. Rooted cosmopolitanism, it appears, can lead to effective action in Canada at the subnational level, especially in jurisdictions where the political economy does not militate against such actions. Even Alberta has seen the expansion of wind energy and a number of other climate change initiatives even though it strongly resists initiatives to restrain tar sands expansion. That particular restraint is crucial to the outcome of Canada's climate change initiatives.

More than that, however, it was *federal* tax concessions for the tar sands in 1996 designed to stimulate the Alberta economy and to soothe oil patch hostility toward the federal Liberals (dating back to NEP days) that undermined the Kyoto agreement within Canada. The growth of this industry even made ratification a great challenge, since by the time the agreement was on the verge of being ratified, compliance was all but hopeless. By the time of ratification, Canada's position on climate change was part of an effort by the federal government to distinguish Canada from the US on a number of fronts, including signing Kyoto – something that an overwhelming majority of Canadians were happy to see take place even if they were not prepared to accept its implications for their continued desire for large suburban houses and big cars.

In short, Kyoto was ratified in a context where the Liberal government sought to place Canada closer to a European perspective on Iraq and multilateral issues generally, and where many Canadians believed that the US was behaving like a rogue hegemonic power. Such an effort required considerable delicacy and balance: send troops to Afghanistan and encourage European nations to do the same, but stand back from the Bush administration's most unilateralist initiatives and, in the case of climate change, its open denial of scientific evidence as a basis for environmental policy making. Worrying at the same time about subjecting Alberta and the oil industry to incremental increases in costs or causing modest delays in tar sands expansion when both the province and the industry were literally swimming in cash flow is the sort of cross-pressure no other national government on earth endures.

It is enough of a challenge to find an autonomous and productively cosmopolitan place in the world when Canada's economy is wholly integrated with that of the United States and that nation is prone to excesses. Those excesses include spending almost as much on arms as the rest of the world combined and being an unrivalled producer of carbon emissions while, in the Bush years, denying that climate change was real. The bizarre compromise in the face of multiple cross-pressures seems to have been to defy the Bush administration by refusing to send troops to Iraq while ratifying Kyoto, but eliminating the possibility of actually complying with the treaty by avoiding effective federal action on large emitters, including the tar sands. Thus, the Canadian government, under both Liberals and Conservatives, has at least appeared to boldly play an autonomous and significant role in the world without daring to offend the provincial governments.

Liberal governments under both Jean Chrétien and Paul Martin were ambivalent about action on climate change and torn by the stark contrast between foreign policy opportunities and domestic political and institutional realities. Stéphane Dion learned the hard way why the two previous leaders felt such cross-pressures (although it is arguable that he failed to win election despite, not because of, his willingness to adopt a strong stance on climate change). In contrast, Prime Minister Harper has resolved the inherent tension between Canada's potential place in the world and domestic pressures on climate change more readily because he instinctively leans away from action. He demonstrates no moral pressure to take an assertive climate change position internationally, but may well be caught in the future in his own special dilemma regarding the issue.

During the Bush years, Harper did not challenge the United States on foreign policy matters. His language on terrorism and wars in the Middle East and Central Asia, for example, often paralleled that of President Bush. Likewise his own views on climate change did not require that he ever challenge the Bush administration on the issue. When Barack Obama was elected, it appeared at first that staying on track with the United States might be more difficult for him. Obama had pledged to alter the US position on carbon emissions and appointed people with an established history of climate change advocacy to all relevant positions.[9] Harper can no longer oppose action on climate change with the convenient excuse that he cannot do more without offending the United States, but has been fortunate that Obama has been blocked by the Congress from taking any decisive actions that might leave Harper looking like the global odd man out.

Day-to-day details and shifting national positions aside, many Canadians remain ambivalent about this issue. This can be true on a personal level, where even those who would prefer action on climate change worry about the high cost of gasoline and heating oil despite the fact that those higher prices will help reduce GHG emissions. Nor is it easy for anyone to abandon plans or hopes for extensive travel or to actively wish for a slowdown in one of Canada's few booming industrial sectors.

Canadians are often torn between their interests and a perspective that hopes that Canada will play a positive and cosmopolitan role in the world. This is especially true for citizens of energy-producing provinces. Most Albertans or Newfoundlanders who are not in the energy business, for example, realize that jobs might be scarcer and taxes higher were it not for the prosperity of the energy sector. Even in non-energy-producing provinces the cost of energy might be higher if coal-fired power plants were phased out, and jobs might be scarcer were it not for the purchase of manufactured items from Ontario and Quebec by Alberta-based oil producers.

That said, Canadians on the whole *are* cosmopolitan in outlook, even if they experience cross-pressures on this issue. As Michael Ignatieff once put it: "Cosmopolitans like myself are not beyond the nation, and a cosmopolitan, postnationalist spirit will always depend in the end on the capacity of nation-states to provide security and civility for their citizens" (Gwyn 1995, 22). Many Canadians want their nation to play a significant and positive role in the world and want their national government to develop foreign policy and engage with the wider world without perpetual interference from provincial governments or particular economic interests. Many are aware that an active and positive role in the world is difficult and delicate enough without Ottawa's continuously having to look over its shoulder at how the provinces or particular interests might react.

This is not to say that Canada's provinces should not have inputs into the policy process in many realms and even dominate in others, but foreign policy *is* different. Canada as a nation is but one voice in that realm and not a particularly powerful one. For any number of reasons, Canada, albeit hesitantly, opted as a nation at the point of Kyoto's ratification to help move a then very fragile global climate change effort forward. But given the power of the provinces with regard to natural resources and the power of oil companies within the nation's economy as a whole, Canada has been unable to honour the international commitments it has made.

Canada's cosmopolitan potential has thus been thwarted by provincial power and to some extent by the institutionalization of dual loyalties within Canada. Those dual loyalties are not unreasonable in matters of culture and language or even a federalist division of powers, but what other nation would allocate a determining role regarding crucial foreign policy matters to subnational governments? And what other nation could do so without strong objections from its citizens, so many of whom simply accede to the normalcy of provincial domination of the national political agenda?

At the national level, particular industrial sectors can be very powerful, but given Canada's particular economic geography some sectors come near to being dominant at the provincial level. Given its importance to the global future and to Canada's position and reputation in the world, climate change policy should fully take into account the views and interests of all Canadians. There should be national policy initiatives regarding areas normally within provincial jurisdiction when and where that is essential to meeting international treaty obligations. Canadian leaders and citizens alike need to be more assertive in this regard, and more open to action on climate change at every level – personal, local, and national.

Provincial and Local Governments and Climate Change Policy Innovation

It was the Canadian government that signed and ratified the Kyoto accord and some provinces that resisted, but there is more to the story of federalism and climate change. As noted, many provincial and local governments have taken strong action to reduce GHG emissions, stronger than the federal government has taken under either the Conservatives or the Liberals. British Columbia's carbon tax makes it arguably the leading North American jurisdiction in this regard. Ontario's support for renewable energy production by small producers is based on the highly successful and widely touted German policy initiative.[10] As well, many Canadian municipal governments, including virtually all of Canada's largest cities, have made major efforts to improve public transit and the number of riders has increased in recent years.[11] Former Toronto mayor David Miller proposed energy-saving retrofitting on the exteriors of many of Toronto's energy-inefficient high-rise apartment buildings, and many municipalities are improving energy efficiency in public buildings, in some cases with federal help.

Most of these governments are without a dominant oil industry, but there is more to explaining these initiatives than that. These initiatives, and indeed most efforts that promote energy efficiency and small-scale renewable energy, are excellent producers of jobs and investment per dollar of public expenditure. From a national perspective, tax breaks for or public investment in the oil industry benefits disproportionately only a few provinces. Energy efficiency and investments in renewable energy can be made virtually anywhere and everywhere in Canada. Pulp mills in trouble in the Maritimes or Northern Ontario could be converted to the production of wood pellets or alcohol as a fuel. The wind blows in the Prairies and on the coasts: east, west, and north as well as along the Great Lakes and in mountain regions. Improvements in energy efficiency can be made anywhere there are people and economic activity.

Funding for such initiatives can come from tax breaks to industry, municipal revenues, infrastructure funding shared by two or three levels of government, carbon taxes, cap-and-trade schemes, stimulus funds, or any number of other policy initiatives. Why Stéphane Dion sought to describe his climate change policy primarily as a tax initiative rather than as a comprehensive program to reduce unemployment and to help every region and community will remain a mystery for the political ages. Action on climate change can also be described as a means of getting Canada to fulfill its global obligations and help lead the world out of a very difficult situation, something we are uniquely equipped to do given bounteous non-fossil fuel endowments and a national capacity for resource development that has existed for centuries. As noted, Canada's political culture may well be open to appeals of this sort.

Canada and the Global Future

Despite a rich array of possibilities, Canada's performance on climate change has been profoundly disappointing. A nation that prides itself on playing a modest but constructive role on the world stage has utterly failed to live up to its obligations. Despite agreeing to behave as a good global citizen, to set a positive example, Canada's GHG emissions today are over 30 percent higher than in the base year – the level from which we have pledged to *reduce* them. At best, short of simply abruptly closing down the tar sands and all coal-fired thermal plants, it is probably impossible to get back even to 1990 emissions levels in less than a decade (we do not replace appliances, cars, and industrial operations more quickly than that and we cannot renovate or replace buildings in sufficient numbers or expand transit systems even that fast).

At the same time, there is now an opportunity, however fraught with complications, to make a significant breakthrough on the future trajectory of global GHG emissions. The reasons for this appear to be well beyond Canada's influence. The United States now has an administration that is open to the possibility of playing a positive role on this issue (although it faces a wide variety of domestic political constraints in this respect). As noted, many other nations now also see energy transformation as a key element in their economic future. China, for example, is moving decisively into the production of advanced solar panels and expanding research on other sources of renewable energy.

Perhaps the greatest challenge that remains is to resolve the differences between the rich nations and the rapidly growing but poorer nations regarding what each of them will do to slow the growth in emissions or reduce them in the future. For this to be resolved, nations must first agree that the issue is per capita emissions, not total emissions. Second, they must agree on how historical emissions are included in any calculus of future emissions. As discussed above, this is an extraordinarily challenging dilemma, one on which Prime Minister Harper's earlier assertions regarding climate change as a socialist plot are presumably based. There are reasonable moral arguments that China and India and Brazil have every right to someday attain the level of per capita income found in the rich nations. Should they, could they, be held back from this hope in order to rectify an atmospheric alteration almost wholly created by the past, albeit unknowing, behaviour of rich nations, including Canada?

This is a central dilemma of our time. If it cannot be resolved, there will be no solution to climate change. To complicate the matter further, rapid reductions in fossil fuel demand by the wealthy nations would hold oil prices down and make rapid increases in fossil fuel use in fast-growing poorer economies all the more likely. Moreover, today's high unemployment rates in the United States will not make it easy for even the most sympathetic administration to institute, for example, carbon taxes or emissions caps while jobs continue to expand in China, India, Mexico, and Brazil even as they are slow to do so in North America. Critics of effective action will not hesitate to play the "undermining the economy card" – even if the measures agreed to are economically beneficial.

During the term of the last Democratic president, with none other than Al Gore as vice president, the United States Senate opposed any and every concession on this issue just prior to the Kyoto negotiations. At the same time, China and India do not want to risk any slowing of their economic momentum for good reason – each must create millions of new jobs each year just to keep pace with population growth. Compromise will not come easily to either rich nations or poor ones. All one can say is that it is clear that the West must do more and first – not just signing agreements but making real reductions in GHG emissions before the poor nations will feel obliged to take significant steps. Even then, poor nations will expect help in meeting their economic goals while simultaneously reducing the rate at which they increase their use of fossil fuels (and ultimately reduce the rate of use itself).

What are the obligations of a wealthy nation, especially one with a cosmopolitan perspective, regarding the resolution of these differences? That is, can Canada make a contribution regarding climate change in today's context, a contribution true to its oft-asserted sense of its character as a nation? Is a significant contribution even possible in the face of Canada's institutional and political realities? The latter two of these questions will be answered in the sphere of domestic and international politics over the next few years. The first question I will attempt to answer here to conclude this chapter.

Nations like India and Brazil, and even China, have only a limited capacity to significantly reduce their GHG emissions while simultaneously continuing the rapid economic growth necessary to provide all of their citizens the possibility of survival, let alone reasonable comfort. Their reluctance to try reflects the political realities that they face. Millions within each of these nations face hunger and large numbers of people live in one small room or in slapdash shelters made of corrugated steel (if they are fortunate). The recent history of these nations saw conditions that were even worse for even larger numbers of their citizens. No government could survive going backward economically if it appeared to be retrogression by choice under pressure from wealthy nations.

The prerequisite to even getting global limits on emissions (let alone reduced emissions) is the achievement of reduced emissions by most wealthy nations – delivered reductions, not promises. Both the US and Canada have been thoroughly unhelpful for years, and the Bush administration's assertions that the US would not act if China did not were patently absurd. What Indians or Mexicans would think of Harper's claims about Kyoto being a plot against Canada, where historical emissions per capita are easily a hundred times the emissions of their fellow citizens, can be imagined.

That is the first step, but only a first step. An extended discussion of the remaining steps is beyond the scope of this chapter, but I will take the discussion just a bit further. Vanderheiden (2008), in his discussion of the issues associated with the moral elements of resolving global climate change obligations, distinguishes between two methods for determining the obligations of historically low per capita emitters. One method distinguishes between levels of per capita GHG emissions, with the line between the two determined in one of two ways (and emissions reduction obligations falling only on those emissions over the line).

One way is to determine a safe (absorbable) level of total historical emissions per capita and allocate that amount globally to nations based on population. A second method is to calculate a basic minimum that people would be "allowed to emit in order to meet their basic human needs and to which all persons would therefore be entitled as a matter of basic rights, even if the world's population producing GHGs at this rate would still contribute to the increasing atmospheric concentrations that cause climate change" (Vanderheiden 2008, 72). Clearly, however, historical emissions are not appropriate as a basis for determining current allowable emissions if they result in a formula that dooms the planet, as they might very well might, given the rate of increase of emissions in China, India, and other fast-growing economies.

The wealthy nations need to appreciate the significance of the fact that poor nations are being asked to contribute to solving a dilemma to which they have contributed marginally at most. Canada has extensive experience in finding federal solutions and resolving differences among regions of differing circumstances, patching them over if that is the only arrangement possible. We have learned how to bend over backward to keep moving forward together. Canadians need to apply those experiences at the global scale. Perhaps Canada can help convince additional wealthy nations that we must go first and do more, and help convince poor nations that they must, with help, also find ways to slow GHG emissions. The help – and Canada would need to take the lead in providing it – would be in the form of technology transfers in alternative energy, energy efficiency, advanced transportation, and carbon capture and storage.

First, then, we need to commit to rapidly deploying all those things here in Canada. Then we need to look to our roots: our historic commitment to public funding of science and technology and infrastructure (through the National Research Council and other endeavours such as transportation and public power). The building of public utilities, the railroads, the Canadian Broadcasting Corporation, and the Trans-Canada Highway were crucial to the creation of a nation. No less crucial now is the need for an energy system far less centred on fossil fuels. Such an effort would also provide the basis for future economic growth as we improve our capacity to export new products, technologies, and non-fossil fuel energy itself to the world.

These exports might include wind turbines designed for climatologically hostile terrain such as might also be found in Russia, Alaska, Greenland, Scandinavia, and elsewhere. They might also include carbon capture and storage systems for tar sands extraction that could be exported to Venezuela. Biomass fuels and the capacity to produce them from wood or algae are another possible export, as are technologies that might produce them from agricultural by-products. We already have Enwave, the system that cools much of downtown Toronto with cold water from Lake Ontario with minimal environmental impact and massive energy savings. Also crucial are new energy-efficient industrial, transportation, and construction capacities. The possibilities are endless and would be part of any national commitment to comprehensive climate change solutions, and, with price or other purchase incentives, part of convincing poorer nations to join in GHG reduction.

Canada has another dimension to its potential on this issue – it is positioned in many ways between Europe and the United States. However well-intentioned the Obama administration may be with regard to climate change, the health care debate suggests that deeply entrenched anti-change forces remain strong in the United States. They are led by ferocious right-wing media and massively funded lobbyists. If Canada were able to join with the Europeans and other traditional US allies to publicly and consistently push for decisive action by all wealthy nations, it might make it easier for the Obama administration to alter the course the US has followed on this issue and to take the lead in seeing through the necessary changes.

To do this, Canadians would have to focus on who we are and what our assets are. Our nation is big and cold; energy is not a luxury for us, but we have in abundance almost every known conventional and alternative form. We need to apply our capacities for organizing political and social life as well as the technological skills that we have developed to live well in a harsh environment. We need to appreciate and utilize all that we have been blessed with: our geography, our abundance, our experience at resolving differences and patching things over. We also need to remember that not all nations have our advantages. Nor do they have our low population densities and thus cannot so easily meet the needs of their populations while at the same time quickly reducing GHG emissions. We should be able to appreciate as well as any nation that seeing this transformation through involves a cosmopolitan willingness to help those that can move ahead only in more limited ways than we are able to move – and now should be more willing to move.

Notes

1 At the time, the tax break seemed necessary to spur production since oil prices were far too low to warrant investment in extraction from this source. When oil prices rose rapidly after 2003, the tax breaks stayed in place despite the fact that investments would have been profitable without them.
2 Mark Kinver, "Arctic Ice Thickness 'Plummets,'" 28 October 2008, BBC News: http://www.bbc.co.uk/news/.

3 BBC News, "Methane Bubbles Climate Trouble," 7 September 2006, http://www. bbc.co.uk/news/.
4 There are numerous polls on this subject over a long period. The 2006 Canadian Automobile Association poll was conducted by Decima Research. See "What Do Canadians Think?" http://www.caa.ca/eco/english/what/canadians.html.
5 Environics, "Canadians Are Critical of the Country's Environmental Performance," 11 April 2007. www.environics.ca.
6 World Public Opinion, "Publics Want More Government Action on Climate Change: Global Poll," http://www.worldpublicopinion.org/.
7 For a discussion of this incident, see Paehlke 2008, 84-85.
8 See CBC News, "Harper's Letter Dismisses Kyoto as 'Socialist Scheme,'" 30 January 2007, http://www.cbc.ca/news/.
9 These appointees include Lisa Jackson, Director, Environmental Protection Agency; Steven Chu, Secretary of Energy; and John Holdren, Advisor to the President for Science and Technology.
10 German-style feed-in tariffs that require the purchase of electricity from renewable sources initially at prices above market rates for electricity were first introduced in Ontario in 2006 and revised upward in 2009. See http://www. powerauthority.on.ca/.
11 Regarding climate change initiatives for Toronto, see "Change Is in the Air," http://www.toronto.ca/changeisintheair; for Vancouver, see "Climate Protection," http://www.vancouver.ca/sustainability/climate_protection.htm.

References

Boyd, David R. 2003. *Unnatural Law: Rethinking Canadian Environmental Law and Policy.* Vancouver: UBC Press.

Gwyn, Richard. 1995. *Nationalism without Walls: The Unbearable Lightness of Being Canadian.* Toronto: McClelland and Stewart.

Harrison, Kathryn. 1996. *Passing the Buck: Federalism and Canadian Environmental Policy.* Vancouver: UBC Press.

Hurrell, Andrew, and Benedict Kingsbury, eds. 1992. *The International Politics of the Environment.* New York: Oxford University Press.

Martin, Pierre, and Michel Fortmann. 2001. "Support for International Involvement in Canadian Public Opinion after the Cold War." *Canadian Military Journal* 2 (Autumn): 43-52.

NRTEE (National Round Table on the Environment and Economy). 2006. *Advice on a Long-Term Strategy on Climate Change in Canada.* Ottawa: NRTEE.

Paehlke, Robert. 2001. "Spatial Proportionality: Right-Sizing Environmental Decision-Making." In *Governing the Environment: Persistent Challenges, Uncertain Innovations,* ed. by Edward A. Parson, 73-123. Toronto: University of Toronto Press.

–. 2008. *Some Like It Cold: The Politics of Climate Change in Canada.* Toronto: Between the Lines.

Vanderheiden, Steve. 2008. *Atmospheric Justice: A Political Theory of Climate Change.* New York: Oxford University Press.

Welsh, Jennifer. 2005. *At Home in the World: Canada's Global Vision for the 21st Century.* Toronto: HarperCollins.

Contributors

Yasmeen Abu-Laban is Professor and Associate Chair (Research) in the Department of Political Science at the University of Alberta. Her research interests centre on the Canadian and comparative dimensions of gender, racialization, migration, citizenship, and rights.

Howard Adelman is Professor Emeritus in the Department of Philosophy at York University and Adjunct Professor, Key Centre for Ethics, Law, Justice and Governance at Griffith University. Two new books are due in 2011: *No Return, No Refuge,* co-authored with Elazar Barkan (Columbia University Press), and *Religion, Culture and State,* co-edited with Pierre Anctil (University of Toronto Press).

Charles Blattberg is Professor of Political Philosophy at the Université de Montréal. His publications include *From Pluralist to Patriotic Politics* (Oxford University Press, 2000); *Shall We Dance? A Patriotic Politics for Canada* (McGill-Queen's University Press, 2003); and *Patriotic Elaborations: Essays in Practical Philosophy* (McGill-Queen's University Press, 2009).

Will Kymlicka holds the Canada Research Chair in Political Philosophy at Queen's University, and is the author of several books on issues of multiculturalism, nationalism, and citizenship, including *Multicultural Citizenship* (Oxford University Press, 1995) and *Multicultural Odysseys* (Oxford University Press, 2007).

Patti Tamara Lenard is Assistant Professor of Ethics in the Graduate School of Public and International Affairs at the University of Ottawa. Her work focuses on the moral challenges that arise from migration across borders, global wealth inequalities, and democratic political participation in multicultural states.

Margaret Moore is Sir Edward Peacock Professor of Political Theory in the Political Studies Department at Queen's University. She is the author of *Foundations of Liberalism* (Oxford University Press, 1993) and *Ethics of Nationalism* (Oxford University Press, 2001), and is currently working on issues of territorial rights.

Robert Paehlke is Professor Emeritus of Environmental and Resource Studies at Trent University. He is a founding editor of the magazine *Alternatives: Canadian Environmental Ideas and Action*. His books include *Some Like It Cold: The Politics of Climate Change in Canada* (Between the Lines, 2008); *Democracy's Dilemma: Environment, Social Equity and the Global Economy* (MIT Press, 2004); and *Environmentalism and the Future of Progressive Politics* (Yale University Press, 1991).

Scott Schaffer is Associate Professor of Sociology at the University of Western Ontario, and the author of *Resisting Ethics* (2004, Palgrave Macmillan). In addition to his work on cosmopolitanism, he writes on social ethics from a French existentialist position, resistance, and development, and is coordinator of the Global Social Thought Project.

Kok-Chor Tan is Associate Professor of Philosophy at the University of Pennsylvania. He works mainly in political and moral philosophy, with special interest in the topic of global justice. He is the author of *Toleration, Diversity, and Global Justice* (Penn State University Press, 2000) and *Justice without Borders* (Cambridge University Press, 2004). Current research projects include a book on distributive justice and papers on associative obligations and toleration.

Joseph-Yvon Thériault is Professor of Sociology at the Université du Québec à Montréal, where he holds a Canada Research Chair in Globalization, Citizenship and Democracy. He is the author of *L'identité à l'épreuve de la modernité* (Éditions d'Acadie, 1995); *Critique de l'américanité, mémoire et démocratie au Québec* (Québec Amérique, 2002); and *Faire société, société civile et espaces francophones* (Prise de parole, 2007). He was elected a member of the Royal Society of Canada in 2004 and received a Trudeau Fellowship (2007-10).

Kathryn Walker is a postdoctoral fellow at the Centre de Recherche en Éthique de L'Université de Montréal (CREUM). She was the Democracy and Diversity postdoctoral fellow at Queen's University in 2008-9, and a postdoctoral fellow at la Chaire du Canada en Mondialisation, citoyenneté et démocratie at the Université du Quebec à Montréal in 2009-10. Her research focuses on questions of global and social justice.

Daniel Weinstock holds the Canada Research Chair in Ethics and Political Philosophy in the Department of Philosophy at the Université de Montréal. He has published widely on a range of issues in political philosophy. Most recently, he has been completing a project on the philosophical issues that arise in the relationship between parents, the stats, and children.

Index

Note: "R2P" stands for responsibility to protect.

Printed and bound in Canada by Friesens

Set in Stone by Artegraphica Design Co. Ltd.

Copy editor: Frank Chow

Proofreader: Sarah Munro

Indexer: Pat Buchanan